Routledge Revivals

The Colonial Agents of the British West Indies

The Colonial Agents of the British West Indies

A Study in Colonial Administration, Mainly in the Eighteenth Century

Lillian M. Penson

First published in 1924 by Frank Cass & Co. Ltd.

This edition first published in 2018 by Routledge
2 Park Square, Milton Park, Abingdon, Oxon, OX14 4RN
and by Routledge
52 Vanderbilt Avenue, New York, NY 10017, USA

Routledge is an imprint of the Taylor & Francis Group, an informa business

© 1924 by Taylor & Francis

All rights reserved. No part of this book may be reprinted or reproduced or utilised in any form or by any electronic, mechanical, or other means, now known or hereafter invented, including photocopying and recording, or in any information storage or retrieval system, without permission in writing from the publishers.

Publisher's Note
The publisher has gone to great lengths to ensure the quality of this reprint but points out that some imperfections in the original copies may be apparent.

Disclaimer
The publisher has made every effort to trace copyright holders and welcomes correspondence from those they have been unable to contact.

A Library of Congress record exists under ISBN:

ISBN 13: 978-0-367-13978-0 (hbk)
ISBN 13: 978-0-367-13981-0 (pbk)
ISBN 13: 978-0-429-02950-9 (ebk)

CASS LIBRARY OF WEST INDIAN STUDIES

No. 16

THE COLONIAL AGENTS

OF THE

BRITISH WEST INDIES

CASS LIBRARY OF WEST INDIAN STUDIES

No. 9.   Henry H. Breen
St. Lucia: Historical, Statistical, and Descriptive   (1844).
New Impression

No. 10.   Sir Robert Hermann Schomburgk
A Description of British Guiana, Geographical and Statistical; exhibiting its resources and capabilities, together with the present and future condition and prospects of the colony   (1840).
New Impression

No. 11.   Richard Ligon
A True and Exact History of the Island of Barbadoes. Illustrated with a Map of the Island, as also the Principal Trees and Plants there, set forth in their due Proportions and Shapes, drawn out by their several respective scales. Together with the Ingenio that makes the Sugar etc., etc.   (1657; 1673).
New Impression of the Second Edition

No. 12.   Edward Long
The History of Jamaica, or General Survey of the Antient and Modern State of that Island; with Reflections on its Situation, Settlements, Inhabitants, Climate, Products, Commerce, Laws, and Government   (1774).
With a new introduction by George Metcalf
New Edition

No. 13.   E. L. Joseph
History of Trinidad   (1838).
New Impression

No. 14.   Alfred Caldecott
The Church in the West Indies   (1898).
New Impression

No. 15.   C. S. Salmon
The Caribbean Confederation. A plan for the union of the fifteen British West Indian Colonies, preceded by An Account of the Past and Present Condition of the European and the African Races Inhabiting them, with a true explanation of the Haytian Mystery (1888).
New Impression

No. 16.   Lillian M. Penson
The Colonial Agents of the British West Indies; a study in Colonial Administration, mainly in the Eighteenth Century   (1924).
New Impression

THE
COLONIAL AGENTS

OF THE

BRITISH WEST INDIES

A Study in Colonial Administration, Mainly in
the Eighteenth Century

BY

LILLIAN M. PENSON

FRANK CASS & CO. LTD.
1971

Published by
FRANK CASS AND COMPANY LIMITED
67 Great Russell Street, London WC1B 3BT
by arrangement

All rights reserved

First edition   1924
New impression   1971

ISBN 0 7146 1944 2

*Printed in Great Britain by Clarke, Doble & Brendon Ltd.
Plymouth and London*

PREFACE

THE work of the West India interest in London has recently attracted considerable attention from historians of the eighteenth century. In particular there is a growing impression that it had an important responsibility for the series of events that led to the revolt of the mainland colonies. In this book I have attempted neither to prove nor assert such claims. My task has been rather to investigate the character and working of this powerful interest, than to discuss the measure of its achievement. At the centre of it stood the agent; his office coming into existence when that interest was born, in the Restoration era, and reaching a position of recognised authority at the time of its highest importance—the administrations of Walpole, the Pelhams, and the elder Pitt. With the Peace of Paris of 1763 the decline in influence began, accompanied as the century advanced by a greater solidarity of organisation; until in the nineteenth century the disappearance of the office is dated only a few years after the final development of that organisation in 1843. The agencies belonged essentially to the eighteenth century: they were a necessary part of the colonial system of the old empire. If they had a share in causing the alienation of the mainland colonies, that alienation in time brought about their downfall.

PREFACE

My attempt here has been to sketch the history of the agents, throughout the two centuries of their office. The title "Colonial Agents" has made unnecessary a detailed treatment of the several variants of the agency existing in the same period. I have dealt with the personal agents of Governors only in the seventeenth century, when they were of considerable influence in developing the office of colonial agent. Of army agents and crown agents [1] I have said little, since they were occupied solely, as far as the West Indies were concerned, with financial functions. For no period in the history of the West Indies have I found the army and colonial agencies combined as they were in the case of certain North American colonies. The history of the colonial agents of Bermuda I have inserted as an appendix, since in the seventeenth and eighteenth centuries the character of their interests separated them in large measure from the agents of the other islands.

In the work of preparation I have incurred great obligations in many directions. I have to express my indebtedness, in the first place, to several owners of private records and others through whom access has been made possible to sources of a private nature. To Sir R. Rutherford, Chairman of the West India Committee, and to Mr. A. E. Aspinall, the Secretary, I am indebted for generous permission to consult the minute-books and letter-books in possession of the Committee and the firm of West Indian merchants now trading as Messrs. Wilkinson & Gaviller. From these

---

[1] i.e. in the eighteenth-century sense of agents nominated by the Treasury. The present office of Crown Agents is referred to in the last chapter.

PREFACE

series of documents, both going back over a large part of the eighteenth century, it has been possible to trace in a manner impossible from official records the activities of the agents and their friends in London. I have also to acknowledge my gratitude to Mrs. A. E. Jeaffreson for the loan of the original letter-book from which Mr. J. C. Jeaffreson compiled his work *A Young Squire of the Seventeenth Century*; and to the Master and Secretary of the Society of Merchant Venturers of Bristol for their permission to work on documents in their possession.

It would be too long a task to thank individually all those who have helped me by suggestions and advice; but I cannot avoid an expression of gratitude to the officers of the Public Record Office, who have frequently aided in my research, and to Mr. E. R. Adair, Mr. C. S. S. Higham, and Mr. H. W. V. Temperley, who have given me much valuable assistance. My work has been done throughout under the guidance of Professor A. P. Newton, and I am glad of this opportunity of expressing my thanks for his constant interest and encouragement during the several years he has directed my research.

That it has been possible to publish this book is due to grants made by the University of London from the Publications' Loan Fund, and by Birkbeck College: to the authorities responsible for the allocation of these grants I must also therefore return my thanks.

LILLIAN M. PENSON.

ABBREVIATIONS USED IN FOOTNOTES

A.P.C. i, etc.	*Acts of the Privy Council, Colonial Series,* vol. i, etc.
B.M. Add. MSS.	British Museum, Additional Manuscripts.
B.M. Egerton MSS.	British Museum, Egerton Manuscripts.
B.M. King's MSS.	British Museum, King's Manuscripts.
B.M. Sloane MSS.	British Museum, Sloane Manuscripts.
Chatham Papers, i, etc.	Chatham Manuscripts in the Public Record Office, Bundle i, etc.
C.O. 1:1, etc.	Colonial Office Records in the Public Record Office, series 1, vol. i, etc.
C.S.P. i, etc.	*Calendar of State Papers, Colonial Series, America and West Indies,* vol. i, etc.
D.N.B.	*Dictionary of National Biography.*
Jeaffreson MS.	Letter-book of Christopher Jeaffreson.
Letter-books of Messrs. Lascelles & Maxwell	Letter-books in possession of Messrs. Wilkinson & Gaviller, 34 Great Tower Street, E.C.3.
Merchants' Minutes, i, etc.	Minutes of Society of West India Merchants, vol. i, etc., in possession of the West India Committee, 14 Trinity Square, E.C.3.
Standing Committee's Minutes, i, etc.	Minutes of Standing Committee of West India Planters & Merchants, vol. i, etc., in possession of the West India Committee.
Stapleton MSS.	Miscellaneous manuscripts in the possession of Sir Miles Stapleton, deposited in the John Rylands' Library, Manchester.

CONTENTS

CHAPTER		PAGE
I.	COLONIAL PROBLEMS AND COLONIAL REPRESENTATION, 1600–1660	1
II.	THE RESTORATION SETTLEMENT.	20
III.	THE EVOLUTION OF THE AGENCIES, 1670–1700	46
IV.	THE PROBLEM OF APPOINTMENT IN THE FIRST HALF OF THE EIGHTEENTH CENTURY.	79
V.	THE NEW AGENCIES OF THE SECOND HALF OF THE EIGHTEENTH CENTURY	98
VI.	THE FUNCTIONS OF THE AGENTS.	114
VII.	CONTROL BY THE ISLANDS	137
VIII.	THE PERSONNEL OF THE AGENCY	158
IX.	AGENTS, PLANTERS, AND MERCHANTS, 1660–1760	174
X.	THE WEST INDIA COMMITTEE	194
XI.	SOLICITATIONS IN WHITEHALL AND WESTMINSTER	215
XII.	THE DISAPPEARANCE OF THE AGENCIES	232

CONTENTS

APPENDIX
 PAGE
I. THE AGENCY OF BERMUDA . . . 247

II. LIST OF WEST INDIAN COLONIAL AGENTS . 250

III. DOCUMENTS ILLUSTRATIVE OF THE HISTORY OF THE WEST INDIAN AGENCIES . . 255

IV. NOTE ON AUTHORITIES—

   I. CONTEMPORARY MATERIALS :

   (A) DOCUMENTS 290

   (B) SUPPLEMENTARY SOURCES . . 300

   II. MODERN WORKS 304

INDEX 311

MAP

THE ATLANTIC OCEAN . *. At end of volume*

THE COLONIAL AGENTS OF THE BRITISH WEST INDIES

CHAPTER I

COLONIAL PROBLEMS AND COLONIAL REPRESENTATION,
1600–1660

THE growth of the British Empire at all stages of its history has been dependent on sea power. In the sixteenth century, when the first indications were given of the future settlements, they are to be found, not in desires for territorial expansion or for the evangelising of native races, but in the exploits of Elizabethan sea rovers, whose aim lay in voyages of adventure and new trade routes. Later, it is true, when the period of exploration was followed by one of planting, new aspects of the movement appeared; but by that time the lines of the future progress had been determined, and so the colonies grew up in places made accessible only by the genius and daring of Elizabethan mariners.

The character of their origin had a lasting influence on the history of these early colonies. They were three thousand miles from England; intercourse was difficult and irregular. In the first years of settlement, insufficient communications led to shortage of supplies and successive threats of starvation; then, later, when the resources available to the colonists had been opened up, the influence was seen in new questions relating to administration. Government from a remote centre was, indeed, a problem with which the English executive was well acquainted in the earlier history of the English realm, for only as internal communications improved had it been found possible to create even in England an efficient system of local government; and it is not without significance that early proprietary charters conferred on the patentee the rights of jurisdiction enjoyed by the Bishop Palatine of Durham. But, while, in dealing with the new territories across the seas, old expedients could be applied, precedent, nevertheless, could not settle all points.

In all systems of local government, and especially those established in growing communities, questions are bound to arise which require to be submitted to the central authority. And so it was with the seventeenth-century colonies. There were differences of interpretation as to the privileges conferred by colonial charters; differences of interest between one colony and another, particularly questions of boundaries; and, as time went on, there were difficulties over the enforcement of the Navigation Acts. The mother-country was ignorant of conditions in the colonies, the colonies were anxious lest their interests should be neglected or overridden by new influences. These were the conditions under which the old Empire grew.

In all the colonies alike, those of North America as well as the West Indies, the situation was met by the appointment of agents. Virginia took the lead, sending over an agent in 1624 to represent on behalf of governor, council, and burgesses, the disastrous consequences of the administration of Sir Thomas

Smith. The other colonies were not long in following her example, and through the whole of the period that terminated in the American Revolution there were, normally, in England representatives of the colonies concerned to care for their interests.

The development into a permanent practice of the seventeenth-century experiments was in a great measure due to the character of constitution established in the colonies. The early colonies had been settled as a result of the grant of charters to one or more proprietors, who became responsible for the administration. During the period of proprietary rule the need for an agency was only sporadic : when the proprietors lived in England, the work of representing the interest of the colony before the home government was borne largely by them, or by some one of their nomination ; when the recipients of the charter were themselves resident in the colony, there was a strong tendency to develop an attitude of independence towards the authorities at home. But as the seventeenth century passed in most cases proprietary rule ceased, and, with the assertion of royal government, the need for a permanent sponsor became felt. The royal colonies were administered by an executive under nomination of the crown, but possessed a representative house which, with the governor and a nominated council, comprised the legislature. Nor were the representative houses in any way content with a merely nominal share in government. As early as 1652 John Bayes, Treasurer of Barbados, explained the difficulties of controlling the island if the governor had not power enough to " lay a curbe uppon our Barbados Parliam^t," for some disaffected persons had already formed the design to

4 COLONIAL AGENTS OF WEST INDIES

make the island "a free state and not to runn any fortune with England either in peace or warr."[1] Forty years later Governor Kendall was complaining that "The Assembly take themselves to be Notable Polititians and some Coxcombs have made them believe they have as many priviledges as a house of Comons in England."[2] Such an accusation was by no means without justification. The colonists had come out from England at a time of great political unrest: they had carried with them the political ideas which made the seventeenth century in England more turbulent than any other period in modern history. The first of colonial assemblies, the House of Burgesses of Virginia, had been established in 1618 as a direct consequence of the supremacy of the Liberal party at home[3]: it was a by-product of the constitutional opposition to the crown in the middle period of James I's reign. The Barbados assembly established in 1639 was not slow to reflect the parliamentary zeal of the years of the personal rule of Charles I: and it kept this character throughout the period of West Indian prosperity. The members of assembly, few though they were in number, regarded themselves as the counterpart of the House of Commons. The same rules governed their debates: the same questions of finance and privilege roused their opposition to the government.[4] To throw off, in

[1] C.O. 1:11, No. 59, Memorial of John Bayes, 30 June 1652.

[2] C.O. 28:1, No. 60, Governor Kendall to the lords of Trade and Plantations, 4 April 1691.

[3] Cf. Osgood: *The American Colonies in the Seventeenth Century*, vol. i. pp. 91–2.

[4] Sir Thomas Modyford described the Council and Assembly of Jamaica in 1670 as "an humble Modell of our high Court of Parliament." C.O. 138:1, p. 87.

measure at least, their subservience to the crown, monopolising the executive as well as the legislative power, this was their aim in the seventeenth century. At a later period, abandoning this struggle, they turned to the control of the executive. In either case they formed a problem difficult enough to a governor, separated from the authority that maintained him, save for intermittent correspondence; without the means for carrying on the government, save with the consent of the assembly. If this system was to be possible, it must be by some reconciling of interests, of the administration and the colonial governor, of the governor and the legislature. There must be some device for bringing together the colonists abroad and the government at home. This was, in brief, the work of the agents, who for nearly two centuries of colonial history acted as liaison officers between colony and mother-country. In large measure it was through them that some degree of smooth working was attained.

The West Indies in 1660.—The history of the West Indian colonial agents may most properly be taken to start with the period of the Restoration. Hitherto, while there had been certain advances in the direction of development, no regular agency had been established, and the lines on which the growth was to take place were as yet not clearly seen. At the Restoration the first attempts were being made to build up in England a permanent system of representation; and, while these were not on the lines of the ultimate progress, there were side by side with them indications of the source of later advance; and there were further, the first signs of a recognition on the part of the home government that the establishment of some form of agency was desirable.

6 COLONIAL AGENTS OF WEST INDIES

The history of the rise of the agencies is confined in great measure to a few only of the West Indian islands under British rule. In 1660 there existed a vital distinction between the nominal and the actual possessions of England in the Caribbean. Grants made in the first half of the century had included in the sphere of control numerous small islands of whose nature little was known, and the settlement of which had never been attempted. Of the islands in effective European occupation the most important belonged to Spain, whose settlements in Cuba, Haiti, and Porto Rico ensured predominance in the Indies. At first, English interest had been confined to the line of small islands circling round from Porto Rico to Tortuga, leaving outposts on the east in Barbados, Tobago, and Trinidad. Here English control was only partial. Towards the north of the line was a little group of islands centring at St. Christopher, the mother-colony of the British West Indies, and including Nevis, Antigua, and Montserrat, later the principal members of the colony of the Leeward Islands ; and then outside the main circle was Barbados, the largest, in early times, of British possessions amongst the islands, and for long the most important in the spheres of commerce and constitutional development. Until nearly the end of the early Stuart period these had been the sole British settlements : but during the troubles of the Civil War and the period of the Interregnum there had come two accessions, one, as yet of little importance, merely a foothold to the north of the Spanish islands in the Bahama group ; the other a gain of great value, the capture of the Spanish colony of Jamaica, an island of greater size and fertility than any of the other islands under British rule. Jamaica, taken in a Spanish war, was an outpost against the aggression of that nation; but for the future the danger lay elsewhere, in the little group of islands where British power was first established. Here, facing them on every side, were the French. In the old days of contest with Spain, Anglo-French rivalry had not been anticipated, and so the two peoples were settled side by side, sharing the island of St. Christopher; and the two centres of English rule in the Leeward Islands and Barbados were separated by the French settlements at Guadaloupe, Dominica, and Martinique, and flanked far to the south by Grenada. Of less ultimate importance was the presence of the Dutch in the extreme north of the line in the Virgin Islands, making itself felt also from time to time in the southerly island of Tobago.

Such was the situation at the return of Charles II, and its features are of considerable importance to the history of the agency. During the Restoration period further British settlements were established in the Bahama group and at Barbuda in the Leeward Islands, while a second addition by conquest was made by the acquisition of one of the Virgin Islands, Tortola, from the Dutch. But these accessions had no effect on the history of the development of the agency. The islands were small in extent, and their economic and constitutional development was long delayed; it was not until the office was firmly established in the other islands that agents for them appear, and so their history belongs to a later period when agencies were founded also in the islands ceded after the Seven Years' War. The growth of the agency in these later times was of a different character, being largely determined by the precedents of the older islands. The main concern is therefore with the older colonies, Barbados, the little group round St. Christopher, and Jamaica, whose size and rapid progress fast compensated for the lateness of its acquisition.

The oldest of all the colonies was St. Christopher, from which settlers had gone out to Nevis, Antigua, and Montserrat. As a result of this early supremacy it had been made the centre of the first general government of the English Caribbee Islands;[1] but this had lasted but a short time. The island was shared with the French, and the early conditions of friendliness, changed soon to a state of neutrality, concealing a fundamental distrust. The French port of Basseterre commanded the best harbour, and if at the time of the Restoration the island was still " the most frequented by Merchants, and the most populous of all the Antilles,"[2] the division between English and French gave less than half the advantage of its prosperity to either of the two nations. When St. Christopher ceased to be the seat of the government of all the islands, the leadership passed to Barbados, where it was fully established before the end of the early Stuart period.

Barbados at the time of the Restoration was well qualified to take the lead in commercial and consti-

---

[1] That under Thomas Warner established in 1625. See C. P. Lucas, *Historical Geography of the British Colonies*. Vol. ii: *The West Indies*, 2nd edition, Oxford, 1905, p. 138. The account of the early settlement of the islands and their constitution has now been revised by Mr. J. A. Williamson in a forthcoming book.

[2] John Davies, *History of the Caribbee Islands*, London, 1666, p. 8. This is a translation of *Histoire naturelle et morale des Antilles de l'Amerique*, 1658.

COLONIAL PROBLEMS

tutional development. At that time it was nearly at the height of the remarkable period of growth which followed the introduction of sugar.[1] Even as early as 1647 the plantations of sugar, cotton, and tobacco had become so extensive that the land was said to be " so taken up as there is not any to be had but at great rates."[2] The population had grown rapidly. On the sea-coast were the towns, the most important, Bridgtown, on Carlisle Bay; here a contemporary writer narrates:

> the Merchants and Factors of the Isle have their storehouses for the negotiation of their Affairs; and from their storehouses or shops the Inhabitants are supplied with such commodities as they have occasion for, in exchange for theirs, which are the product of the Isle.[3]

The coast towns were frequented by numerous vessels sent out by the great merchant adventurers of London, Bristol, and other ports. During the Civil War a large part of the trade passed to the Dutch merchants,[4] but from the beginning of the Commonwealth period Englishmen, aided by the deliberate policy of the government, started to regain their predominance.[5] These merchant adventurers consigned their goods to their factors in the islands or to local merchants who acted as middlemen between them and the

---

[1] C. P. Lucas, *Historical Geography of the British Colonies.* Vol. ii: *The West Indies*, 2nd edition, Oxford, 1905, pp. 187–8.

[2] Thomason Tracts, 669, f. 11/115, *Declaration by James Earl of Carlisle*, 22 November 1647.

[3] Richard Blome, *Description of the Island of Jamaica*, London, 1672, pp. 79–80.

[4] G. L. Beer, *The Origins of the British Colonial System*, New York, 1908, pp. 357–9.

[5] Beer, *Origins*, pp. 384–94.

planters.[1] The factors and merchants made the best sales they could, and returned the proceeds in sugar, cotton, tobacco, or some other product. At this date it was emphatically the English merchants who took the initiative in building up the trade between England and the colonies; they advanced the goods necessary for commencing a plantation, waiting for a return until the crops on the lands could be realised. They were making no idle boast when they asserted in the middle of the seventeenth century that it was to their enterprise that the islands were indebted for their early prosperity.[2]

The London Merchants.—The character of the relationship between the merchants and the islands changed completely during the century following the Interregnum. In the eighteenth century it was the planters in the islands who consigned the goods, principally sugar, to the merchants at home, and in return they requisitioned from the merchants the commodities they needed for their plantations. This reversal of the system of trade was due in great measure to two factors both in operation at the time of the Restoration.

The process was fostered in the first place by the policy of the Navigation Acts. Although it is true that the earlier acts were not as rigidly enforced as that of 1696, from the year 1650 onwards there was

---

[1] Ligon, *op. cit.*, pp. 108 *et seq.*, where an account is given of the establishment of a plantation in Barbados.

[2] "The state of yᵉ Difference as it is pressed between yᵉ Merchants and yᵉ Planters in relation to free Trade att yᵉ Charibee Islands And yᵉ meanes of Reconciliation and generall satisfaction proposed." (Letter-book of Thomas Povey, B.M. Add. MS. 11411, ff. 3–5. The document is undated, but the letter-book relates to the years 1650–5.)

COLONIAL PROBLEMS

a definite movement towards the exclusion from the trade of the British plantations of all except English and plantation merchants. The chief rivals in the seventeenth century were the Dutch, and they gradually disappeared as the acts were made effective. But this policy, although contributory to the end, was by no means the sole cause. Side by side was another development wholly different in character, but working with it from the point of view of West Indian trade. Gradually, more and more, sugar was outstripping tobacco and cotton as the staple product: the West Indian islands were becoming the sugar colonies, and the West Indian merchants in England, granted a practical monopoly of the West Indian trade by the terms of the Navigation Acts, became at the same time specialists in sugar. When these two forces had been for a short time in operation, there grew up in England, and especially in London, a class of merchants, no longer like Maurice Thompson, Martin Noell, and Thomas Povey, the great merchant adventurers of the Interregnum, interested in all branches of plantation trade, but restricting their enterprise to trade with the West Indian islands, an intercourse that on one side was predominantly concerned with sugar.

As to the steps by which this change was effected, it is impossible to make any definite statement. The process was of necessity gradual, and the most that can be said of the position in the Restoration period is that there were evidences of the way in which it was brought about. From very early days in the history of the islands, the planters were not wholly dependent on the local merchants and factors for the supply of commodities required on their estates.

As was natural, they had friends and relatives at home, some of them merchants, to whom they could apply for goods to be sent out to them. Thus, Thomas Verney in 1638 and 1639 sent from Barbados a list of his needs to his father, Sir Edmund Verney.[1] Thus, forty years later, Christopher Jeaffreson of St. Christopher wrote constantly to his cousin William Poyntz, "at the sign of 'the Goat' in Cornhill."[2] As the plantations in the islands become more settled, no doubt such relations increased in frequency and, as the conditions of trade changed, developed into the system of intercourse prevailing in the eighteenth century.

In the seventeenth century this friendly correspondence had another significance, also a foreshadowing of later conditions. The repeated exchange of letters, while it aimed at securing for the planters the commodities they wanted, incidentally ensured that there should be in England persons who were in frequent receipt of information from the West Indies. There is evidence, further, that this correspondence was not merely of a commercial or domestic character. The various members of the family of Povey maintained during the Interregnum constant communications with one another. The most famous member of the group was Thomas Povey, a barrister of Gray's Inn and a merchant with widespread interests, well known for the influence he exerted in colonial matters.[3]

[1] F. P. Verney, *Memoirs of the Verney Family during the Civil War*, London, 1892, vol. i, pp. 147-53.

[2] J. C. Jeaffreson, *A Young Squire of the Seventeenth Century*, London, 1878, vol. i, pp. 231, 236, etc.

[3] *Vide sub nom.* D.N.B.; also C. M. Andrews, *British Committees, Commissions, and Councils of Trade and Plantations*, 1622-1675, J.H.U.S. Hist. & Pol. Sc., XXVI, i, Baltimore, 1908, pp. 51-3.

COLONIAL PROBLEMS

His brother Richard was Secretary and Commissary-General of Provisions at Jamaica; another brother, William, was Provost-Marshal at Barbados. The brothers in the colonies acted as factors in the mercantile enterprises of Thomas Povey and his friend Martin Noell, while Thomas looked after the interests of his brothers at home. In 1655 he wrote to William in Barbados that it would be impossible for him to remain in reputation in the island unless he had " one foot in England," and he added, " I beare att least as much of ye stress and weight of y^r affaires heere as you may bee judged to doe upon ye place."[1] Three years later he wrote to his brother Richard deprecating the " briefe and Contracted " nature of the letters he received from him;

> as if ... dated from the Exchange to Graies Inne, and were rather some hasty notes, and hints of busyness, to be farther debated and discoursed on at the next meeting, than solemn correspondencies of ffriends & Brothers and Persons concern'd in busyness, at a distance so remote. ... Nor is it for my reputation that I remaine soe unknowing in all the matters that relate to Jamaica whilest it is known I have a Brother there, and that I am diverse waies Interested therein.[2]

It appears probable that the relation fulfilled by Povey towards his brothers was undertaken by someone on behalf of most of the prominent persons in the islands, for Povey in a letter to the Governor of Barbados in 1673, describing the activities of certain members of the assembly, refers to their " Correspondencies ... on the Exchange "[3] as a matter of political significance.

[1] B.M. Add. MS. 11411, ff. 8-9, letter dated 10 Nov. 1655.
[2] B.M. Add. MS. 11411, ff. 68-70, letter dated 20 July 1658.
[3] B.M. Egerton MS. 2395, ff. 487-9, letter dated 15 March 1672/3.

It was not long before the action of the government at home gave added importance to this development. The value of the merchants as a source of information in colonial affairs had been recognised before the Interregnum, but it is interesting to find in the " Overture " drafted by Povey in 1654, which became the model for the Instructions to the Restoration Council for Foreign Plantations of 1st December 1660, that the proposed Board should " call to its Advice and Consultations . . . any well experienced Persons, whether Merchants, or Seamen, or Artificers."[1] From this time consultation of the merchants became a recognised feature of colonial administration.

The Planters.—In the Instructions of 1660 another class of persons was added : the planters of the islands.[2] At the time of the Restoration the group of planters was, like that of the merchants, particularly powerful. The Civil War and the Interregnum had brought troubles to the outlying parts of the Empire as well as to the mother-country, and, in the West Indies, Barbados and Antigua, after some fluctuation of faction, had shown marked loyalty to the losing side. The political strife in Barbados was of a most embittered character. The royalists, when, soon after the arrival of Lord Willoughby, they obtained the predominance in the island, proceeded on the policy already inaugurated of banishing their opponents. Many of the planters, to escape such penalties, voluntarily absented themselves from the island, coming home to England and maintaining a constant intercourse with the home government ; prominent among them Captain John Bayes,

[1] Andrews, *British Committees*, pp. 69-70.
[2] A precedent for this can be found in 1643 (see also Ligon *op. cit.*, pp. 22, 96).

COLONIAL PROBLEMS

then holding the office of Treasurer.[1] The downfall of Lord Willoughby's administration and the establishment of a Commonwealth governor in 1652 resulted, despite the terms of the surrender, in the banishment of a group of royalists, and these, together with others who voluntarily left their estates, formed again a circle in England, not as yet acting together in political matters, but waiting only for more favourable times for this end.

The presence of planters and merchants at home known to possess information as to the colonies was a situation charged with possible difficulties for the Governor in the islands. The factions of Barbados, led by Thomas Modyford and aided by his friends at home, caused considerable anxiety to Daniel Searle, the Governor established in Barbados by the Commonwealth. In 1658 he had suspended from his judicial office a relative of Modyford, Colonel Colleton, a member of a family conspicuous in the early annals of the Barbados agency; and, as Povey told him, he was in danger of losing the favour of the Protector through the agitation raised by Colleton's friends.[2] Nor was the factious state of Barbados alone responsible for such conditions. Differences of interest did not take long to develop in Jamaica: for in 1662 Colonel D'Oyley, on his return from the island, described as one of the difficulties with which he had to contend in his government "the Crying up Merchants and trade & there being heard here &

[1] Bayes laid claim in 1653 to having come over to look after the affairs of the island. C.O. 1:12, No. 2. At about this time he was summoned by the Committee for Foreign Affairs on the business of Barbados, e.g. 10 Jan. 1652/3, S.P. Dom. Inter. i. 132, p. 38.

[2] B.M. Add. MS. 11411, ff. 58-60.

countenanced against the Governor who at that distance cannot speake for himselfe." [1]

The Governors' Correspondents.—The situation thus created was met by Governor Searle of Barbados by the solution it most obviously suggested, the appointment of someone at home to safeguard the interests of the Governor against misrepresentation. Of such appointments Thomas Povey may be regarded as a professional promoter. He wrote to the Governor and Council of Virginia,[2] he wrote to Colonel Temple at Nova Scotia,[3] and to Governor Searle at Barbados. Moreover, he was apparently willing to perform the functions of an agent first before any discussion of remuneration had taken place, a valuable quality in the building up of an office. In 1659 he obtained his reward as far as Barbados was concerned, for in that year Governor Searle appears to have invited him to a " Correspondencie," and to have suggested some definite scheme of payment. It is difficult to tell in what way his more official position affected his activities.[4] He continued to work in conjunction with Searle's staunch supporters Colonel Drax and Martin Noell, and when he made the suggestion that the Governor should write letters occasionally " civilly acknowledging and importuning . . . favour " the task of adding " the superscription or direction thereof " was to be left, not to Povey alone, but to all his friends at home.[5] Nevertheless Povey desired a letter

[1] B.M. Add. MS. 11410, f. 21.
[2] The letter to Virginia is undated and unsigned, but it is in Povey's letter-book (1655–60), B.M. Add MS. 11411, ff. 19–20.
[3] B.M. Add. MS. 11411, ff. 27–8, letter dated 3 April 1660.
[4] The first letter written in this new relation was dated 9 June 1659.
[5] B.M. Egerton MS. 2395, ff. 176–81. The same letter is in B.M. Add. MS. 11411, ff. 90–5.

"upon everie shippe that comes," and his report to the Governor at the end of 1659 shows a considerable care of the Governor's concerns.[1]

Embassies from the Islands.—There was before the time of the Restoration yet another type of representative whose activities point forward to later developments. The "principal correspondent" of the Governor and the merchants and planters in England all lacked any form of official position recognisable by the home government. From the earliest times before the outbreak of the Civil War, there had been felt from time to time the need for some official sponsor at home: and to meet this situation there appeared so-called agents acting on behalf of their islands as a whole. How these agents were appointed it is not clear, but it seems probable that, while they were as a rule residents of the islands coming home on their own business and entrusted with the cares of the colony before their departure, in times of great urgency they were specially sent home to represent the islands. Thus, in 1640 Edward Cranfield and Edward Shelley attended "his Ma^{ty} and their Lo^{ps} from the Inhabitants of Barbados."[2] Later, in the troubled times that followed the death of Charles I, Captain George Martin came to England from Barbados, on a mission variously described as to gain for Lord Willoughby a commission from the Parliament, and to invite, perhaps with doubtful honesty, the return of those adherents of the Parliamentary party who had fled from the island.[3] For the other islands the evidence of such embassies is

---

[1] B.M. Egerton MS. 2395, ff. 176-81.
[2] C.O. 1:10, p. 47, 10 Jan. 1639/40.
[3] C.O. 1:11, No. 25, 25 Nov. 1650.

18 COLONIAL AGENTS OF WEST INDIES

still more incomplete. In 1659 there appeared one Captain Roger Morton, described as "Agent for the Island of Nevis."[1] A little earlier in 1656 the Governor of Antigua, Colonel Christopher Keynell, came home "by y? desire of his Councell & y? whole Inhabitants ... wholely upon his owne Charge to give an account of the said Island and to sollicit his Highnes on theire behalfes."[2] And at the time of the Restoration two members of the Army in Jamaica, Captains Thomas Lynch and Epinetus Crosse, were in England partly on their own concerns and partly on the business of the island.[3]

When Charles II returned to England, therefore, several distinct indications foreshadowed the growth of the agent's office. There were the merchants, whose power during the Interregnum had been so conspicuously great, and there were West Indian planters, temporarily or permanently absentees from their estates: both regarded as repositories of knowledge on colonial matters. There was the Governor's correspondent, permanently residing in London, employed to look after his personal interests; and there had been from time to time special agents sent over from the colonies who were regarded as representing the islands as a whole. The Restoration period with its important decisions in connection with the islands brought about a coalescence of these

---

[1] C.O. 1:13, No. 67, 10 Feb. 1658/9. It seems likely from the context that Morton was defending Governor Russell and his predecessors from certain aspersions cast upon them.

[2] C.O. 1:13, No. 7, 15 July 1656.

[3] C.O. 1:14, No. 52, 28 Nov. 1660. They stated that they had received their furlough to come to England "about Eight months since."

COLONIAL PROBLEMS

elements, so that there appeared for the first time agents who, like the Governor's correspondent, were permanently resident in London, and like the agents who came over from the colonies looked to the whole island for their directions.

CHAPTER II

THE RESTORATION SETTLEMENT

THE years immediately following the Restoration are of extreme importance in the history of the British Empire. In the east they saw the acquisition of Bombay, in the west the transfer from Holland to England of the Middle Colonies, New Jersey and New York. But, more significant than this, they were characterised by consolidation, the settlement on a firm basis of problems, which had, indeed, hardly been so pressing in earlier times, but which were, nevertheless, inherited from the years of the Interregnum and the reigns of the early Stuart kings.

It is easy to exaggerate the degree to which the period of the Interregnum constituted a break in colonial development. In matters of imperial administration, of local government, and commercial regulation there were tendencies continuous throughout the seventeenth century. In the time of James I and Charles I, when the control of the plantations first became a practical problem, the machinery employed was the Privy Council, the immediate circle of the king's advisers; and when business required, committees of the council had been appointed.[1] With the downfall of the royal power, the function of the Privy Council of necessity ceased, and for a short

[1] Andrews, *British Committees*, pp. 13-20.

THE RESTORATION SETTLEMENT

time the Long Parliament undertook the whole management of colonial matters through a commission of its own members.[1] This system was, however, quickly abandoned. As soon as a settled executive was established in the Council of State, the direction of the colonies fell under its purview, and the treatment accorded by the Council and its committees was very similar to that of preceding times.[2] Later, when it was thought necessary to commission separate boards to deal with trade and the plantations,[3] precedent can be found, if not in Laud's council of 1634, which was in reality a committee of the Privy Council,[4] at any rate in the successive Commissioners for Virginia of 1623–31,[5] and earlier still in the Tudor councils established to control outlying parts of the mother-country.

In the history of the government of the islands there can be traced the same continuity despite apparent change. The authority of the Proprietor of the Caribbee Islands, represented by the Earl of Carlisle's lessee, Francis Lord Willoughby of Parham, was abrogated by the terms of the surrender to Sir George Ayscue in 1652 :[6] the islands were in consequence brought for the first time since their settlement under the immediate control of the English government; in each island the governor was directly responsible to the Council of State. Yet the change

---

[1] *Ibid.*, pp. 21–3.
[2] *Ibid.*, pp. 32–3, 43–5.
[3] *Ibid.*, pp. 37–47.
[4] *Ibid.*, pp. 61–7.
[5] *Ibid.*, p. 14.
[6] B.M. Add. MS. 11411, ff. 95–7. The articles are printed in N. Darnell Davis, *Cavaliers and Roundheads in Barbados*, Georgetown, 1887, pp. 251–5, and Schomburgk, *History of Barbados*, pp. 280–3. Paragraph 19 of the articles disposes of the proprietary claims.

was not so sudden as it appears. As far back as the reigns of James I and Charles I the tendency may be seen towards the substitution of royal for proprietary government, culminating in the confirmation by royal commission of the appointment of proprietary governors.[1] Thus the abolition of the rights granted under the Carlisle patent may be regarded as a progression on lines already marked out, made more rapid by the troubles of the times.

Again, in connection with the commercial system there is no real revolution. The act of 1650, forbidding the trade of the colonies with foreign powers,[2] and the subsequent Navigation Act of 1651,[3] placed the restriction of plantation trade for the first time on a parliamentary basis. But at the same time the principles underlying the acts were by no means new, being implicit in the imperial scheme of the early Stuart kings.[4] A study of colonial development in the Interregnum forces into prominence the principle that the broad lines of evolution are determined, not by the wit of legislators, but by unrecognised forces latent in the circumstances of the time.

The Problems of the Restoration.—Despite this, however, the passing from the rule of the Protectorate to that of the returned Stuarts constituted a real epoch in colonial history. If the policy of the In-

---

[1] Francis Lord Willoughby received the confirmation of his appointment from Charles Prince of Wales in 1647. On the general tendency see H. L. Osgood, *American Colonies in the Seventeenth Century*, New York, 1904-7, vol. i, pp. 26-8.

[2] C. H. Firth and R. S. Rait, *Acts and Ordinances of the Interregnum*, 1642-60, vol. ii, London, published by His Majesty's Stationery Office, 1911, pp. 425-9, especially p. 427.

[3] *Ibid.*, pp. 559-62.   [4] Beer, *Origins*, pp. 220-40.

THE RESTORATION SETTLEMENT 23

terregnum had proceeded on lines indicated in earlier times, there had been nevertheless considerable and important change. The movements which formerly had been tendencies hardly noticed by contemporaries, had now received a definite and formal recognition. It was necessary that, in connection with the problem of trade, the principles of the Navigation Act should be again enunciated or wholly abandoned: it was necessary that the claims of the Proprietor of the Caribbee Islands should be re-established, or else finally disallowed; while in addition there was, almost equally pressing, the question of making some decision as to the fate of Jamaica, whether it should be retained by England, and if so what should be the form of its government. And for the solution of such problems there was, as an immediate result of the return of the king, no machinery in existence.

Such a situation was well calculated to galvanise into activity the various groups of persons at home who were interested in the West Indian colonies. In the history of the agency the true interest of the ten years that followed the Restoration lies in the activities of these groups. There, it is possible to trace the gradual growth of an element of permanency in the representation of the islands at home. Throughout the period of development the exercise of functions preceded formal recognition, and a large measure of importance therefore attaches to the unofficial solicitations carried on by these planters and merchants. Slowly during the course of this decade the link between the islands and these voluntary sponsors became more definite, until finally, immediately after its close, there appeared for Barbados an agency recognisably similar to those of later years.

As yet for some time the most marked development was that connected with Barbados. To that island in 1660 belonged the greater number of the absentee planters in England, many of whom had been banished during the successive revolutions of the Interregnum, and there, also, lay the greater part of the trade of the London merchant adventurers, who, although they had been in high favour during the previous decade, remained to exert a great influence on the settlement of the Restoration.

But, while these groups were predominantly interested in Barbados, the other islands were not without spokesmen. Even Jamaica, despite its very recent acquisition, could look for support from friends at home. It was early determined that Jamaica should be retained by the restored monarchy, and during the last few months of the year 1660 and the early part of the following year it was provided that a civil government should be established under Cromwell's military governor, Colonel D'Oyley. And while these decisions were being made, not only were there still in England during the first few months the two captains Crosse and Lynch,[1] but, when in September it was ordered by his Majesty in Council that the business of Jamaica should be considered,[2] there were other persons who could be consulted, those "that have been imployed unto, or have traded thither."[3] For the Leeward Islands, too, there were in 1660 certain planters in England whose estates lay in the islands,

---

[1] *Vide supra*, p. 18.

[2] The machinery constituted was a sub-committee of the Council for Foreign Plantations, *vide infra*, p. 34. The sub-committee met at the Grocers' Hall.

[3] *A.P.C.* i, No. (489), p. 298, 5 Sept. 1660.

THE RESTORATION SETTLEMENT 25

and there were merchants who traded thither. But in neither case was their influence comparable to that of the partisans of Modyford or the merchants who sought to dictate the policy in relation to Barbados. In the struggle of the years immediately following the king's return, although the Leeward Islands and Barbados were alike concerned, only a small part is taken by any of the planters and merchants but those concerned in Barbados. The settlement of Jamaica was too little advanced for a prominent place to be taken by its affairs, and the Leeward Islands were still as yet many years behind Barbados in economic development.

Nevertheless certain planters and merchants concerned in the Leeward Islands were the first of all the groups of the West India interest to take action after the return of Charles. The matter was one of personnel: the appointment and confirmation of the governors of St. Christopher and Nevis. Captain Philip Ward had been granted a commission by the Council of State as governor of St. Christopher in 1659, after some discussion of his appointment in the place of Colonel James Russell in Nevis;[1] but the matter had been postponed pending the restoration of Charles.[2] It was therefore petitioned in June 1660 that Russell should be continued in Nevis and the appointment of Ward confirmed for St. Christopher. One of these petitions was referred to the Privy Council; and while no decision on their subject was reached, the important result followed of the creation of the first piece of machinery for the control of the colonies established after the Restoration, a standing

[1] *C.S.P.* i, pp. 474-9. [2] *Ibid.*, p. 482.

committee of ten members of the Privy Council appointed on 4th July.¹

It had no doubt been expected that other problems more fundamental in character than those raised by the planters and merchants of Nevis and St. Christopher would soon come up for solution. And it was not long before this was so. On 9th July Lord Willoughby was directed by the king to take up his responsibilities as governor in Barbados and the other Caribbee Islands, in accordance with his position as lessee of the Earl of Carlisle's rights, and orders were sent to the islands that his claims to authority should be recognised.² No sooner had this been done, however, than interested persons in England commenced to protest, and on 16th July the first hearing was given by the Committee for Plantations of Lord Willoughby on the one side and " severall Merchants Planters in the Barbadoes " on the other.³ The hearing of the two parties was continued through July and August, being complicated by the claims registered by the son of the first settler of Barbados, Sir William Courteen.⁴ On 30th August the committee reached its decision :

> It is the opinion of the Comittee that the Lord Willoughby ought to be restored to the Governm^t of that Island & to

¹ C.O. 1:14, No. 15, and *A.P.C.* i, No. [484], p. 295. See also Andrews, *British Committees*, pp. 61–3. The Committee was directed " to meet and sitt as a Committee every Munday and Thursday at Three of the Clock in the afternoone, to receive heare, examine, and deliberate upon any Peticions, propositions, Memorialls, or other Addresses wch shall bee presented or brought in by any person or persons concerning the Plantacons, as well in the Continent or Islands of America."

² C.O. 1:14, No. 18 (*C.S.P.* i, p. 483).

³ C.O. 1:14, No. 20 (*C.S.P.* i, pp. 483–4), and *A.P.C.* i, No. (485), p. 296.   ⁴ C.O. 1:14, No. 35, Aug. 1660.

THE RESTORATION SETTLEMENT 27

be there placed in the same condition as when he was dispossessed of it by the illegal power of Cromwell etc. As for the validity of the Pattent, whereby Mr. Kendall & the rest doe claim, they are to be left to the Law.[1]

In accordance with this ruling Lord Willoughby resumed the exercise of his responsibilities with regard to the islands, and took the first action in this connection by issuing a commission in October to Colonel Watts to be governor of St. Christopher.[2]

Barbados.—With reference to Barbados, round which the main interest still centres, no steps were as yet taken. There, on 16th July, instructions had arrived from the Council of State requiring the deposition of Daniel Searle from the government and the instatement of Colonel Modyford, an end achieved by the joint intrigues of Modyford's friends in England led by John Colleton and aided by the favour of General Monk.[3] At the same time, however, there came the news of the restoration of the king, and Modyford's position was thus from the beginning rendered insecure.

The change of governors proceeded peaceably, and Modyford immediately issued a proclamation recognising the authority of the king. Nevertheless, not without some cause, he desired further measures to strengthen the foundations of his power, and accordingly on 1st August

> The Governor and Councell did ... press the gen^n of the assembly to consider of and provide for something

---

[1] C.O. 1:14, No. 42, 30 Aug. 1660.
[2] C.O. 1:14, No. 50, 27 Oct. 1660 (*C.S.P.* i, p. 490).
[3] Both Colleton and Monk were relatives of Modyford. *Vide sub* Modyford in *D.N.B.*

to bee sent to the King's most Excellent Majestye as a present, as alsoe for an Agent to bee sent home to England in behalfe of this Island. . . .[1]

With neither of these suggestions the assembly appear to have been willing to comply, but on the same day at a joint meeting of governor, council, and assembly, it was decided to send home addresses to the king. It was at first proposed that Peter Watson should be asked to present them, but the governor and council stated their opinion

> that the addresses may bee Joyntly p^{r}sented by John Colleton, James Drax, Thomas Kendall, Jonathan Andrews, Tobias Frere, Edward Walrond, and Peter Watson Esq^{rs} so many of them as are willing, and that m^r Watson if hee pleaseth and the Gentlemen of the Assembly desire it, may bee the Convayor of it home. . . .[2]

Instructions signed by Modyford on behalf of himself and the council together with the speaker of the assembly were given to Watson to communicate to " our Loveing ffrends " in England.[3]

With these measures Modyford and his council were not satisfied, and they proceeded to recommend that a sum of money should be sent home to forward their petitions. The reason assigned was the possibility of a reimposition of proprietary rights: if it was too late to prevent this, the money would still be needed to secure from the holders of the patent certainty of tenure for their estates and freedom from impositions: if the decision was in favour of a royal government it might be necessary to purchase a

---
[1] C.O. 31:1, Minutes of Council in Assembly of Barbados, p. 22.
[2] C.O. 31:1, Minutes of Council in Assembly, p. 26.
[3] C.O. 31:1, Minutes of Council in Assembly, p. 27.

charter from His Majesty to guarantee the privileges enjoyed by New England and Virginia. The assembly, however, refused : news had reached the island that a royal governor was sailing for Nevis, and that another was coming to Barbados. If this were so, probably the patent had already been declared void; at the same time, if proprietary government was restored, the certainty of their tenure was already assured under an act passed by Lord Willoughby during his first government. Finally, they asserted that any purchase of privileges would require more money than the island could raise.[1] No more official responsibility for the action of the planters and merchants at home can be assigned to the legislature of Barbados than that involved in the instructions to Peter Watson and his associates.

The embassy of Peter Watson was much on the lines of those of former occasions. One item of his instructions is, however, of especial importance in connection with later developments. It required " that you & our said friends take all opportunityes to improve the good & freedome of this place and from time to time give us advice thereof." Opportunity was thus given for the planters and merchants to claim the authority of the island for negotiations not mentioned in the addresses.[2] But the main significance of the appointment is the association in the

[1] C.O. 31:1, Minutes of Council in Assembly, pp. 28–30.

[2] The main purposes of the address seem to have been to secure protection from a rumoured attack by Spain, and free trade, the latter probably referring to the possibility of the grant of a Mandamus to certain merchants in England to " ingross the trade of this Island : and in fine make us as poor and comfortless as the unfortunate Bermodans at this day are." On these two points special stress was laid in the instructions: C.O. 31:1, Minutes of Council in Assembly, pp. 28–30.

affairs of the island of a group of planters in England, perhaps the first of the many such connections in the history of the early agency of Barbados. The colonists in the islands looking for some means by which they could make clear their wishes to the government at home, had found the most obvious instrument in their fellow-planters. As yet there was no idea that at home or in the island their interests could be anything but the same. Of their own number some were ready on the spot to represent their views, and to them they naturally turned, trusting to common interest to produce action that they would approve. Henceforth, the key to the rise of the Barbados agency was to be the actions of this group, reaching the zenith of their importance in 1671-2, and retaining considerable influence during the remainder of the seventeenth century.

The planters and merchants at home, even before the arrival of this authorisation from Barbados, continued their representations regarding the patent. The decision of the committee on 30th August, confirming the action already taken by the king, did not end the dispute: for the appearance of rival claimants, the heir of the Earl of Carlisle and the representative of an earlier grant, James Earl of Marlborough, permitted the reopening of the whole matter, and Kendall, Colleton, and their friends had again an opportunity of pressing their case for a royal government.[1] It was during these renewed hearings that Kendall proposed the grant to the king of an export duty, a proposal which, though instantly disavowed by his

[1] Details of the whole of the negotiations are given in C. S. S. Higham, *The Development of the Leeward Islands under the Restoration*, 1660-1688, ch. i, pp. 1-26.

THE RESTORATION SETTLEMENT 31

fellow-planters, was a determining factor in the voiding of the patent, and led to the imposition of the much hated 4½ per cent. duty. By March 1660/1 it was clear that the decision would be adverse to the claims of the proprietors; but that at the same time Lord Willoughby would be continued in the government, the remaining two years before the verdict was given being absorbed in the apportioning of the payments to the various claimants under the patents.

Meanwhile in the island important changes were taking place. The addresses sent over by Modyford together with his council and assembly had been received with favour by the king, who appears to have considered the desirability of retaining him as governor,[1] but Lord Willoughby, acting in accordance with the royal authorisation of 9th July, despatched a commission in September to Humphrey Walrond, as President of the Council, to take over the government.[2] After some demur on the part of Modyford this change was carried out, and Modyford, returned a member of assembly at the session commencing in January 1660/1, once more led the opposition in the island.[3]

The change in government naturally altered the relations between the legislature and those who had been commissioned during Modyford's government to care for its interests at home, and brought into existence a desire to secure more effective representation. In May, Walrond and his council urged

> That the genⁿ of the Assembly would seriously consider with themselves and joyne with the President and Councell

[1] C.O 1:14, No. 58 (*C.S.P.* i, p. 492).
[2] C.O. 31:1, Minutes of Council, pp. 37–40 (*C.S.P.* i, p. 494).
[3] *Ibid.*, pp. 38–40 (*C.S.P.* ii, p. 1). He was elected Speaker of the Assembly in July 1661: *ibid.*, pp. 61–2 (*C.S.P.* ii, p. 49).

in makeing sume publique addresses to his Majestie, or the Lords of the Councell or Com^rs appointed by his Ma^tye, for forreigne Plantations, that noe . . . pson or psons whatsoever und^r any pretext or colour may be received or admitted to act anything in the behalfe or the name of the Inhabitants of this Island in any matter or cause whatsoever with(out) the approbation and consent of the Genn^rll Assembly of this Island for the time being.[1]

The assembly delayed to take such action: two months later news reached the President from Sir James Drax describing Kendall's offer of an export duty and giving information as to the recent Navigation Act.[2] The President thereupon made certain propositions to the assembly:

    1. That a pettičon bee forthwith drawne up unto his Ma^tye against the Act of Trade, soe farr as referrs to the transporting of sugars and against the propositions of four p ceñ now at home; . . .

    2. That a hansom present bee prepared and sent from the country unto his Ma^tye along with the said Pettičon.

    3. That the aforesaid Pettičon bee sent by a Confident of our owne imployed from heare to Negotiate our business and give us acco and that hee bee Enabled with a Competent Sume of money to make his Address in Court and prepare friends to his Majestye in our behalfe.[3]

But the assembly was no more favourable than they had been under Modyford. They replied that "they did conceive many things in the . . . proposalls to be good, yet they did not Judge the present time

[1] C.O. 31:1, Minutes of Council, p. 44, 9 May 1661.

[2] It is noteworthy that protests against the Navigation Act formed only a small part in the action taken by the island at this time. Its full significance in West Indian trade does not seem to have been recognised at this early date. Representations were made later on this point. *Vide infra*, pp. 125–6.

[3] C.O. 31:1, Minutes of Council, p. 53, 4 July 1661.

THE RESTORATION SETTLEMENT

convenient."[1] The President had warned them that a dissolution would follow if they persisted in refusal, their action being held to indicate complicity with factions at home.[2] The assembly, however, brushed aside this reflection upon them, protesting against the threat of the President.[3] The result was the dissolution of the assembly, and the sole objection raised by the proprietary party in the island against the voiding of the patent and the imposition of the export duty was Walrond's letter of the 29th March 1661, dissociating himself and the island from the intrigues and promises of Kendall, Colleton, and others, who were, as he asserted, really working for the reinstatement of Modyford.[4] In 1663, when Lord Willoughby finally reached Barbados, the strife of parties in the island and the action of the planters and merchants at home caused as much trouble to him as they had to Daniel Searle a few years earlier.

By this time considerable advance had taken place in England. The negotiations regarding the patent were all conducted before the Committee for Plantations appointed in July 1660. This committee was probably in existence for some years, reappearing in the re-

[1] C.O. 31:1, Minutes of Council, p. 55.

[2] "Wee feare there is a faction in this Assembly, wch will not permitt any proceedings in prejudice of the designes . . . against the people of this Island, at home, who care not to sell the hearts of his Ma^{tyes} Subjects here by Evill Ends, to obteyne his favor and opinion of them there " (C.O. 31:1, Minutes of Council, p. 54).

[3] " As to the Joyneing with any persons you call Agitators in acting anything privately for their owne Ends to the prejudice of the Inhabitants of this Island, wee doe perfectly abhorr and detest " (C.O. 31:1, Minutes of Council, p. 55).

[4] C.O. 1:15, No. 36, 29 March 1661, letter from Walrond to Secretary Sir Edward Nicholas.

34 COLONIAL AGENTS OF WEST INDIES

organisation of 1668,[1] but during the period 1661 to 1665 its significance in all matters except the voiding of the patent was overshadowed by that of the Council for Foreign Plantations nominated in December 1660. The membership of the Council was varied, including, besides the Secretaries of State and other members of the Privy Council, a number of experts; amongst them Lord Willoughby, the Earl of Marlborough, and several West Indian planters and merchants, Sir Peter Leare, Sir Andrew Riccard, Sir James Drax, Thomas Povey, John Colleton, Edward Walrond, Martin Noell, Thomas Kendall, Thomas Middleton, and William Watts.[2] And these, despite their individual differences of interest, worked side by side during the four or five years of the Board's activities.

The Council for Foreign Plantations shows some evidence of Povey's influence in its attitude to the agency. In the seventeenth century there is very little record as to the attitude taken by the home government to the developments in this direction, but in 1661 a definite policy was formulated by the Council. Early in that year two letters very similar in content were written to Barbados and Virginia, and another two months later to New England. In the letters to Virginia and New England, of the former of which drafts exist in Povey's handwriting,[3] there were inserted recommendations for the granting of powers to some persons at home:

[1] Andrews, *British Committees*, p. 87.
[2] The Commission is in C.O. 1:14, No. 59, 1 Dec. 1660. The "Orders and Proceedings" of meetings from 10 Dec. 1660 to 24 Aug. 1664 are in the same document. Povey and Noell were amongst the most frequent in attendance. See Andrews, *British Committees*, p. 64.
[3] B.M. Egerton MS. 2395, ff. 335, 336.

THE RESTORATION SETTLEMENT 35

And because it wilbe difficult to make any certaine judgm^t of affaires of such a varietie and at such a distance unless some persons experienced and interested therein be employed by you here who may be able to give a ready answer and accompt of such matters as may arise in consultačon and debate here. This Counsell doth advise and direct it as a thing very expedient that you doe appoint and instruct some Planters or such others as are knowing and concern'd in your affaires that are either now here or shall come from Virginia who may be able to represent and agitate such things as may tend to the advantage of his Ma^{ty} and of you his Collonie of Virginia.[1]

The corresponding letter to Barbados did not include this exhortation, no doubt on the ground of the unsettled state of its government.

The letter indicates the attempts Povey was making at this time to secure his own appointment as agent. During the greater part of the period covered by the meetings of the Council for Foreign Plantations Povey's influence continued hardly diminished from the time of the Interregnum. As in the days of Searle's governorship, he hoped for the development of an agency from the relation of personal correspondent to the governor. Nor was he without indications that his scheme would succeed. In February 1660/1 Lord Willoughby wrote to Colonel Osborne and Colonel Russell, Governors of Montserrat and Nevis, recommending them to address themselves to Povey in the event of his own absence from England on " ye Affaires of the Collonie or yor more particular Concernments."[2] At St. Christopher Povey's old partner William Watts was in command of the government, and in June 1661

[1] C.O. 1:14, No. 59, 18 Feb. 1660/1. The letter to New England differs somewhat in wording.
[2] B.M. Add. MS. 11411, ff. 31-2, 19 Feb. 1660/1.

he received a letter from him acknowledging his great indebtedness;[1] and again the next month Povey, writing to his brother Richard in Jamaica, spoke of his friendship with the new governor of that island, Lord Windsor, and said he supposed he would be left at the governor's departure " his principall Correspondent and that the Affaires of Jamaica will from time to time (be) transacted heere by mee, as intrusted by his Lo^{pp} and ye Island."[2]

Yet Povey, despite his multifarious activities and painstaking negotiations, can lay little claim to a place among the early agents of the islands. Except for the short period when he was the paid correspondent of Daniel Searle, he does not seem ever to have had other than honorary charge of the affairs of any governor in the islands, and with the assemblies there is no evidence of any intercourse at all. The Barbados assembly, in the years immediately following the Restoration, was dominated by a party with which Povey was prohibited from intercourse by his alliance with Lord Willoughby. By the time the assemblies of Jamaica and Leeward Islands started to take an interest in the agency, his power had declined.

The period during which Povey's influence was at its height ended about the year 1663. In that year there came to light the intrigues of a rival candidate for the Barbados agency. On the departure of Lord

---

[1] " Yo^r favo^r have been soe many that I blush to think how ungratefull & remissive I have been to you, my time hath been very little here yet & my Expence very greate yet when I shall be in a Capacitie to enlarge myself & pforme my obligations I shall not be wanting. . . . I begg yor ffurther Correspondence." B.M. Egerton MS. 2395, ff. 303-4, 19 June 1661.

[2] B.M. Add. MS. 11411, ff. 33-4, 14 July 1661.

THE RESTORATION SETTLEMENT

Willoughby from England a recommendation was made to him :

> That some Discreet and able person residing here in England neere unto o^r Court should be enterteyned by yo^u to sollicite and negotiate yor concernem^{ts} wth Us our Councell and Principall Secretaries of State . . .[1]

And, it was added, since it was understood that no one had yet been appointed, Colonel Philip Froude, the Secretary of the Council for Foreign Plantations, would be a suitable choice. Nor was Froude content with this testimonial. He had secured the support of Modyford's party in the Assembly, having obtained " letters from ye Lord Bartlet & others, whoe desire (by Modiford) of o^r Assembly y^t he may be there Agent, & not his Co-rivall & Antagonist Mr. Povey." [2]

The competition was unfortunate for Povey's ambitions. His brother William told him that the assembly " intend to raise five hundred pounds for a present to there agent," and that he would certainly be the favoured candidate; for " they all Cry, no Westmistry man, wch was an affront to Modyford." But the result appears to have been that no agent was appointed.

At the time when Colonel Froude was prosecuting his ambitions for the agency, Povey was absent from the meetings of the Council for Foreign Plantations.[4]

---

[1] C.O. 1:17, No. 36, 5 June 1663. Draft endorsed " Mr. Frowd etc. w^n ye L Will. goes." A fair copy is in Dom. Entry Book, Chas. II, vol. x, pp. 86–7.

[2] B.M. Egerton MS. 2395, f. 383, letter from William Povey to Thomas Povey.   [3] *Ibid.*

[4] In the " Orders and Proceedings " of the Council there are recorded eight meetings between August 1662 and December 1663. Povey

And during the following years 1664 to 1666 he must frequently have been out of London on his work as surveyor-general of the victualling department. This period marks the end of Povey's dominance in the affairs of Barbados. Throughout the rule of Francis Lord Willoughby, and later in that of his brother William,[1] Povey maintained the intimacy he had begun in the days of Willoughby's exile; but its political significance was diminished. The two governors maintained a personal agent, John Champante,[2] and although the co-operation of Povey was sometimes asked,[3] it was Champante who appeared in public to defend their patron.[4]

Some revival in the political significance of Povey's correspondence took place apparently in the last two years of William Lord Willoughby's governorship. In 1672 Lord Willoughby wrote to him

> I have discourse my minde in Order to yor service to severall of my friends here & doe finde most inclinable to engage you before any in theire concerns, I shall omit noe opportunitie to promote that & by ye next conveyance doe hope to give you some account of that Matter.[5]

was present at a meeting of 11 August 1662 and again on 11 December 1663, but at none of the intervening meetings. C.O. 1:14, No. 59, pp. 46-54.

[1] Francis Lord Willoughby, governor 1660-6, died at sea in 1666. His brother, William Lord Willoughby, succeeded him as governor, 1667-72.

[2] Champante was a clerk in the Grand Excise Office; *vide* his own statement C.O. 1:19, No. 103, 2 Sept. 1665. This is the first notice of his agency.

[3] e.g. in 1670. B.M. Egerton MS. 2395, f. 470. Lord Willoughby to Thomas Povey, 24 Sept. 1670.

[4] Notably in 1667; *vide infra*, p. 43.

[5] B.M. Egerton MS. 2395, f. 484, 29 Dec. 1672.

THE RESTORATION SETTLEMENT 39

But Lord Willoughby's influence was insufficient for the purpose. Three months later no further instructions had reached Povey. He had presented the letters as directed to the Lord Chancellor and the Earl of Arlington, but he had been able to do nothing further.

> Each of them would have entered upon some Discourses of matters to which it seems yor letters related: but quickly finding the ignorance you thought fitt to continue mee in, by the reservedness of y^r Lo^{ppe} to mee, they said little to mee, supposing and rightly enough, that I was noe otherwise concern'd in y^r affairs, then to bee the Deliverer of the Letters.[1]

From this time no more is heard of Povey's candidature for the agency, for Lord Willoughby returned to England, and with his successor Povey had established no relations.

The explanation of Lord Willoughby's failure to secure Povey's appointment as agent was the old difficulty in Barbados of faction in the assembly. The removal of Modyford to Jamaica in 1664 did not destroy the power of the party he had built up to oppose first Searle and then Willoughby. In 1660 Modyford on his accession as governor boasted that it was his " great contentment " that he was the first who from a planter became a governor.[2] And this remained for many years the keynote of his party. By the time of Willoughby's letter of 1672/3, the assembly under the guidance of Modyford's followers had taken definite action with regard to the agency. But before that their

[1] B.M. Egerton MS. 2395, f. 487, Thomas Povey to Lord Willoughby, 15 March 1672/3. The greater part of this letter is printed in the Appendix, *infra*, pp. 257–8.

[2] C.O. 31:1, Minutes of Council of Barbados, p. 13, 1 Aug. 1660.

activities can be seen, working in conjunction with their old friends at home. In 1661, when the discussions as to the Carlisle patent were at their height, Francis Lord Willoughby had written to the Council of Barbados referring to the action of the planters and merchants in England who were opposing the re-imposition of proprietary government as " the stirrings of some Persons heere; who undertake to represent the Collonie; and having some privat ends of their own to bee assisted thereby."[1] And the representations of this group, despite its fluctuations in membership, as planters returned to their estates or came over to England, remained to cause considerable anxiety to Willoughby's brother. From his first arrival in the island in 1667 he was faced by difficulties in his assembly. There were certain " factious and seditious spirits" who presented an opposition to his policy. They maintained Modyford's tradition of a local patriotism :

> Their correspondents in England are Sr Peter Colleton a Chip of the old blocke Sr Paul painter formerly a worthy cobler Sr Peter Leare all Baronets and subtle M^r fferdinando George, who pretends kindness to me and is only for a Planter Governo^r in hopes to Arive to that Hono^r.[2]

It was from this group of absentee planters continuing in London the work of Kendall and John Colleton,

[1] B.M. Egerton MS. 2395, ff. 329–30.

[2] C.O. 1:23, No. 23. Account of Lord Willoughby's proceedings from his first arrival at Barbados, 23 April 1667 to 13 July 1668, signed W. Willoughby, 22 July 1668. In October 1668 the Assembly concurred in a proposal from the Council to send thirty butts of sugar to England for the presentation of addresses. C.O. 31:1, Minutes of Council in Assembly, p. 173, 17 Oct. 1668. It does not appear to whom they were to be sent, but later events suggest that it was to this group of absentees. *Vide infra*, pp. 47–8.

their history going back to the period of the Interregnum, that the agency was to develop, irrespective of the carefully laid schemes of Thomas Povey.

Yet in the history of the agency the work of Povey had by no means been in vain. In his endeavours to build up an office for himself he had demonstrated the uses to which the office might be put : when the agency appeared, its features for over a century and a half remained in a great measure those which he had foreseen. Further, in this early period when communications between one colony and another were extremely difficult, the ambitious designs of Povey, extending over several colonies, form an important connection to bind together in one the various lines of development scattered in different parts of the New World.

The Leeward Islands.—For some years after the Restoration, Barbados retained its position as commanding the largest share of interest in connection with the agency. Before the first decade was passed, however, signs appeared that for the Leeward Islands also a system of representation was being constructed. There, as in Barbados, there was growing up a political consciousness. In Barbados the spirit of local patriotism had shown itself in the " planter party," the opposition to the governor from England whether he was a Cromwellian or a Stuart nominee. In the Leeward Islands it took the form of a desire for separate government, in revolt at first against the rule of Lord Willoughby from Barbados, and, when this point had been satisfied, against the general government of the Leeward Islands established to take its place. As yet the first tendency only was to be seen. At the time of the dissolution of proprietary rule, no objection appears to have been raised to the supremacy allotted to Barbados, but as the decade wore on a vigorous opposition showed itself. The crucial event in the period was the French War of 1666. St. Christopher, Antigua, and Montserrat fell into the hands of the French, and much blame was attached to the government at Barbados for the insufficiency of the defence. It was, indeed, no easy matter to organise a defence of the Leeward Islands from Barbados as a centre,[1] and immediately following upon the disaster of the French War there commenced an agitation for separation.

The situation thus ensuing gave opportunity for George Marsh, an absentee planter of St. Christopher, to intrigue to obtain a position of honour for himself, by securing the separation of the islands from the government of Barbados and his own appointment as independent governor.[2] Like Modyford in 1652–60 he attempted to make the widespread feeling among the colonists serve the gratification of his own interest, but he did not experience even the brief period of triumph enjoyed by Modyford. In January 1666/7 the Privy Council Committee for Plantations discussed the rival representations put forward by Marsh and his friends and in answer by Lord Willoughby's agent John Champante, inclining to consider the case against Lord Willoughby as the better.[3] No definite action was, however, taken,[4] and some months later the planters and merchants in the Leeward Islands led by Marsh returned to the attack. The "proposalls"

[1] For an account of the geographical conditions making such an attempt difficult, see Higham, *op. cit.*, pp. 9–13.
[2] *Cf.* Higham, *op. cit.*, pp. 75–6.
[3] C.O. 1:21, No. 8, 23 Jan. 1666/7.   [4] *Ibid.*

THE RESTORATION SETTLEMENT   43

they offered to the king for the improvement of the government of the Leeward Islands[1] came up in October before the Committee for Plantations,[2] and, as before, John Champante was called upon to reply. Despite, however, Champante's answers[3] to the accusations against the Barbados government, the matter remained unsettled. In the winter of 1667–8, when William Lord Willoughby was visiting the Leeward Islands on his way to England, he secured from them some kind of repudiation of the representations then being made on their behalf,[4] and upon his arrival in England he was granted a renewal of his commission as governor of all the islands.

The question of the restitution of St. Christopher and reparation to be granted by the French gave opportunity in 1670 for the revival of the whole matter. Fresh petitions of the planters and merchants resulted in a rehearsing of the claims before the newly founded Council for Trade and Plantations.[5] Lord Willoughby, representing the interest of Barbados, was aided by various of the Barbados planters and merchants in England, including Sir Peter Colleton and Edward Drax, but the Leeward Islands' interest triumphed. In September the Council for Trade and Plantations

[1] B.M. Egerton MS. 2395, ff. 455–6.
[2] Probably referred by Council to Committee 2 Oct. 1667. *A.P.C.* i, No. 726, p. 441.
[3] B.M. Egerton MS. 2395, ff. 457–8.
[4] *C.S.P.* ii, Nos. 1665, 1668, 1676, 1688, 1692–4.
[5] Higham, *op. cit.*, pp. 74–5, where a carefully documented account is given of the whole matter. *Cf.* Schomburgk, *History of Barbados*, p. 293. Schomburgk was enabled to use a source at present not available in England: the minutes of the Councils of Trade and Plantations of the years 1670 to 1674. *Vide infra*, Appendix III, p. 297.

made report in favour of the separation of the government,[1] and despite subsequent negotiations, during the course of which Lord Willoughby sought to obtain again a repudiation from the islands,[2] this decision was upheld.[3] In January 1670/1 Sir Charles Wheeler was appointed first Governor-General of the Leeward Islands.[4]

The appointment of Sir Charles Wheeler closes the period during which the first beginnings of the agencies can be traced. As yet there had been no agent of the normal type, resident in England, in the constant employment of the islands. But with the opening of the year 1671 the first such appointment was only a few months distant. By that date for Barbados and the Leeward Islands the conditions governing the development had become manifest, bred in the changes and troubles that marked the Restoration in the islands.

In Barbados the governors had found the strength of that party at home which maintained a constant intercourse with the most difficult section in the assembly. The little group at home, too, had grown in community of feeling during the years of common action, despite its frequent changes in personnel. The growth of this group and the recognition paid to it by the Barbados legislature in 1660 are important factors foreshadowing the coming developments. And there is, moreover, another significant feature. In 1660, when the king returned, the most influential element in the West India interest was the circle of merchants whose rise

---

[1] *C.S.P.* iii, No. 268, 22 Sept. 1670.
[2] C.O. 31:2, Barbados, Journals of Assembly, pp. 21–3. Letter from Lord Willoughby to Colonel Codrington, London, 7 Nov. 1670.
[3] *C.S.P.* iii, No. 339, 17 Nov. 1670.
[4] *Ibid.*, Nos. 392–7, Jan. 1670/1.

THE RESTORATION SETTLEMENT 45

to power had been caused mainly by the share they took in the Western expedition of 1655. By the end of that decade their action had become no longer of paramount importance. The interest of Noell had early left the West Indies, and Povey's schemes disappear after the death of the second governor, Lord Willoughby. Povey's ambition set forth in his letter of 1672/3 of building up an agency of the whole island out of the correspondency with the governor was already impossible to be realised. For many years to come the governors were to maintain personal agents, but their political significance vanished as there grew up, first in Barbados and then in the other islands, political consciousness demanding a principal share, if not a monopoly, of the control of the agent. The Leeward Islands were not long behind Barbados. The separation of their government had given opportunity for the expression of separatist tendencies, and the history of the rise of their agencies during the following period is one of the fight of these sentiments for predominance against the ever-present fear of French attack. The character of affairs in Jamaica had hardly yet become visible; but the rapid commercial progress of the island had enabled it, already, nearly to overtake the older colonies in development, and the civil settlement had made way for the development of the constitutional position out of which the agency arose.

CHAPTER III

THE EVOLUTION OF THE AGENCIES, 1670–1700

THE last thirty years of the seventeenth century saw the establishment of agencies in all three of the larger West Indian colonies. By the opening of this period the most significant of the acts of settlement had been accomplished. Barbados and the Leeward Islands were no longer under proprietary rule; the government of the Leeward Islands had been separated from that of Barbados; a system of civil government had been set up in Jamaica. Moreover, in all three colonies there were vigorous representative institutions whose adherence to their traditional principles was to play a large part in the building up of the agency. By this time, too, many of the similarities that bound together in the history of the islands the periods of the Restoration and the Interregnum were beginning to disappear; and led by Barbados, the colonies were settling down to the commercial conditions and political interests which were to mark them in increasing measure through the eighteenth century.

Barbados.—The first indication of the attainment of this more advanced stage in the history of the agency was occasioned by the first of several organised fights against a threatened imposition on sugars. In 1670 Charles II was greatly in need of supplies, and it was proposed to lay additional taxes on several com-

THE EVOLUTION OF THE AGENCIES 47

modities, amongst them sugar.[1] At that time William Lord Willoughby was still in England carrying on correspondence with his agent Champante, and to some extent with Thomas Povey, regarding the claims which were put forward by the Leeward Islands; he was also soliciting the grant of the petitions entrusted to him by the Barbados assembly on his departure from the island in 1668. Lord Willoughby's representations had not met with any great success, and in November 1670 the assembly fell back on the expedient to which recourse had been made ten years earlier during the governorship of Modyford. On 17th November two letters were written by the speaker of the assembly, one to Lord Willoughby and the other to " the Gentlemen Planters in London."[2] The former of these, having set forth the gratitude of the island for Lord Willoughby's efforts on its behalf,[3] went on to describe the new measures the assembly was taking to secure attention to its interests:

> And for that wee are not Certaine of you^r Lordshipps stay in England, or that some other of you^r weighty affairs may in some measure not pmitt such Attendance from time to time as our affaires may Require wee have Requested some Gentlemen Planters o^r ffreinds Resident in London to afford their uttmost assistance in Accomplishing o^r Desires to his Matie by yor Addresses. . . .

The assembly were evidently apprehensive lest their action should be construed as a reflection on Lord

---

[1] *Cf.* letter dated 1 May 1671, printed in Appendix III, *infra*, pp. 262-5.

[2] Both letters are entered in full in the Journals of the Barbados Assembly: C.O. 31:2, pp. 11-13.

[3] In October the Council and Assembly voted to Lord Willoughby 1,000 lb. of sugar in recognition of his services. C.O. 31:2, pp. 2-4, 21 Oct. 1670.

Willoughby's services, for they " earnestly desire " him to take it " in Good part " and that he will " bee theire Director as in you^r Grave wisdome shall seeme meet and Convenient."

The idea in the minds of the colonists was no doubt the same as that determining their procedure in 1660. The Gentlemen Planters in London were not only to represent the specific addresses entrusted to them, but they were to exercise a general care over the interests of the island :

> And if at any time you may find opportunity of Presenting anything on our behalfes to his majestie or Committees whatsoever, that you will with all due Care & Industry be mindefull of us, And if at any time anything may be started that may be prejudiciall to this place you worke them to a prevention & by all opportunity let us Know how all things move, that wee may still apply ourselves to his Excellency and your selves. . . . And what Charge in prosecution may be expended wee will with hearty thankes & due acknowledgement Discharge to Content, out of the first goods shall be Raised for any Publique use. . . .

The terms of the request showed little development from the time when Peter Watson brought over the petitions of Modyford and his council and assembly in 1660. Several, too, of those empowered at that time were still prominent amongst the group at home, Colleton and others of those who troubled Lord Willoughby in 1668, Sir Paul Painter and Ferdinando Gorges. In the intention of the assembly there seems to have been no desire for any more definite relations with the planters at home than those established on previous occasions.

The letters written in November, however, had not yet reached London when events at home pre-

THE EVOLUTION OF THE AGENCIES 49

cipitated an important advance. In a letter written on 14th December the planters in England, after some friendly advice as to the interests of the island, gave an account of the threatened danger of a sugar tax, so adjusted as to raise the menace of foreign competition.[1] The conditions at home were unfavourable to the cause of the opposition. The Court was in urgent need of supplies: the refiners in England wished to exclude from their province the producers of sugar in the islands, and therefore sought to vary the rates on the different grades of sugars so as to penalise any attempt at refining on the estates. The merchants trading to Portugal wanted to ensure that no preference should be shown to plantation goods. And the Barbados merchants, angered by the laws made by the colonial legislature concerning debts, had been induced to support the refiners.[2] The position was one that demanded the greatest efforts from those whose prosperity depended on the success of the sugar plantations.

The Gentlemen Planters in their letter of December pointed out the burdens they were attempting to bear: constant attendance in Westminster, and, moreover, considerable expenses. They doubted how long they would " thinke it our Interest at our particular charge to withstand a General Inconveniency."[3] They suggested a remedy for this situation. In the

[1] The letter reached Barbados in March, being entered in the Journals of Assembly under date 7 March 1670/1. C.O. 31:2, pp. 15–17. The most important section of the letter is printed in Appendix III, p. 259.

[2] An account of the whole negotiation was given by the Gentlemen Planters in London in May 1671. C.O. 31:2, pp. 45–9. *Vide infra*, Appendix III, pp. 262–5.

[3] C.O. 31:2, p. 15.

first place, as had been proposed in earlier years, the island should " Lodge some Stock in England . . . for defraying the Charges." The supplies were to be entrusted to certain persons nominated by the colonists without whose orders no expenditure should be undertaken. But the advice went further:

> wee doe also desire that you would allow a Sallary to a person of some quallity who shall Constantly attend the General Councelle & from time to time give notice to us what is in Agitation Relating to Barbados.

It was this suggestion that constituted the innovation, the first proposal for the empowering of an agent resident in London responsible, not, as had been the idea of Povey, to the Governor, but to the assembly of the island. It was an important step forward in the development of the agency.

The letters written by the assembly in November reached London almost immediately after the Gentlemen Planters had despatched their letter to Barbados;[1] and were welcomed by the circle in London as an authorisation of the action taken on the island's behalf. In their next letter written in February they gave " humble thanks for the great trust and Confidence " shown in them, and assured the assembly of their zeal in the interests of the island.

Moreover, immediately they took further action,

[1] The letter to Lord Willoughby seems to have arrived the same day; and he communicated it on the 15th December to Colonel Henry Drax, the only one of the Planters who attended him when he asked their advice. Letter from Lord Willoughby to the Deputy Governor dated 20 December 1670, C.O. 31:2, pp. 17–18. The letter to the Gentlemen Planters was said by them to arrive after the dispatch of theirs of the 14th December. Letter dated 17 Feb. 1670/1, C.O. 31:2, pp. 33–5.

THE EVOLUTION OF THE AGENCIES 51

looking upon the instructions they had received as tantamount to approval of the schemes propounded by them. On 28th January the Gentlemen Planters in England, together with Lord Willoughby, constituted themselves a committee " to Consider of the best way how to promote your Petitions." The committee, later known as " the Committee for the Concern of Barbados," was to meet regularly "for the Business of Barbados " : one of the group was nominated as treasurer and the committee was enjoined " to Imploy such person or persons as they shall see Convenient " for their service. A former colonist of Barbados, Colonel Edward Thornburgh, was chosen for the time to attend the affairs of the island; and the Planters wrote in their letter of 17th February:

> Wee . . . doe humbly Recommend him to you as a fitt person to be Continued in that employment with a Sallary Convenient takeing into your Consideration ; that Buisness in this great Town is not (to) be done without great expense. . . .

Once more the letter from London was crossed by one from Barbados. The assembly had taken some time to consider what action was required in connection with the proposals of the Gentlemen Planters. At last, in April, information was sent to London that their advice had been accepted, and one of their number, Ferdinando Gorges, had been chosen

> to be our Solicitor who at all times and on all occations is Desired to appeare, in our behalfes before his Majestie Council & all Committees & an account of all proceedings there (in Relation to our Interest) to Render to you . . . for whose paines and Care we have by vote allowed him one hundred pounds sterling for one yeare. . . .[1]

[1] Journals of Assembly, C.O. 31:2, pp. 26–30. Letter dated 20 April 1671.

At the same time a letter of authorisation was sent to Gorges requesting him to take upon himself the duties of soliciting the business of the island.[1] The difficulty of the double appointment thus made was met by the resignation of Gorges and a further recommendation of Thornburgh, who was thereupon accepted by the assembly as their solicitor for the year then in progress.[2]

In the tale of the Barbados agents the first place may most properly be assigned to Edward Thornburgh. The manner of his nomination was, it is true, peculiar in that it was first suggested by the Barbados interest in London; and his instructions came similarly through this medium. Further, the assembly alone and not the whole legislature was concerned in his appointment. But despite these deficiencies the position of Thornburgh was far more closely allied to that of the later agents than was that of anyone who had previously acted on behalf of Barbados. He was resident in London, receiving a regular salary from the island; and he appeared on behalf of the colonists of Barbados, and not, as had Povey and Champante, merely to defend the reputation of the Governor.

The history of the Barbados agency from the end of the first year of Thornburgh's office was nevertheless still for some years broken in character. The system established by the co-operation of the assembly and the group of their friends in London broke down through a lack of unanimity over the question of appointment. At the end of 1671 the assembly,

[1] Letter dated 15 June 1671 addressed to the Speaker of the Assembly, C.O. 31:2, pp. 79–80.

[2] Letter dated 6 Dec. 1671 from the Assembly to the Gentlemen Planters, C.O. 31:2, pp. 87–91.

THE EVOLUTION OF THE AGENCIES 53

wishing no doubt to keep the nomination of the agent in their own hands, made choice for the next year of one Thomas Hinchman, who had, as he himself stated, " noe inheritance " in the island;[1] and in a letter dated 6th December 1671 the Speaker sent him instructions for him to act in conjunction with the Gentlemen Planters. In London, however, this action was viewed with disfavour. The committee of planters appointed on 28th January 1670/1 was still in existence, and when on 12th March Hinchman's appointment was discussed the matter was postponed upon the plea that Lord Willoughby was not present. Upon his attendance on 7th June 1672 Lord Willoughby left the whole matter to the planters, who thereupon decided that the position of solicitor should be entirely suspended

> till such time as wee shall Receive more particular Orders from the Assembly of Barbados, after the Arrivall of his excellency there, or further orders from them, except urgent occasions, require in the meane time. . . .[2]

In fact, however, Thornburgh continued his functions as before, as no doubt had been the intention of the planters from the first.

The attitude of the planters to the appointment of Hinchman caused some breach between them and the assembly, for after this incident little correspondence took place between them until the year 1675. Then their renewal of intercourse again resulted in divergency of opinion. The planters on this occasion

[1] Letter dated London, 11 March 1671/2, from Thomas Hinchman to Speaker and members of Assembly. C.O. 31:2, pp. 96-7.
[2] Meeting of the Committee for the Concern of Barbados, 7 June 1672. C.O. 31:2, pp. 108-9.

were asked by the whole of the legislature to undertake addresses to the king.[1] They received an apology for the recent neglect of correspondence; and a gift of twelve butts of muscovado sugar to pay the expenses of the solicitations; " the nomination of Coll. Edward Thornburgh " was agreed.[2] Every effort seemed to have been made to secure successful cooperation.

But again difficulties arose. In 1677 Thornburgh, together with Sir Peter Colleton, who had recently returned from Barbados, presented a petition to His Majesty from " the planters & merchants concerned in . . . Barbados " for the shipping of pikes for defence in case of a French war. They experienced some difficulty in securing a favourable report from the recently constituted committee for trade and plantation affairs, the Lords of Trade, because no mention had been made of the necessity for pikes in the last letter from Sir Jonathan Atkins; but at last at a meeting of the King in Council at Whitehall on 23rd May 1677 the necessary order was obtained.[3] The

---

[1] " The House Repairing to his Excellency was by him, Desired to Adjourne till tomorrow morning, in order to Preparing a Letter, to the Gentlemen Planters in England Desireing theire Assistance in Presenting & prosecuting the Petition of the Councell, & Assembly to his Ma^{ty} for Removall of theire Grievances." C.O. 31:2, p. 176, 15 April 1675.

[2] " Wee Leave itt to you to appoint Coll Edward Thornburgh or what other person you shall thinke fitt, to sollicite the Buissness under you." The Assembly prevented the creation of an undesirable precedent by including in the vote of approval for the letter " the Nomination of Coll Edward Thornburgh." Letter dated Barbados 16 April 1675 from Council and Assembly to the Gentlemen Planters in England, C.O. 31:2, pp. 182-3.

[3] *A.P.C.* i. No. (1139), p. 707. See also C.O. 31:2, pp. 274-5.

THE EVOLUTION OF THE AGENCIES

news of this action caused immediate protest from the island. In a letter to the Lords of Trade it was stated that the pikes were entirely useless, that the planters had acted "wthout the least Authority or Direction from this place," and a request was made

> that noe such persons, may draw any mischiefe upon us, or be heard in ou^r behalfes, without ou^r particular Address to you^r Lord^{ps} for that purpose, or the Recommendation of ou^r noble Governo^r Sr Jonathan Attkins. . . .[1]

This second failure of the attempt to establish representation at home through the group of Gentlemen Planters with Thornburgh as agent for a time discredited this method of procedure. As yet the tradition of the office had not been established: the measure of responsibility reposed in the agent had not yet been determined. And it is significant of the incomplete recognition of the agency that the Lords of Trade, in considering the protest of Sir Jonathan Atkins against the action of Colleton and Thornburgh, laid it down as a principle

> That, his Matie will suffer any person to represent the state of things, in those parts, where their private interest, or knowledge, renders them apprehensive of danger and more especially when they are called upon to express their thoughts. . . .[2]

A further period of experiment was needed before the position of the agent was established.

A necessity for renewed representation arose in 1679. This time a more direct channel was set up, two members of the Planters' Committee, Sir Peter

[1] C.O. 31:2, p. 280, 3 Oct. 1677.   [2] C.O. 391:2, pp. 205-6.

Colleton and Colonel Henry Drax, being empowered to attend the island's business. They were requested

> that in all matters that Concerne, the Island of Barbados, you will appeare in our name & behalfes, before his Majestie & Councell, & in all other places where you shall Judge It needfull & Convenient, wee doe wholly rely upon your ffaithfullness, Care & Conduct. . . .

Any fear of independent action was thrown aside, for the agents were assured that much was left to their own " Judgement & Discretion (especially in Suddaine Emergencies) " ; although they were at the same time urged to " take notice of such particular Desires & Instructions, as we shall commande . . . from time to time."[1] Colleton and Drax accepted the trust given to them, and appeared as the agents of Barbados whenever the affairs of that island were in question.[2]

To some extent, the agency of Colleton and Drax constituted an advance on that of Thornburgh a few years earlier, since they were placed in more direct relation with the legislature ; but, on the other hand, in other respects their position bore less resemblance to that of later agents. No mention was made of salary, or of the term of their office, and it appears

---

[1] C.O. 31:2, pp. 344–5, 16 April 1679. This letter came from the Assembly alone, but another of the same date to somewhat similar effect was agreed by Council and Assembly. *Ibid.*, pp. 338–43.

[2] Entries in the Journals of Assembly regarding the agency of Colleton and Drax occur under dates 22 October, 20 Nov. 1679, 15 April, 19–20 October 1680, 27 April 1682. C.O. 31:2, pp. 359–63, 367, 382–6, 401, 402, 481–2. In 1683 the Council sent for the accounts of the money expended by these agents on the island's behalf. It appears from this entry in their minutes that Colonel Drax was by that time dead. C.O. 31:1, p. 598, 7 Nov. 1683.

THE EVOLUTION OF THE AGENCIES

that their appointment was rather on the lines of the powers granted to the Committee for Barbados than on those of later agencies.

Six years later fear of an increased duty on sugar again called forth a desire for representation. Sir Peter Colleton and several other absentees were appealed to for aid, and requested to stir up William Blathwayt, Secretary to the Lords of Trade, in behalf of the colonists.[1] Again in 1689 a recurrence of similar conditions resulted in similar action, and once more an appeal was made to Sir Peter Colleton and the other planters then in London.[2] This time it was suggested by the assembly that a solicitor should be appointed to aid the planters, following upon the precedent of 1670. In 1685 the applications against the increased duty on sugar had been made with the full approbation of the governor,[3] and a share in the solicitations had been taken by his personal agent, Thomas Robson; and now when the representations at home were again considered necessary it was suggested that Robson should be chosen agent " in this affaire " if he " continue An Active Man at Court and a manager of business there and else where as formerly."[4]

The group of planters and merchants to whose direction Robson was referred contained several

[1] Letter dated Barbados, 16 Sept. 1685, from Speaker and Assembly to Sir Peter Colleton, etc. C.O. 31:3, pp. 134-5.

[2] Letter dated Barbados, 8 Oct. 1689, from Speaker and Assembly to Sir Peter Colleton, etc. C.O. 31:3, pp. 203-6.

[3] In 1685 an Act was passed requiring £500 sterling to be paid to the governor, Sir Robert Dutton, " to Defray the Charges of Sollicitting the Comutation of the Duty of ffour and halfe p cent, and other Occasions of the Country." C.O. 30:5, pp. 113-14, Act dated 3 June 1685.

[4] Letter dated 8 Oct. 1689, C.O. 31:3, pp. 203-6.

members not formerly included amongst those acting on behalf of the island. One of the most prominent in the negotiations was Edward Littleton, the author of the pamphlet *The Groans of the Plantations*, published to set forth the point of view of the colonists; another was John Gardner, a merchant who is later described by Oldmixon as having, together with an older member of the group, Sir John Bowden, " the largest Commissions from Barbados of any Merchants in England, and perhaps the largest that ever were lodg'd in one house in the West India Trade."[1] And further there was James Kendall, soon to be appointed Governor of Barbados, the first planter governor since the brief rule of Modyford.

The representation of this group was the last of such activities in the history of the Barbados agency. As in 1675, it was quickly followed by the more specific appointment of two agents to act directly under the control of the island. In 1691 Edward Littleton and William Bridges were chosen to transact the affairs of the island, a manifest injustice, Oldmixon asserts, to the merits of John Gardner, who had done considerable service to the island by unofficial representations.[2] But while in this appointment the precedent of 1679 was being followed, an important change occurred in the manner of payment. The new agents, like Thornburgh twenty years earlier, were to receive

[1] J. Oldmixon, *The British Empire in America*, London, 1708; vol. ii, pp. 53-4. The wording suggests that the change in the system of trade indicated above (pp. 10-12) had already started.

[2] *Ibid.* Oldmixon infers that Gardner had been proposed as a rival candidate in 1691. If this was so there is no record of it in the extant proceedings of council and assembly. The negative vote on his appointment took place on a later occasion in January 1693-4. C.O. 31:3, p. 361.

THE EVOLUTION OF THE AGENCIES

a regular sum each year, in their case £250 sterling each; and this was provided by a formal act of the legislature. The act was passed in September 1691,

> declaring in what manner the Sallary and expences of Edward Littleton and William Bridges Esqr (Agents in England appointed for the solicitting the affaires of this Island) shall be paid.[1]

In reality it was the first act of Barbados for appointing agents, and its successor in 1695, following closely on its model, included the appointment of the agents in its title.[2]

The Leeward Islands.—At about the same date a similar stage of development was reached in the history of the agents of the Leeward Islands, although the process of growth had been on somewhat different lines. Here, as in Barbados, forces applicable to all the colonies were working for the growth of the agency: the distance from the mother-country and difficulties of communication, the zeal of the colonists lest their interests should be overlooked by the authorities at home.

In the details of the development there are, however, certain differences, in the main attributable to divergency of conditions in the two colonies. In the Leeward Islands, throughout this period, and for some generations to come, fear of the French constituted an important factor in the islands' politics. In 1670, at the time of the establishment of the separate government of the islands, the negotiations regarding the restitution of St. Christopher in accordance with the terms of the Treaty of Breda were still in progress, and during the remainder of the century there was frequent

[1] C.O. 30:5, Act dated 1 Sept. 1691. [2] *Vide infra*, p. 81.

apprehension of French attack. The islands were defended by an English regiment, and received assistance from the English fleet in time of danger, but the fear of capture remained. There was, moreover, a further difference in the form of constitution. The several Leeward Islands were grouped in a single colony, and the existence of two governments, one general and one for each island alone, complicated all institutional growth. And lastly there was a personal factor. In 1672 the first Governor-General of the Leeward Islands, Sir Charles Wheeler, was succeeded by Sir William Stapleton, who remained in office until 1685. Stapleton was a man of great power, capable of influencing the course of events in the islands by his own personality, and his attitude was a matter of considerable importance in the development of the agency.

The Governors of the Leeward Islands, like those of Barbados, found it necessary to maintain a personal agent at home. The place taken by Champante and Robson in relation to governors of Barbados was filled by a succession of persons during the long rule of Stapleton: Ferdinando Gorges down to 1676, William Freeman from 1675 to 1682, Patrick Trant from 1681 to 1685. Unlike Champante and Robson, these agents were men of some importance in the history of the islands. Gorges was a member of a family already famous in colonial annals,[1] a prominent planter of Barbados, and the first choice of the Barbados assembly as agent in 1670. Freeman and Trant were London merchants trading to the islands, and Freeman was in addition the owner of estates in Montserrat. Their position approximated more closely to that

[1] *Vide sub nom.*, Ferdinando Gorges, *D.N.B.*

THE EVOLUTION OF THE AGENCIES 61

of Povey than Povey's successors as " principal correspondents " of the governors of Barbados. The activities of these agents were, it is true, very largely personal in character. Their main function was to receive the Governor's salary; but further they saw that the goods needed by the Governor in the island were sent out; the expenses of his family in England were paid; sundry gratuities were distributed amongst persons of importance in plantation affairs; and the Governor's interest was defended before the Lords of Trade. But, at the same time, some functions were performed which were of more concern to the islands as a whole : solicitations were made for the pay of the troops as well as for that of the governor; questions of reparation of forts, and the supply of labour, came occasionally under the hand of the agent; and he was called upon from time to time by the Lords of Trade, largely in his capacity as one with interests in the islands, to give information and advice in matters in which they were concerned. Whatever the functions, however, the agents remained responsible to the Governor alone, maintaining careful accounts with him, and charging to him a percentage on all business transacted.[1]

This measure of representation, although undoubtedly of value to the islands as safeguarding their concerns from neglect, was not sufficient for their needs. And, as had been the case earlier in the history of the islands, the circumstances were met by the sending home of agents. At some time in the years 1670–80 Captain John Symes was despatched to

[1] See Higham, " The Accounts of a Colonial Governor's Agent in the Seventeenth Century," in *American Historical Review*, January 1923, pp. 263–285.

obtain guns and ammunition.¹ In 1675 the arrears of pay due to the soldiers were so heavy and the resulting situation so dangerous that one Lieutenant Greatbach was sent to secure their payment.² His death early in 1676 cut short the period of his agency, and greater importance is to be attached to the appointment of Captain Joseph Crispe in 1678 and Captain Jory a little later. In April 1678 Stapleton received a fresh offer from his French neighbours of a Treaty of Neutrality to guarantee the continuance of peace in the islands despite the fortunes of diplomacy at home. The Treaty was concluded by Stapleton and the French Governor, de Blenac, and it was arranged that out of the hostages given by the two powers for the observance of the terms, one of each party should be sent home to obtain confirmation of their agreement. Crispe, a member of the council of St. Christopher, was sent home to represent the English colonists,³ and Captain Jory, a merchant resident in London, was employed later to assist him.⁴ The business of the

¹ The following entry occurs amongst the accounts of Montserrat: "Goods sent to Nevis to ye value of 7788^{lb} at 1^d p lb. is £32. 9. 0. ... to bear part of Capt. John Symes charges who was Imployed home to prcure y^{ee} guns and ammunition." Stapleton MSS.

² C.O. 391:1, p. 45, 2 Dec. 1675, and p. 69, 3 Feb. 1675/6; and Jeaffreson MSS., letter dated 22 June 1676 (J. C. Jeaffreson, *A Young Squire in the Seventeenth Century*, London, 1878, vol. i, pp. 193-4).

³ Minutes of Council and Assembly of St. Christopher, C.O. 1:28, No. 69, 26 June 1678. Although the appointment originated with St. Christopher it was agreed by the whole colony, *cf.* Stapleton's letter of 29 June 1678, *C.S.P.* v, No. 741, pp. 262-8.

⁴ There is no record of Jory's appointment; but in the journals of the assembly of Nevis under date 13 April 1682 there is the following entry: "That Capt Jory be paid his disbursem^{ts} on the articles of Neutralitie, the rest of the islands in the Generalls government

THE EVOLUTION OF THE AGENCIES 63

treaty was long protracted and eventually came to nothing, and Crispe while he was in London tended to assume in England the position of an accredited agent,[1] acting as spokesman for the islands in the question of the farm of the 4½ per cent. duty.[2]

The employment of Crispe and Jory was temporary in character, and for some time permanent appointments were delayed by a conflict of interests similar to that which deprived Povey of the agency. Governor Stapleton, like Lord Willoughby, desired the appointment of an agent who would attend to his personal concerns and also represent the whole island : and at first he met with success. In 1674 the islands, feeling their need of representation at home, sent commissions to Stapleton's agent Gorges to act on their behalf as well as for the Governor-General,[3] and provision

haveing paid their proportion." C.O. 1:48, No. 23. A similar motion was carried later, *ibid.*, No. 79. The island of Nevis paid in "Disbursem^{ts}" in soliciting the Treaty of Neutrality" in the period 1678–81 sugar to the value of £402 10*s.* 2*d.* currency. Stapleton MSS.

[1] The scope of Crispe's mission is not clear. St. Christopher, at any rate, seemed to intend his mission to be general. He was " to Goe for Europe for Hostadge and promoteing the Country as aforesaid and other Affaires of this Island." C.O. 1:28, No. 69, 10 Jan. 1678.

[2] C.O. 391:3, p. 46. The Barbados agents, Colleton and Drax, were dubious of Crispe's authority : " upon Inquiry wee Cannot finde that Crispe hath any power to treat in behalfe of the Leeward Islands, about this matte^r." C.O. 31:2, pp. 359–63.

[3] Gorges appears to be the agent referred to in the following extract from " The Humble Petition of the Representatives of his Majesties Islands, St. Christophers, Nevis, Mountserrat & Antigua : " . . . wee humbly supplycate y^r Maj^{tie} to Lend a ffavourable Eare to o^r Agent who hath received full & plenary Instructions from us, to Attend y^r Maj^{ties} Commission^{rs}, on that behalfe, whose Actings therein, on o^r behalfes, shall be a unviolated tye upon us for ye Just and true performance thereof." C.O. 1:31, No. 29, 26 March 1674.

was made for payment out of the public money.¹ The experiment was, however, unsuccessful. Gorges gave little attention to the interests of the islands, and he was dismissed from their employment.²

The dismissal of Gorges gave opportunity for the growth of agencies for which the employment of Jory had provided precedent, but which differed from this in that they concerned one island only. The first proposal on record for the maintenance of a permanent agent at home for any one island relates to St. Christopher. In that island in the year 1679 a serious attempt was made to secure the appointment as agent of Colonel George Gamiell, the father-in-law of a prominent planter of the island, Christopher Jeaffreson.³ The assembly proposed to allow him £100 sterling per annum as salary. But the unanimity of the local legislature was not sufficient to secure the

---

[1] The Accounts of Montserrat contain the following entry under date 1674 :

"To yᵉ publique stock of nevis for sugᵃʳ disbursed to pay Capt. Georg pʳ ordʳ of his Excellency as pʳ accᵗ from Capt Jnᵒ hugh Treasurer of Nevis 12000 sugʳ." Stapleton MSS.

[2] *Cf.* J. C. Jeaffreson, *The Young Squire of the Seventeenth Century*, i, p. 194 : "yᵉ Governor was pleased to discourse to me something concerning Capt. George whom yᵉ Island did imploy to act for them at home and allowed him two or three hundred pounds p Annum for wᶜʰ he did litle and when they ordered him to petition for a frigate or two to be sent hither for yᵉ security of yᵉ Islands and theire Trade . . . he sent them Answer yᵗ in tymes of peace they had noe occasion for such a security and in tyme of warre his Majestie had soe much to doe with his shippes yᵗ he could not spare one soe it is thought yᵗ they have withdrawn theire allowance to Capt. George." Letter dated 22 June 1676.

[3] Jeaffreson gives an account of the negotiations in his letter-book under dates 10 July, 9 Sept. 17 Nov. 1679, and 24 July 1680. It can be traced in J. C. Jeaffreson, *op. cit.*, i, pp. 228–42.

appointment. "Nothing of this nature is to be done without yᵉ consent of oʳ Generall," and so the Deputy-Governor was commissioned to secure leave " to employ a friend to take care of yᵉ affaires of this Island in perticular." After an initial agreement Stapleton refused his consent,¹ and, as Gamiell refused to serve on any less official basis, the scheme failed.

The next attempt to establish an agent for St. Christopher was more successful. In August 1682 Jeaffreson left the island to return to his English estates. Before going he had an interview with the Governor-General, and arranged to carry on certain negotiations on behalf of the island with respect to the transportation of convicts to assist in the peopling of the settlements. On his arrival, in accordance with his instructions, he approached William Blathwayt, the Secretary to the Lords of Trade, to obtain official approval of his scheme. He met with certain difficulties. Some were common enough, incidental to the solicitation of any public business at the time: constant waiting upon officials and the payment of heavy fees and gratuities before any advance could be made. But there were also others of a personal nature. After four or five months of negotiation Jeaffreson wrote:

> I am Labouring to doe something for oʳ Island tho it be a little against yᵉ hare for a private person to act in a publick concern unlesse otherwise capacetated that I am. . . .²

Again, a little later he reported his inability to do

---

¹ His opposition was probably due to his desire that the island should employ his personal agent, William Freeman.

² Jeaffreson MSS. Letter dated London 1 February 1682/3 (J. C. Jeaffreson, *op. cit.*, ii, p. 29); *cf.* the solicitation of Colleton and Thornburgh for Barbados in 1677 (*supra*, p. 55).

anything. Blathwayt had insisted that letters were necessary from Governor-General, Deputy-Governor, council, and assembly, to confirm and support his applications.[1]

At last in the year 1684 Jeaffreson was placed in a more favourable position. The Deputy-Governor and council in September 1683 recommended his services to the assembly:

> Whereas Capt Christopher Jeaffreson hath bin and still is very Active for the interest, and Promotion of the good of this Island more especially for the late recruit and for Cannon and other necessaries for his Maj^{ties} ffort on Cleverleys Hill, which he hath always negotiated at his owne Charge which could not be small he being a Stranger at Court It is therefore proposed that thankes be returned him for his great Care and good servis therein and that a Gratuity may be presented him in Consideration of the same or the reimburse his Expences.[2]

At first the assembly did not feel able to carry out the suggestion, the country being much in debt, but early in the new year Jeaffreson received a notification from the island that the Governor-General had consented to his appointment as " Agent for that Island of St. Christopher."[3] A present of £50 accompanied the notification, and, although Jeaffreson said he should spend this sum solely on the charges of solicitation,

[1] Jeaffreson MSS. Letter dated London 16 May 1683 to Deputy Governor Hill (J. C. Jeaffreson, *op. cit.*, ii, p. 59).

[2] Minutes of Council of St. Christopher, 20 Sept. 1683, C.O. 1:51, No. 98.

[3] Jeaffreson MSS. Letter dated London 25 August 1684 (J. C. Jeaffreson, *op. cit.*, ii, pp. 119–20). At the same time the Council of St. Christopher notified the Lords of Trade of the appointment. C.O. 391:4, p. 288, 7 May 1684. It is not clear to what extent the assembly participated in the appointment.

he may be regarded from this time as the official paid agent of St. Christopher. He remained in the employment of the island for at least two years, and probably until 1690.

Almost contemporary with Jeaffreson's period of office was the first agency of Antigua. Here the growth of the agency was dictated not, as in the case of St. Christopher, by the desire for immigration and defence, or, as in that of Barbados, by the need to defeat threatened duties on sugar, but by the requirements of the island in connection with their laws. The instructions to Governors required the sending home of all acts passed by the colonial legislatures for review by the King in Council, and in the twenty years following the Restoration obedience to this injunction became general. After the establishment of the Lords of Trade in 1675 a great increase in care was shown by the home government in the review of legislation,[1] and in February 1683/4 the first successful attempt was made to secure the confirmation of laws through the maintenance of an agent. In that month the Governor and council of Antigua recommended to the assembly that they should agree

> in Chooseing an Agent to serve this Island on all occations in England and Chiefely to sollicite for his Maj^s Royall Confirmation of our Lawes and desire your Concurrence therein.[2]

[1] Before this very little seems to have been done. In Feb. 1677/8 no acts had been confirmed except those granting the 4½ per cent. duty. C.O. 138:3, p. 182. Upon the downfall of Clarendon in 1667 some of the colonial acts were said to have been lost. C.O. 138:1, p. 98.

[2] Minutes of Council and Assembly, 27 Feb. 1683/4, C.O. 1:50, No. 81.

The assembly readily consented, fixing upon a member of council, Major William Barnes, as a suitable person for the office, and suggesting that he should be allowed £100 sterling per annum as salary. Major Barnes arrived in England shortly after this appointment and remained in the employment of the island probably until the year 1686,[1] acting in some of his negotiations in conjunction with Christopher Jeaffreson.[2]

The history of these earlier agencies of the Leeward Islands[3] shows the existence of two tendencies of importance in later development. The repeated services rendered by planters and merchants in England, either voluntarily or as definitely commissioned by the Governor-General or the legislatures of the islands, bear witness to the presence in London of a circle of persons interested in the islands similar to that which earlier

---

[1] In 1683 Barnes appeared on behalf of an act of Antigua before the Lords of Trade in opposition to certain merchants. C.O. 391:5, p. 138, 27 April 1685. In 1686 there was a motion regarding his payment in the council and assembly. C.O. 1:59, No. 49, 25 and 26 March 1686.

[2] Jeaffreson MSS. Letter dated London August y* 25th 1684 (J. C. Jeaffreson, *op. cit.*, ii, pp. 119–20).

[3] There were other temporary appointments of minor importance. In 1680 Colonel Bastian Bayer, a London merchant, was employed by Antigua to receive and expend money for the purchase of guns. He acted under instructions from the Governor and some of the Council. Minutes of Council of Antigua, 8 Dec. 1680 (Stapleton MSS.). In 1684 a planter of Nevis, Colonel Nethways, attempted to secure recognition as agent of that island. He took part in the presentation of the island's addresses and then requested for remuneration for his services. The assembly at first was inclined to refuse his claims, but finally it was agreed to give him " twenty Guinneys out of the publick stock to buy him a gelden, and to be noe farther concerned wth the publick busines." Journal of Assembly of Nevis, C.O. 1:53, No. 4, 4 August 1684.

THE EVOLUTION OF THE AGENCIES

came into prominence in connection with Barbados. And as in the case of Barbados, this group provided an element of permanence in the system of representation lacking in the sporadic empowering of agents by the councils and assemblies. Secondly, it is to be noted that while the islands in the group frequently acted separately in the caring for their interests at home, there had been from time to time when matters of special urgency were under consideration general agents commissioned by all the islands at the same time, and receiving remuneration of which all the islands provided a share.

The outbreak of the French war of 1689, bringing with it common dangers in which all the islands shared, brought to a head the development of a general agency. As early as 1682 Sir William Stapleton, in accordance with his policy of emphasising the general government of the colony in opposition to the particularist sentiments of the islands,[1] recommended at a meeting of the General Council and Assembly of all the Islands that a salary should be allowed to an agent at home; but the proposal was refused immediately by both Council and Assembly.[2] Seven years later, however, the French war changed the attitude of the islands, and at a general meeting of the Legislature of all the Islands it was decided to make formal provision for representation at home. Accordingly in November 1690 an act was passed

> appointing Commissioners and an Agent to Negotiate and Manage the Affairs of the Leeward Islands as also for settling

[1] Stapleton's policy is indicated in Higham, *op. cit.*, pp. 229-34.
[2] Minutes of General Council and Assembly at Nevis, 15 Nov. 1682, C.O. 1:50, No. 83.

of a Fund for the defraying of the Expence and Charge of such Negotiation.[1]

Five commissioners were named in the act: Bastian Bayer, formerly employed by Antigua; Jeaffreson, the agent of St. Christopher; Jeffry Jefferies and Joseph Martyn, both London merchants; and Richard Cary, another merchant soon to establish a long-standing connection with Nevis. This little group bears decided resemblance to the Committee for the Concern of Barbados of twenty years earlier. Their position was, however, more formal, constituted as it was by an act of legislature. The act laid down their functions and provided for the nomination of an agent, Samuel Gilliam, to act under direction from the commissioners. In 1694 Richard Cary was appointed to take the place of Gilliam as agent,[2] but little differentiation is possible between his functions and those of his fellow-commissioners, who appear together to have acted as the islands' agents during the period of the French war.

The system established in 1690 was not permanent in character; it lasted only for the duration of the war. Nevertheless in the Leeward Islands, as in Barbados, the period between the constitutional settlement of 1660–70 and the early years of the French war had seen the gradual development of the agency. The need for representation was fully appreciated, and the method of appointment, although not yet fully established, had received some recognition. Moreover, the act of 1690 constitutes a definite step forward, for the precedent of this more formal method

[1] C.O. 154:4, pp. 64–9, 8 Nov. 1690.
[2] Plantation Register, vol. i, pp. 300–2, Act dated 31 Aug. 1694.

THE EVOLUTION OF THE AGENCIES

of appointment was not allowed to slip by when the maintenance of general agents ceased.

Jamaica.—For Jamaica the course of events had been of quite a different character. There the development was not so rapid, and hardly began until the second decade after the Restoration. In 1660, indeed, two captains in the Jamaica army were in England soliciting at their own charge the affairs of the island; but there appears to have been no repetition of their activities. Possibly the successive governors of the island maintained personal agents. In 1676 a reference exists to one John Bindloss, agent to Sir Henry Morgan.[1] In the next year there appeared Sir John Griffith, described, as "Agent for Jamaica,"[2] but no details are available as to the character of his agency. The most significant fact is that during this period a circle of planters and merchants interested in Jamaica began to grow up, as they had for Barbados and the other islands. In 1680 the merchants and planters of Jamaica were heard by the Lords of Trade regarding disputes with the Royal African Company,[3] and two years later the Jamaica merchants took the leading part in certain actions concerted by those interested in all the islands as to regulations for the transportation of servants.[4]

The central event, however, in the development was the attempt by the home government in the years 1677 to 1680 to reorganise the method of legislation in Jamaica. The constitutional position

[1] Journals of the Lords of Trade, C.O. 391:1, p. 255, 24 Nov. 1676.
[2] *Ibid.*, p. 292, 6 Feb. 1676/7.
[3] C.O. 391:3, p. 229, 4 Nov. 1680.
[4] Jeaffreson MSS. Letter dated London 25 November 1682 (J. C. Jeaffreson, *op. cit.*, ii, pp. 5–6).

in the island had long been unsatisfactory. An assembly had met in 1664,[1] but the laws sent home for confirmation were not returned by the home government, and constitutional uncertainty was the result. The attempt of Sir Thomas Lynch as Governor in 1673 to persuade the assembly to employ someone " to sollycite for us " failed,[2] and repeated dissensions in the island justified the feeling at home that reform was necessary. The colonists, however, had no desire for a change. They regarded their legislative privileges as their " Magna Carta,"[3] and they were quick to resent any infringing of their claims. Their " just and inherent right " was asserted against " His Majesty's right of dominion," and one or the other it seemed must give way. The proposal of 1677 aimed at settling the contest in favour of the Crown. Henceforth Jamaica was to be governed on the principle of Poyning's Law :[4] the assembly was to be little more than a registering body. The new system was to be brought into force by a new Governor, Lord Carlisle, and in 1678 he reached the island to accomplish this task.[5] It proved too great for him. No party in the island would accept the scheme, and finally he sent home Major-General Sir Francis Watson to report his failure, and to seek to turn the minds of the administration from their purpose.[6]

The opposition in the island was led by Colonel Samuel Long, a member of one of the most famous

---

[1] C.O. 1:43, No. 172; cf. C.O. 138:1, p. 97.
[2] C.O. 1:30, No. 58, 12 Aug. 1673.
[3] C.O. 1:27, No. 21.
[4] C.O. 1:40, No. 71, 138:3, pp. 162–3, etc.
[5] C.O. 138:3, pp. 216–41, Instructions to Earl of Carlisle.
[6] C.O. 1:43, No. 48.

THE EVOLUTION OF THE AGENCIES

families of Jamaica; and in March 1679/80 it was determined by the Lords of Trade that Colonel Long ought to be sent home to answer the charges against him.[1] Long reached England in September and was duly heard, together with his accusers, before the Lords of Trade.[2] Together with several planters and merchants of the island then in England, Long represented the need for a return to the old system of making laws, and in November new instructions were drawn up for the Earl of Carlisle re-establishing the powers of the legislature on "the Barbados model."

The struggle and its issue showed clearly the dangers of a government so far removed from its source. Little over a month of negotiations had been enough to convince the administration that their plan was fruitless. A short period of personal contact had done what long correspondence could not do. It was obviously desirable that some attempt should be made to make permanent this personal relation, and the colonists were not slow to see it. Their end achieved, Long and his friends turned to other matters of concern to their island; in the same month a list of requests was handed to the Lords of Trade, and included amongst them was the grant of leave to the people of Jamaica to raise money in the island to pay the expenses of the solicitations of their affairs in England. The request was favourably received. On 16th December, upon the attendance of "the Earl of Carlisle, Coll Long, Mr Beeston and others Merchants and Planters of Jamaica" the Lords of Trade recommended

> that the Governor bee impowered to consent to a Law for Raising Money in order to the better carrying on the sollici-

[1] *C.S.P.*, v, No. 1318, p. 496.
[2] *Ibid.*, Nos. 1501, 1503, 1509, 1517, pp. 597, 599–600, 606.

tation of the Publick Affairs in England. Provided such levy doe not exceed 300¹ yearly. And in case the Governor shall not think fit to agree to such law, that then the persons concern'd may be permitted to make voluntary contributions for discharging the expence of their sollicitations provided such contributions doe not in any one year exceed the summe of three hundred pounds.[1]

And from this time until the close of the long struggle over the agency in the eighteenth century a clause to this effect was inserted in the instructions to the Governor.

The reference of the Lords of Trade to "a Law for Raising Money" no doubt suggested to the legislature of Jamaica the desirability of making their levy by formal act of legislature. And therefore in 1682 and again on later occasions an Act was passed "for raising money for soliciting the affairs of this his majesty's island in England." The act of 1682 received the royal assent from Governor Sir Thomas Lynch on 7th October 1682,[2] and Sir Charles Littleton and Colonel William Beeston were requested to undertake "to sollicit the Affairs of the Island in England, to dispose the money raised for that purpose, as they shall see reason."[3] The period of Littleton and Beeston's agency is uncertain. In September 1683 the Governor in his speech to the assembly referred to the "Great obligations to our friends in England . . . particularly Sir Charles Littleton and colonel Beeston."[4] And probably Beeston was still acting as agent in 1687, in

---

[1] C.O. 391:3, pp. 239-43, 16 Dec. 1680. *Cf.* Instruction to Governors, 24 Aug. 1702, printed in Appendix III, pp. 265-6.

[2] *Journals of the Assembly of Jamaica*, i, p. 63.

[3] C.O. 140:4, 5 Oct. 1682, Minutes of Council of Jamaica.

[4] *Journals*, i, p. 66.

THE EVOLUTION OF THE AGENCIES

which year the accounts of his charges for his services appear in the minutes of council.[1]

The next soliciting act that passed the legislature was that of 1688, which received the royal assent from the Governor on 18th September.[2] On this occasion no agents in England were chosen to act in accordance with its provisions, but a member of council, Ralph Knight, was appointed by the assembly with the council's concurrence

> to go for England, to present to his majesty the address from the council and their house, and to solicit the passing of the laws now sent home, and other affairs of this island.[3]

The passing of another act for solicitation was delayed by disagreements in the island.[4] At last in 1693 an act was passed, appointing as agents three Jamaica merchants, Gilbert Heathcote, Bartholomew

[1] " His Maj^{ttes} Acc^t Curr^t D^r 1687
" July 4 To D° Remitted Coll Wm Beeston for ye ball of his disbursements 28 : 4 : 3 with allowance of 15 p Cen p Order of Gover^e & Councill—32. 8. 10½." Minutes of Council of Jamaica, B.M. Sloane MS. 1599, p. 212, 26 Nov. 1688.

[2] *Journals*, i, p. 130. This act was cancelled by the death of the Governor: in October of the same year a new bill was therefore passed which, although it formed the basis for solicitations, was "unfixed from the broad seal and cancelled" in 1693 as a result of disallowance by the Crown. The disallowance was dated 22 Feb. 1688/9. *Journals*, i, p. 146. It was disallowed together with all other laws passed at the same time, on the ground that the assembly then sitting was illegal. *A.P.C.* ii, [277] p. 123.

[3] *Journals*, i, p. 132, 22 Sept. 1688.

[4] *Journals*, i, pp. 141–2, 28 Jan. 1691/2. "Account of the calling, proceedings, and dissolution, of the assembly summoned by the Earl of Inchiquin." The Governor suspected that the bill was "to solicit against him." In his speech on 9 June 1691 the Governor had urged the passing of a soliciting act. *Journals*, i, p. 138.

Gracedieu, and John Tutt,[1] and for a period of eleven years this act remained the basis of the agency.

To some extent it is true the agency of Jamaica was earlier developed than that of any other island, since the first act of appointment was passed in 1682 instead of 1690 and 1691 as for the other colonies. But in reality little evidence can be found of an agency organised on the lines of later years until 1693. Of the earlier agents, Knight was only temporarily sent over from Jamaica; Littleton and Bridges, although resident in London, apparently acted without regular salary, charging, as did the personal agents of Sir William Stapleton, a commission on business transacted by them. Although, by the acts of 1682 and 1688, the provision of supplies was rendered secure, the actual details of the office of agent had to be worked out in Jamaica as in the other islands by a succession of experiments. And in the case of Jamaica, even more than in that of the other islands, it is true that the system established at the end of the seventeenth century did not remain in operation without many and repeated difficulties.

The Agency in Working Order.—Despite the lack of finality in the stage of development reached in the last decade of the seventeenth century, it is possible from this point to regard the agency as an office actually in working. It was no longer merely a matter for experiment. There was in large measure a general recognition that agents were not only desirable but necessary. All three colonies had suffered experience as to the evils that could result from

---

[1] Plantation Register, i, pp. 249–53, 10 Aug. 1693.

THE EVOLUTION OF THE AGENCIES

lack of support at home. Their interests might be subordinated to those of some section at home : their defence might be neglected : the foundation of their liberty might be destroyed. They were liable to misrepresentation from any who claimed to speak on their behalf. With such dangers before them they had laid the foundations of a common system, and henceforth this system was to have general recognition. At the close of the century the newly constituted Board of Trade and Plantations made recommendations for the appointment of agents to Virginia, Maryland, and New York, comparable to those made at the Restoration to Virginia and New England. But in the interval the idea of the method of representation had become crystallised, and the advice was now more definite in character: " Barbados and other places," the colonies were told, " have Agents constituted . . . by Acts of those General Assemblies," and they were desired to follow their examples.[1] Not only the need for representation but the method of supplying it was by this time certain.

The policy of the home government, as suggested by this instruction and that to Jamaica in 1681, had operated in conjunction with the rapid constitutional development in the islands to bring the agencies of all the three larger colonies in the West Indies to similar positions by the close of the century. Henceforth, throughout the eighteenth century, although there were many difficulties, the general conception of the office changed hardly at all. As other colonies grew to maturity or were added by the issue of diplomacy and war to the empire, new agencies

[1] Board of Trade Journal, C.O. 391:10, pp. 310-11, 15 Oct. 1697.

appeared; but no organic change took place in the character of the office, and the history of later developments was to a great extent merely the definition and establishment on a firm foundation of the position reached by the end of the seventeenth century.

CHAPTER IV

THE PROBLEM OF APPOINTMENT IN THE FIRST HALF OF THE EIGHTEENTH CENTURY

THE value of the agent from the point of view of the government at home depended largely on the method of appointment. He must be properly accredited, or his actions might later be disavowed; he must represent the whole island, or some conflicting party might resent his power. Hence no doubt the suggestion in the instructions to Jamaica in 1681 and to Virginia, Maryland, and New York in 1697, that appointment should be by act of the colonial legislature. The precedents, however, of the seventeenth century were not uniformly followed in succeeding years. The passing of an act demanded a large measure of unanimity in the legislature, and this was very frequently lacking. Very early in the history of the agency Jamaica found the difficulties of securing legislative action,[1] and similar experiences were not long delayed for the other islands. They were, indeed, an inevitable result of the constitutional situa-

[1] The President and Council in a letter to the Lords of Trade, dated 28 Jan. 1691/2, described their difficulties " Unless a Govern' could be Perswaded to pass a law according to their Maj^ties Instructions to Raise three hundred pounds a year to be Employed in the Publick Affairs of this Island . . ." C.O. 140:5, Minutes of Council 28 Jan. 1691/2.

tion. Between the Governor and his council there was some measure of correlation, for both were appointed by the home government, and the recommendations of the Governor contributed largely to the decision of the membership of the council; but between the Governor and council and the assembly no link existed. The assembly was representative of the planters and merchants of the island, and owing to the system of annual elections was normally very closely in touch with the constituencies; the council, although chosen from among the colonists, was wholly dependent on the Crown, and, in its executive character, worked in unison with the Governor without any dependence on the assembly. So long as there were representative institutions with an executive entirely irresponsible disputes were bound to arise. They occurred in Massachusetts, where for some considerable period of time there were maintained in consequence two agents in England, one representing the council and the other the assembly.[1] And they reappeared in the history of the later development of the agency in the nineteenth century in Lower Canada, where the greater measure of success secured by the assembly indicates the trend of development.[2] In the West Indies a working agreement was reached by the middle of the eighteenth century, but no formal decision was made and there remained the same problems to be faced by later colonies.

The Struggle in Barbados, 1694–1732.—In Barbados

[1] E. P. Tanner, " Colonial Agencies in the Eighteenth Century," in *Political Science Quarterly,* March 1901, p. 43.

[2] " General Report of the Commissions for the Investigation of all Grievances affecting His Majesty's Subjects of Lower Canada." *Parl. Papers,* 1837, xxiv (50), 1, p. 188.

THE PROBLEM OF APPOINTMENT

the struggle began with the expiry of the first agency act in 1694. The tradition of the Barbados agency was bound up with the most independent section of the assembly, the "planter" party, and perhaps it had not been realised in 1691 that the use of legislation in connection with the agency gave opportunity for the Governor and council to take a share in the choice of the agent. The dispute of 1694 raised the question at once. The assembly, upon the expiry of the former act, nominated two agents to succeed those of 1691 and drew up a bill for the payment of salary.[1] The council thereupon voted the addition of a third agent: the assembly refused to concur and the bill fell to the ground. The difficulty was met by the introduction of a new bill, including amongst the agents the one favoured by the council,[2] but the assembly was not prepared to give way on the question of nomination. In 1696 a bill was sent up to the council, immediately to be rejected, "for yᵉ Assembly to establish agents,"[3] and this was the beginning of a long struggle on the part of the assembly to secure recognition of their monopoly of appointment.

Six months later the question was revived and a

[1] C.O. 31:3, Journals of Assembly, p. 395, 13 Nov. 1694, and pp. 397, 399, 27 Nov. and 11 Dec. 1694.

[2] The Assembly Journals are missing from 13 Dec. 1694 to 15 Feb. 1697/8; extracts for the months June–August 1695 are in C.O. 28:2, No. 109. The Minutes of Council record the failure of the 1694 Bill, C.O. 31:5, pp. 58–9, 14 and 19 July 1695. The second Bill was sent up to the Council 27 Dec. 1695 and passed the next day. *Ibid.*, p. 77. The second Bill is printed in full in *The Laws of Barbados . . . by William Rawlin now Clerk of the Assembly of the said Island*, London, 1699, No. 408, pp. 193–4.

[3] C.O. 31:5, p. 169, Minutes of Council, 2 Dec. 1696.

joint conference of council and assembly was held. The members for the council proposed a compromise :

> When the assembly shall think it needfull to have agents in England, they may present to the Governor and Councill the names of four persons out of which number the Governour and Councill to choose two, and they to continue for what time the assembly shall thinke fitt, not exceeding two years at once to be paid £250 p annum for their sallary out of the excise, by Warrant of the Governo^r and Councill. The Agents to be corresponded with by a Committee of three of ye Councill, and five of the Assembly, or any five of them.[1]

The measure was moderate, the assembly virtually retaining the pre-eminence, but it was refused.

A month later another conference was held and the assembly continued to hold its ground :

> The Assembly Conferrees concede that they be paid by Warrant of the Governo^r with the advice and consent of the Council but insist upon having the sole Nomination of the Agents exclusive of the Governo^r & Councill.[2]

Neither side would give way. Yet it was not at all desirable that the agency should be vacant : sugars had fallen in price, a new duty on sugar was threatened.[3] In August the assembly presented a memorial setting forth their claim to sole appointment, and the council responded by a new offer of compromise. It was hardly so conciliatory as the last. There were to be two sets of representatives : one nominated by the assembly, as to whom the council offered

> that £500 be paid to such person or persons out of the Excise to transact such matters before the King in

---

[1] C.O. 31:5, pp. 222-3, Minutes of Council, 9 June 1697.
[2] *Ibid.*, p. 225, 7 July 1697.
[3] C.O. 31:5, pp. 231-2, Minutes of Council, 8 Aug. 1697.

THE PROBLEM OF APPOINTMENT 83

Councill, as may be for the service of the Countrye, for two years, (but not under ye denomination of agents) ;[1]

the other to last also for two years, "the Publick Agents of ye Island," either those already appointed under the last act or such others as the Governor and council should nominate:

> to doe such Acts and things as they shall be directed by the Governou^r and Councill, or the Governou^r, Councill and Assembly, when they shall thinke fitt to unite.[2]

The assembly agreed that they would substitute for the title of agents that of solicitors or commissioners, but they refused to have their agency limited to two years, or to allow the appointment of other agents.[3]

Meanwhile an expedient, to become well-worn in later years, had presented itself to the assembly. The supplies required to pay the expenses of representation in England were derived from the excise on wines and other liquors levied in accordance with an annual act, in which a clause appropriated a part of the duty to the payment of agents. In 1697 the assembly made an addition to the usual wording of the act:

> A Paragraph wherein the Assembly reserved to themselves a power of Choosing and employing some separate agents to transact matters in England without the privity or approbation of the Governor and Councill.[4]

The council thereupon refused to allow the bill to pass. In September, however, shortly after the failure of the second compromise offered by the council, information was received which determined

[1] C.O. 31:5, pp. 231-2, Minutes of Council, 5 Aug. 1697.
[2] Ibid.
[3] Ibid.
[4] C.O. 31:5, pp. 244-5, Minutes of Council, 21 Sept. 1697.

the issue in favour of the assembly. Several ships arrived in Barbados on the 28th of that month; they had, it was said, touched at the Madeiras on their way, and "brought great quantities of Wyne from thence, and alsoe other Liquors"; if their cargoes were discharged before the Excise Bill was passed a great loss to the public would follow. The assembly remained obdurate to the argument, intent on gaining their end. The council, more heavily burdened with the responsibility of administration, could not hold out any longer; and so they passed the Excise Bill, with the agency clause, comforting themselves that "the Bill was to last but one yeare."[1]

They were not so easily to rid themselves of the assembly's triumph. In December, it is true, the council once more threw out a bill "Impowering the Generall Assembly . . . to nominate and Establish . . . agents,"[2] but the expiry of the Excise Bill of 1697 did not terminate the assembly's claims. In 1698 and each year to 1705 a similar clause was included reserving to the assembly the agents' appointment. In consequence agents were chosen by the assembly alone: in November 1700, William Bridges, Francis Eyles, and Robert Heysham;[3] in August 1704 Sir John Stanley, William Bridges, and Melatia Holder,[4] to whom William Cleland was added two weeks later.[5] Unquestionably the protraction of the assembly's success was due in part to the political conditions of the time. Sir Bevil Grenville arrived as Governor in 1703, and became involved in disputes

[1] C.O. 31:5, pp. 244–5, Minutes of Council, 21 Sept. 1697.
[2] *Ibid.*, p. 262, 8 Dec. 1697.
[3] C.O. 31:7, Journals of Assembly, 8 June 1702.
[4] *Ibid.*, 24 Aug. 1704. [5] *Ibid.*, 6 Sept. 1704.

THE PROBLEM OF APPOINTMENT 85

with his council in which he gained the assembly's support: the agents nominated by the assembly were employed in his defence at home against accusations from the council, and one of those appointed in 1704, Sir John Stanley, was his own brother-in-law. Thus in the middle of their struggle the assembly had unexpectedly the adherence of the Governor.[1]

Before long, however, reports of the state of the island reached the home government, and in March 1704/5 a letter was written to Sir Bevil Grenville in which he was rebuked for his action in countenancing the appointment of agents by the assembly alone.[2] The result was a return to the procedure of appointment by act. In 1705 an act was passed[3] which, although it formed the model for its successors, had in comparison with them certain peculiarities which aimed at safeguarding the assembly's claims. There had been, it stated, some doubts as to the validity of appointment by the assembly except for the actual period of the session :

> wch uncertainty as well as often Changeing of The Agents have been and may be very great Discouragem^ts to such Gentlemen whose Qualificačions render them to be propper persons for the negotiation of so great trusts.

The assembly's appointment, therefore, was "ratified approved and confirmed" by the whole legislature, the issue of instructions to the agents being left in the hands of the assembly alone.[4]

---

[1] *Cf.* R. H. Schomburgk, *History of Barbados*, London, 1848, pp. 310–12.

[2] The latter was dated 6 March 1704/5, C.O. 29:9, pp. 207–8.

[3] C.O. 30:6, pp. 481–4, 7 Aug. 1705.

[4] This appears from the fact that the operation of the existing Committee appointed for this purpose was extended.

When once the practice of passing an agency act had been started again the council attempted to increase its share in control. In September 1706 a new act was necessary, and the council before passing it suggested several amendments stipulating for the cooperation of council and assembly in the instruction of the agents, and adding another name to the agents appointed by the act. At first they met with a definite refusal from the assembly; later, however, a conference was held, and while the additional agent was still refused the other amendments were accepted, that relating to the control of the agents only by equality of votes.[1] In this form the act became law.[2]

The assembly, however, was not satisfied, and before another act was passed the whole question was brought up again. The same claims were made by the assembly and repudiated by the council: the same expedient was tried with the Excise Bill. But this time it was the assembly that had to surrender. At conferences held in March 1707/8 the assembly resolved

> that from the first constitution & appointment of Agents in England for the Publick service of this Island The Right of appointing such agents was and is in ye Representative body of this Island,

but they agreed that for the sake of avoiding losses they would pass the Excise Bill without the clause regarding agents.[3]

The council had now grown bolder. A proposal

[1] An account of the negotiations relating to the act is given in C.O. 31:6, Journals of Assembly, 1 Oct. – 15 Oct. 1706.
[2] The text is C.O. 30:6, pp. 573–5, 29 Oct. 1706.
[3] C.O. 31:10, Journals of Assembly, 19 March 1707/8.

THE PROBLEM OF APPOINTMENT 87

from the assembly that two of the agents should be nominated by the assembly and one by the council was refused; and they even tentatively put forward a claim to appointment by Governor and council alone.[1] The assembly proceeded as before to choose agents for themselves, but, without any provision for payment, this arrangement could not prove lasting; and so in 1709 an act was passed safeguarding like those of 1705 and 1706 the claims of the assembly.[2] This act led to the temporary settlement of the dispute. It was sent home for confirmation, and the authorities at home had by this time heard sufficient of the quarrels in the island to inquire into the matter with some care. The Board of Trade, after a detailed examination of the history of the agency, reported that the act embodied the assembly's assertion of a right of nomination exclusive of the Governor and council: a recognition of such a claim would be most pernicious, for it would lead either to the existence of rival agencies in England or to a mere agency of the assembly whose representations would have to be checked by consultation with the Governor. The act was therefore disallowed, and it was insisted that appointment should be " by the joint consent of the Governour Council and Assembly."[3]

[1] *Ibid.*   [2] C.O. 30:6, pp. 695–6, 12 May 1709.
[3] The report of the Board of Trade is in C.O. 29:12, pp. 39–45, 9 Nov. 1709. The policy embodied in the report is of some importance. The difficulty it sought to solve recurred persistently in the history of the agency. In 1767 the House of Representatives of Massachusetts Bay attempted to establish " a Right to chuse an Agent for themselves," and a report on the claim was made by the Board of Trade, 4 Feb. 1768. The ruling was on the same lines as that of 1709, which was quoted *verbatim* as a precedent. C.O. 325:1, (Tracts relative to Colonies.)

The settlement even now, although thus so strongly established, was not permanent. A short struggle in 1723[1] was followed by a revival of the whole dispute in 1728.[2] The history of the contest is much the same as that of earlier times and lasted for four years. The "Countrye's Interest," said a member of the assembly in 1730, "lyes a bleeding for want of agents."[3] At last in 1732 the assembly receded from its claims and an act of appointment was once more passed, this time with none of the features to which objection was made in 1709: and henceforward no further difficulty arose. In reality the assembly retained much of the advantage for which it had been contending; for the nomination of the agent took place in the assembly, and only at rare intervals did the council quarrel with their choice.

The Struggle in Jamaica, 1704-1732.—Meanwhile difficulties of a similar nature were occurring in Jamaica. Here they started early in the eighteenth century and continued without intermission for nearly thirty years, creating the longest gap on record in the histories of any of the West Indian agencies. The act of 1693 expired in 1704,[4] and before its expiry the administration at home had reminded the

[1] C.O. 31:16, Journals of Assembly, 21 May 1723.

[2] C.O. 31:18, Journals of Assembly, 29 Aug. 1728. The same expedient as before was attempted with the Excise Bill, but without success.

[3] C.O. 31:20, Journals of Assembly, 23 Dec. 1730.

[4] Although it appears from the Board of Trade Journal that two at any rate of the "sollicitors" nominated by the act functioned as agents throughout this period, the terms of the act were not always rigidly observed. In 1696 the fund arising from the act was voted to "be appropriated to the maintenance of parties to suppress rebellious negroes." *Journals*, i, p. 164, 11 June 1696. In 1698/9 a committee

THE PROBLEM OF APPOINTMENT 89

Governor of the coming necessity for a new act; the instruction, worded like those of 1681 and the following years, was to the effect that he was empowered to assent to an agency act, or, failing this, to the raising of a voluntary subscription to carry on the affairs of the island at home.[1] For some years, however, despite the introduction into the assembly of agency bills in 1705 and 1708/9, no provision was made for solicitation in England, and the concerns of Jamaica were left to the care of such absentee planters and merchants trading to the island as chose voluntarily to fulfil some of the functions of an agent.

Early in 1712/13 some disputes arose in Jamaica, as to the character of these unofficial services,[2] and it was therefore determined to revive the practice of passing an act. Accordingly a bill was brought in early in 1714, and, having passed the assembly, was sent up to the council. It was found, however, to contain objectionable features,[3] and the council proposed radical amendments, to which the assembly would not agree.[4] A new bill passed by the assembly in November 1715, giving the assembly entire control of the islands' representatives, was again rejected

of the House reported that it was " very much for the advantage of the island that it be continued for the use it is raised for, but that some other person or persons in England be employed there." *Ibid.*, p. 193, 24 March 1698/9.

[1] The instruction is printed in Appendix III, *infra*, pp. 265–6. An account of the history of these instructions and their effect is given in a report of the Board of Trade in C.O. 138:15, pp. 148–53, 16 Oct. 1716.

[2] *Journals*, i, pp. 81 *et seq.*, 105, 107, 168.

[3] It is probable that this act is the one mentioned from 1721 onwards in the Instructions to the Governor of Jamaica. *Vide infra*, Instructions of 16 March 1721/2. Appendix III, p. 266.

[4] *Journals*, ii, p. 132, 17 Feb. 1713/14.

by the council, their committee reporting that "it tends to the utter subversion of the constitution of the island."[1] The assembly, refusing a counter-proposal from the council,[2] had recourse to the expedient of a voluntary subscription ; and the former agent, Sir Gilbert Heathcote, was entrusted with the control of a fund of £1,100 so raised.[3] Meanwhile the Governor referred this dispute among others to the authorities at home, asking that some directions should be sent him as to his own attitude to it.[4] The result was a new instruction empowering the Governor to pass an agency act on the basis of that of 1693, conferring on a joint committee of council and assembly the control of the agent.[5] Thus, the claims of the assembly were refuted.

Ten years passed before the difficulties altogether ceased ; but henceforth the disputes were matters of personnel. The assembly, despite the alteration in the Governor's instructions, appointed agents for themselves : Alexander Stephenson in 1724, Edward Charlton in 1725/6, Charles Delafaye in 1728,[6] the

[1] *Journals*, ii, p. 169, 20 Dec. 1715.

[2] *Ibid.*, pp. 172-3, 23 Dec. 1715.

[3] *Ibid.*, pp. 162, 170, 15 and 21 Dec. 1715. See also Board of Trade representations. C.O. 138:15, pp. 148-52. The amount raised was contrary to the instructions, which imposed a limit of £300 per annum.

[4] Memorandum from Governor Pitt, C.O. 138:15, pp. 1-6.

[5] Plantation Register, v, p. 247. The instruction is printed in Appendix III, *infra*, pp. 265-6.

[6] *Journals*, ii, p. 548, 28 Oct. 1725 ; p. 563, 28 Jan. 1725/6 ; p. 677, 15 Feb. 1728/9. It is noteworthy that despite the theories of appointment enunciated by the Board of Trade in 1709 the activities of these agents were accepted without question. As a rule no inquiry was made into the credentials of the agents, and possibly the lack of authority for these agents was not realised. It appears also that James Knight acted as agent in 1727/8, although there is no record of his appointment :

last continuing as the formal agent for the colony upon the passage of an agency act in 1731/2.[1] From this time, with the exception of a short repetition of the controversy in 1732/3, there was no contest over the agents' appointment, the long agency of John Sharpe, commencing in 1733/4, being in large measure responsible.

Constitutional Difficulties in the Leeward Islands.—The history of the Leeward Islands agencies was on somewhat different lines from those of Barbados and Jamaica. In their case the importance of the first part of the eighteenth century lies not so much in the adjudication between rival claims within the legislature as in the settlement of more fundamental questions as to appointment delayed on account of the complications of their government. The act of 1690,[2] unlike the contemporary acts of Barbados and Jamaica, did not establish a precedent. It was an emergency measure occasioned by the outbreak of war with France; and it had in consequence no successor.[3]

he was a prominent absentee planter. *Ibid.*, p. 677, 14 Feb. 1728/9. The main difficulty was in providing for payment. *Ibid.*, ii, p. 501, 30 Jan. 1723/4; p. 564, 29 Jan. 1725/6.

[1] C.O. 139:13, No. 49, 11 Feb. 1731/2.

[2] It was entitled "An Act for appointing Commissioners and an Agent to Negotiate and Manage the Affairs of the Leeward Islands as also for settling of a Fund for the defraying of the Expence and Charge of such Negotiation and procuring of Divers Necessaries for the Use and Benefit of the said Islands." C.O. 154:4, pp. 64-9, 8 Nov. 1690. There is another copy in Plantation Register, i, pp. 163-5.

[3] The act of 1690 was limited in operation to three years. Before its expiry, however, it was extended for the duration of the war by an act of 1692. C.O. 154:4, p. 103, 12 Aug. 1692, and Plantation Register, i, p. 190. In 1694 a further "explanatory Act" was passed, Plantation Register, i, pp. 300-2, 31 Aug. 1694.

When the Peace of Ryswick terminated its operation, the General Council did indeed resolve in favour of the continuation of an agent in England, but already there were seen the separatist tendencies of the islands constantly recurrent in the early eighteenth century, and there was no General Assembly to take action on the motion. Thus the five "Commissioners" appointed in 1691 were the only permanent agents for all the islands.[1]

The "Commissioners" ceased their functions on behalf of the colony the autumn of 1697;[2] and each island was free to take its own course. Alone among them Antigua proceeded to pass an appointing act; Montserrat allowed the agency to lapse for nearly fifteen years;[3] St. Christopher apparently chose an agent, although there is no record of his appointment;[4] Nevis proceeded by the less formal method of passing resolutions of council and assembly,[5] a practice which was continued throughout the first half of the eighteenth century.

[1] In 1705 a temporary agent was nominated by the General Assembly to secure the confirmation of the acts passed at those meetings. C.O. 155:3, Minutes of General Assembly of all the Islands, 25 June 1705.

[2] Nevis received a letter from the Commissioners to this effect on 10 Feb. 1697/8. C.O. 155:2, p. 458, Minutes of Council. The letter was dated 19 November 1697: the Treaty of Ryswick was concluded on 10 September.

[3] The General Council in May 1705 referred to the absence of an agent for Montserrat. C.O. 155:3, Meeting of General Council, 28 May 1705. The first notice of an agent is in 1711/12.

[4] The General Council of May 1705 resolved that St. Christopher "should be put in mood to pay their agent what's due to him." In 1706 Stephen Duport was the agent. C.O. 155:5, Minutes of Assembly of St. Christopher, 16 July 1717. Duport's accounts are here given for the years 1706–16.

[5] C.O. 155:2 pp. 490–1, Nevis, Meeting of Council and Assembly.

THE PROBLEM OF APPOINTMENT 93

The histories of these agencies were marked by no such struggles as those of Barbados and Jamaica. Nevis and St. Christopher were happy in an entire absence of any interruption in the continuity of their agencies. In St. Christopher the line of agents is unbroken from 1706;[1] while in Nevis the whole of the first half of the eighteenth century was covered by only three agents. Somewhat more difficulty occurred in Antigua and Montserrat. But here, with the exception of one occasion in Antigua, the disputes were purely personal in character: Governor, council, and assembly could not agree on any agent to whom all would be willing to entrust the island's business. For this reason, in Antigua there was a vacancy of nearly three years commencing in 1713,[2] and thirty years later a similar dispute[3] occasioned a longer interval which did not end until 1751, when a nominee satisfactory to all parties was found in John Sharpe, already agent for Jamaica and Barbados. Similar disagreements occurred in Montserrat over the appointment of William Nevine in 1718,[4] and during the years 1729 to 1736, when a satisfactory solution was found in the appointment of the agent of Antigua, John Yeamans.[5]

[1] See lists of agents in Appendix II, *infra*, p. 252.

[2] The council wished to appoint William Popple and the Assembly Archibald Hutchinson. During part of this period Hutchinson was temporarily employed, although not as a " proper agent." *Ibid.*, 7 Jan. 1713/14. The next agent regularly appointed was William Nevine in 1716.

[3] The Council wished to appoint Samuel Martin and the Assembly Thomas Kerby. C.O. 9:16, Journals of Assembly, 21 March 1743/4.

[4] The appointment of Nevine was a victory for the Council. C.O. 155:5, Montserrat Journals of Assembly, 12 Nov. 1715, 8 Sept. and 15 Oct. 1716, 29 March and 1 April 1718.

[5] C.O. 155:7, Minutes of Council of Montserrat, 26 March 1729. The assembly desired to appoint William Gerrish, who during Nevine's

The absence of more fundamental disputes in the Leeward Islands was due partly to the more harmonious relations between council and assembly and partly to the absence of a tradition of appointment by assembly so conspicuous in Barbados. In Antigua, however, there was on one occasion an attempt made by the assembly to oppose the claims of Governor and council on the ground of an alleged ancient custom. The incident occurred in February 1711/12. A year earlier it had been suggested at a meeting of the General Legislature of all the Islands that the appointment of a general agent should be revived. The General Assembly disapproved of this proposal, and in its place asked that the Governor-General should recommend to each island some one person to serve as agent.[1] Accordingly the Governor-General recommended a near relative of his own, Sir John St. Leger. He made the suggestion to Antigua in terms that appeared to minimise the share of the assembly in the appointment,[2] and to obviate any disregard of their rights the assembly put forward what they described as "the usage & Custome upon making an Agent." It was the same practice as was

agency had been concerned in the island's public affairs. C.O. 155:6, Minutes of Council of Montserrat, letter dated 13 Oct. 1722. The dispute was repeated later. C.O. 177:2, Journals of Assembly, 28 March 1733, 25 April and 13 Sept. 1734. In 1736 the Governor-General complained of the disadvantages of the continued lack of an agent. The assembly recommended William Gerrish once more. C.O. 177:2, Journals of Assembly, 5 June 1736. John Yeamans was finally appointed. C.O. 177:3, Journals of Assembly, 9 Nov. 1736–2 Aug. 1737.

[1] C.O. 9:2, Minutes of General Council and Assembly, 3 and 8 March 1710/11.

[2] C.O. 9:2, Journals of Assembly, 4 Feb. 1711/12.

THE PROBLEM OF APPOINTMENT 95

adopted for the election of members to a General Assembly.

> All the freeholders of the Island to be summoned to appear in some convenient pasture & vote for a fit pson to serve in that Station who being ellected by majorities of voices his sallarye was then setteled by an Act.[1]

They did not offer any instances in which this method of election was followed, and when the Governor replied that the council said it had never been put into practice and urged once more the passing of an act, the assembly immediately gave way, and two days later the required measure was passed.

The Agency Acts.—In the series of acts passed by the various islands, there were certain main features in common. They opened with a preamble setting forth the need for an agent; there followed next the enacting clause naming the agent or agents chosen, and the remaining part of the act prescribed the authority in the island from whom the agent was to receive instructions and to whom he should report on his activities, and made provision for payment of salary and necessary disbursements. With one exception alone the acts were temporary in character, remaining in operation as a rule for one year in the case of Barbados, three in that of Jamaica, and varying periods in the other islands.

The exception is the island of Antigua. Here the act of 1698[2] was without limitation of time, and

---

[1] C.O. 9:2, Journals of Assembly, 4 Feb. 1711/12. The election of members for the General Assembly of all the islands was made at a meeting of all freeholders " at Bayes pasture in New North Sound " in 1709/10. C.O. 9:1, Journals of Assembly, 17 Jan. 1709/10.

[2] C.O. 8:1, No. 109, pp. 89–91, 22 Dec. 1698. There are other copies in *Acts of Assembly passed in the Island of Antigua, from* 1668–

remained the basis of the agency throughout the period of its history. Unlike all other agency acts it named no agent, prescribing instead the method of nomination by " the Commander in Chief Governor, or President for the time being . . . by, & with the Consent of the Council & Assembly." There was, therefore, in fact no necessity for any subsequent act, but, although the agent was on several occasions appointed by resolution of council and assembly in accordance with this provision,[1] frequently the more formal procedure of passing a supplementary act was adopted; and, with the exception of the first of such acts in 1716, the fundamental act of 1698 was invariably cited in the preamble.

Although the act of Antigua of 1698 was the only attempt made by the islands to establish the machinery of appointment on a permanent basis, there was no less finality in the system of appointment evolved for the other islands. In the seventeenth century the agents' office had grown into being to meet the needs of each colony as they arose, and the following half-century of development was necessary before the main attributes of the agency became recognised. In this process a great measure of influence is to be assigned to the struggles over appointment. They caused the enunciation of principles by the conflicting parties, most of which had to be abandoned: they made necessary the investigation by the home government of the

1730, London, 1740; in Bodleian MS. Rawlinson A 272, f. 308, among the papers of John Champante, and in Plantation Register, ii, pp. 13–14. The act is printed in Appendix III, *infra*, pp. 267–9.

[1] *e.g.* in 1698, when the first agent under the act was appointed. C.O. 155:2, p. 289, Antigua Minutes of Council and Assembly, 20–22 Dec. 1698.

THE PROBLEM OF APPOINTMENT

principles on which the agency was based, and led up to the firm establishment of the attitude already indicated before the close of the seventeenth century. The period was in the history of the agency one of consolidation, and its value is easily apparent in the narrative of succeeding years. In 1750 the appearance of agents for colonies other than Barbados, the Leeward Islands, and Jamaica was only a few years distant; and, although to some degree it is true that each island had to solve by experience its own difficulties, the precedents established in the older islands were a determining factor in guiding the development of the new agencies.

CHAPTER V

THE NEW AGENCIES OF THE SECOND HALF OF THE EIGHTEENTH CENTURY

In the latter part of the eighteenth century the history of the West Indian agents is extended to include the representatives of several groups of islands which had hitherto stood outside the general course of development. The early years of the agency in these islands show a marked contrast to those of the other colonies. Before they started, the conceptions of the agent's office had already been formed, and in each island in turn the need for an agent was no sooner felt than measures were taken to secure an appointment, the full powers of an agency being immediately developed without the experiments through which they had been evolved in earlier times. In only one of these new agencies can any parallel be found to the early imperfect forms through which the agent's office passed in the other islands, and in this case the final development was entirely separate, due to the imitation of established precedents.

The islands, which in the later eighteenth century added new agencies to those already in existence, fall naturally into two classes. Two groups, although their agencies were nearly a century later in development than those of Barbados, the Leeward Islands, and Jamaica, date the beginning of their existence under British rule from the same period in West Indian history. The others, in spite of some fluctuation in their position, were never finally established under British control until in the mid-eighteenth century the sea-supremacy of England gave opportunity for the assertion of her claims.

The two groups of the first class are the Bahamas and the Virgin Islands. In the seventeenth century, at the time when Barbados, the Leeward Islands, and Jamaica were growing to maturity, English settlements existed also in the long stretch of the Bahama Islands extending along the northern coast of the Spanish colonies, and in the Virgin Islands, the cluster of unfertile rocks that blocked the way of navigation to the north-west of St. Christopher. In the Bahamas, by the time the Barbados agency had come into being, there were two main settlements, Eleutheria and New Providence, both the result of expeditions from the Bermuda group; while, in the Virgin Islands, Dutch buccaneers had in the middle of the seventeenth century established their headquarters at Tortola, to be ousted only a few years later by Englishmen of the same type. In neither group was there any semblance of settled government or any attempt to further cultivation.

The Bahama Islands.—In the latter part of the seventeenth century, however, both the Bahamas and the Virgin Islands received the attention of the Restoration Government. The Bahama Islands were the subject of a grant to certain of the proprietors to whom the province of Carolina was granted in 1670;[1] the Virgin Islands were brought under the direct rule of the Crown, being included in the

[1] *C.S.P.* iii, No. 311, pp. 132-3, 1 Nov. 1670.

commission to Sir William Stapleton in 1672 as part of the Leeward Island colony.[1] In neither case, however, did the succeeding half-century bring settlement and progress. The proprietors of the Bahama Islands made little provision for their defence; and in the successive wars of the late seventeenth century they were frequently ravaged by Frenchmen and Spaniards; in 1704 they were reported to be entirely depopulated.[2]

The Spanish Succession War, however, marked the end of this period of neglect. As soon as the inhabitants returned, after their dispersal in 1703, representation was made to the home government of the negligence of the proprietors. The colony, it was asserted, formerly contained on New Providence alone one hundred and fifty families, and now on all the islands they totalled no more than twelve.[3] And, before long, confirmation was gained of the need for improvement by the receipt of news that the French and Spaniards had once more seized the islands.[4] In themselves they were considered, as the Board of Trade stated in 1697, of little consequence.[5] They were not fertile, the soil being thin and the surface rocky; they could not profitably produce the articles of West Indian commerce so much valued in the neighbouring islands. But their effective control by England was a matter of serious moment. They were the strongholds of pirates. " War is no sooner

[1] The Commission conferred upon Stapleton authority over all the islands leeward of Guadaloupe as far as St. John de Porto Rico.
[2] *A.P.C.* ii, p. 343, 3 Aug. 1704.
[3] *Journal of the Commissioners for Trade and Plantations*, pp. 583-5, 28 Jan. 1708/9.   [4] C.O. 391:21, p. 144, 29 June 1709.
[5] C.O. 391:9, pp. 328-9, 6 Jan. 1696/7.

THE NEW AGENCIES

ended," it was said in 1707, " but the West Indies always swarms with Pyrates."[1] The inhabitants of the Bahamas were constantly subject to molestation, and when they avoided dangers for themselves by complicity with the pirates the matter became even more serious for the other islands.[2]

During the early years of the eighteenth century, frequent representations of agents, merchants, and planters interested in the other islands set forth the dangers to trade incurred from these continued disorders.[3] In 1715 the matter at last moved forward to a decision : at a meeting of the Board of Trade in November the question of the Bahama Islands was " mention'd in discourse," and the representatives of Barbados who were attending at the Board, " Mr Heysham and the other Gentlemen," set forth the great benefit which would result to trade if a settlement were made of the government, especially in New Providence.[4] The result was a speeding up of the consideration which had already lasted for some years.[5] And, in 1716, it was decided that the charter

[1] John Graves, *Memorial : or a Short Account of the Bahama Islands*, London, 1707 (?), p. 6. Graves had been for twenty years collector of customs in the Bahamas.

[2] *Ibid.*, p. 7.

[3] *e.g.* " Petition of Merchants and Commanders of ships trading to and living on the Continent of America, and on the Island of Jamaica, and also of the distressed Inhabitants of the Bahama Islands." *A.P.C.* ii, No. (1060), p. 550.

[4] C.O. 391:25, p. 284, 24 Nov. 1715.

[5] On 24 May 1706 the Board of Trade reported to the Privy Council in favour of the establishment of a royal government. *A.P.C.* ii, No. (1004), pp. 507–9. See also *Journal of the Commissioners for Trade and Plantations*, p. 259. On 3 February 1708/9 the Board of Trade again reported to the same effect, and the Privy Council, after referring

of the proprietors should be resumed, and the islands taken under the direct rule of the Crown;[1] following upon this, in 1718 the famous navigator, Captain Woodes Rogers, was sent out as Governor with special powers for the suppression of pirates.

The difficulties of the period of proprietary rule, and the negotiations leading to the establishment of royal government, had not passed without bringing into existence some attempts to secure representation of the islands at home. The proprietors were all resident in England, and they maintained an agent to care for their interests before the Board of Trade and other authorities, an office executed over a large part of the period by one of their own number named Thornburgh. But there was, in addition, another type of representative: as in the case of other islands there came to be a class of persons in England whose interests lay in the islands, not indeed, as in the other colonies at this time, a closely organised group of merchants, but similar rather to the sponsors of Jamaica in 1660, those " that have been imployed unto or have traded thither."[2]

During the last ten years of the proprietary government the most important of these was John Graves, formerly collector of customs in the islands. His first appearance before the Board of Trade seems to

the matter to the Attorney- and Solicitor-General and to the Board of Ordinance, decided in November 1710 that an engineer should be sent from Jamaica to estimate the cost of fortifying New Providence. *A.P.C.* ii, No. (1060), pp. 550–1.

[1] *A.P.C.* i, No. (1232), pp. 698–700, 22 Feb. 1715/16.

[2] *Vide supra*, p. 24. The Bahama Islands were not sugar-producing colonies. Salt was their chief product: at the beginning of the nineteenth century cotton was of some importance.

THE NEW AGENCIES 103

have been in April 1706,[1] and from that time he was frequently present, urging the decayed state of the islands in consequence of the neglect of the proprietors. In 1707 he tried without success to prevent royal confirmation of the appointment of Robert Holden as Governor. He alleged that Holden had been heard to say " after he came out from the Lords Proprietors " that he had no intention of resettling the island of Providence during the war, and that he desired the government only to be able to make profit out of his patent for " Fishing for Wrecks and Whales."[2] In this case Graves failed in his object, but unquestionably his repeated solicitations, aided by the publication of a manifesto,[3] had a large influence in bringing about the final decision. Graves, moreover, did not always act alone: in December 1708 a petition was referred to the Board of Trade regarding the fortification of New Providence, from " divers merchants, commanders of ships, and inhabitants of the Bahama Islands," and Graves, with several others, was heard in its favour in opposition to the representatives of the Lords Proprietors.[4] A little later he was requested by the Board to discuss the question of establishing a royal government

> with such Persons as he thinks best acquainted with the State and Condition of them, and let the Board have as soon as possible the joint opinion which may be the best method for facilitating the settlement.[5]

[1] *Journal of the Commissioners for Trade and Plantations*, p. 248, 12 April 1706.
[2] *Ibid.*, p. 373, 9 June 1707.   [3] *Vide supra.* p. 134, n. 4.
[4] *Journal of the Commissioners for Trade and Plantations*, pp. 573, 583–5, 7 and 28 Jan. 1708/9.
[5] C.O. 391:22, pp. 66–7, 15 Sept. 1710.

And such consultation was repeated on several occasions during the six years that passed before the patent of the proprietors was cancelled.

With the establishment of royal government, however, the solicitations of persons at home did not develop, as might be expected on analogy from the other islands, into a system of agency. Woodes Rogers and his successor, George Phenney,[1] who together governed the colony from 1718 to 1728, were mainly concerned with the strengthening of defences, the restoration of order, and the introduction of a settled condition of affairs favourable to the economic progress of the country. Neither of them, despite a representation from the " Governor Council and Principal Inhabitants of the Bahama Islands " in 1722,[2] was granted the power of summoning assemblies. Upon Rogers' second appointment, however, in 1728 provision was made in his commission for the election of an assembly, and the first meeting was held in September 1729.[3] Even then, however, the progress of the colony was slow. The inhabitants were so poor that, during Rogers' second governorship, not only did he forego the salary which he was expected to derive from the colony, but he agreed to postpone the building of a prison court-house recommended in his instructions, " the Colony being at present too poor for such works." [4]

In 1732 Rogers died, and there followed a period

---

[1] Phenney, unlike Rogers, was far from popular, exacting large sums of money from the inhabitants. *Journal of the Lower House of Assembly of the Bahama Islands*, vol. i, p. 28.

[2] C.O. 391:31, pp. 89–91, 3 May 1722.

[3] *Journal of the Lower House of Assembly of the Bahama Islands*, vol. i, p. 1.   [4] *Ibid.*, pp. 34–5.

THE NEW AGENCIES

marked by repeated difficulties between Governor and assembly, when the peace of the island was frequently disturbed by private brawls.[1] The reputation of the colony for constant disorders prevented any great immigration. In 1741 the population was estimated as two thousand three hundred, about half being Europeans.[2] Fourteen years later a report from Governor Gambier gave the population as only two hundred above this figure.[3]

The condition of the colony during these years of turmoil, coupled with its slow economic progress, forbade the appointment of a regular agent. The governors indeed maintained personal agents, and these appeared from time to time at the Board of Trade, as had nearly three-quarters of a century earlier the personal agents of Lord Willoughby and Sir William Stapleton:[4] upon occasions also the Governor sent home some one from among his supporters to answer allegations made against him, as when in 1744 Governor Tinker sent home his secretary, John Snow.[5] Further, in the early years of royal government, Governor Woodes Rogers with his Council and " several of the principal Inhabitants " had entrusted an address to the King to one Beauchamp, Secretary of the Colony and Lieutenant of the Independent Company,[6] who

---

[1] See the description given by P. H. Bruce, who visited the islands in 1741. Bruce, *Memoirs* . . . , London, 1782.

[2] Bruce, *Memoirs* . . . , p. 428.

[3] B.M. King's MS. 205.

[4] C.O. 319:35, pp. 343-4, 17 Nov. 1726. and 37, pp. 210-12, 216-19, 27 Aug. and 10 Sept. 1728.

[5] Bruce, *Memoirs* . . . , p. 430.

[6] C.O. 23:13, p. 31, Minutes of Council, 19 May 1719, and C.O. 23:1, A 29 Minutes of Council (undated rec'd 26 Oct. 1719).

was going home to England: later, the internal disputes of the islands made such action difficult.

In 1758, however, William Shirley was appointed to the government of the Bahama Islands.[1] He had been previously Governor of Massachusetts, where an agency had been in existence since the end of the seventeenth century.[2] Upon his arrival in the Bahamas, finding that they had "no Standing Agent in London to solicit the affairs of these Island," he proposed to the council and assembly that an agent should be appointed. The usefulness of such a representative had been proved, he said, by long experience in other colonies, and, even if the Bahama Islands had at that time no very urgent business to represent before the administration at home, probably their interests would develop, and such a sponsor would be of the utmost value.[3] The assembly accepted the recommendation without demur, and proceeded to vote to the prospective agent a salary of one hundred pounds sterling. They then asked the Governor to suggest a suitable candidate, and, upon his nomination of Richard Cumberland, resolved his appointment, and proceeded to name a committee to issue instructions. The collaboration of the council was secured, the committee comprising three members of each house, and a bill for the provision of salary was passed. Richard Cumberland continued as agent for over twenty years, his appointment being confirmed from

[1] *A.C.P.* iv, p. 776.

[2] E. P. Tanner: "Colonial Agencies in England during the Eighteenth Century," *Pol. Sci. Quarterly*, March 1901.

[3] *Journal of* . . . *Bahama Islands*, ii, pp. 38-40. Shirley's speech is printed in Appendix III, *infra*, pp. 266-7.

time to time by subsequent resolutions. His successor in 1785 was appointed in a similar manner, although some increase of formality was obtained by the inclusion of the resolution amongst the island's acts sent home for confirmation. After this date the agent was appointed by an act, in form resembling the acts of other islands.

The Virgin Islands.—The establishment of an agency was not reached so early in the Virgin Islands. This little group, transferred to England upon the cession of Tortola from the Dutch, developed more in accordance with the usual course of the history of the West Indies than did the Bahamas. Here, sugar and cotton could be cultivated, and trade was therefore opened with England in much the same way as in the more important colonies.[1] For a long period, however, the islands, very small in extent, mountainous over a large portion of their surface, were not suited to rapid development. They were included in the general government of the Leeward Islands, but their rule was desultory in character.

In 1707 Governor-General Parkes appointed as Lieutenant-Governor one Captain John Walton; but he, after a short stay in the islands, came home to England to lay before the Queen a report on their condition, and being unable to obtain a hearing remained there for nearly ten years. Finally he was successful in bringing his case before the Privy Council,

---

[1] George Suckling, in his *Historical Account of the Virgin Islands*, London, 1780, states that the merchant creditors of the Virgin Islands belonged to Liverpool: a fact of some interest in connection with the circumstance that one of the agents for the Virgin Islands belonged to Liverpool, being the only West Indian agent who came from an outport. *Vide infra*, pp. 109-10.

and the Board of Trade was required to furnish a report. They stated, after examining Captain Walton and " other Persons who have been at the s⁴ Virgin Islands," that only one of the islands, Spanish Town, was fertile, most of the rest being little more than rocks. There were very few inhabitants, and, if it was attempted to establish a settlement there, it would be necessary to protect the islands from pirates and buccaneers and to keep stern watch against illegal trade with the Danes of St. Thomas : there was the danger also of the arrival of runaway servants from the other Leeward Islands.[1] The result of this report was the dispatch of a commission to investigate conditions in the islands.[2] After this time the Virgin Islands made greater progress economically, but their government remained as before, under the control of a Lieutenant-Governor appointed by the Governor-General of the Leeward Islands.

In 1773, however, the colonists secured the co-operation of the Governor-General to petition the King for leave to summon an assembly, promising to pass an act making grant of the 4½ per cent. duty. The required permission was obtained, and on 1st February 1774 the first assembly met.[3] The island almost immediately became involved in disputes over the laws concerning debts and very little business was done.[4] No taxes were raised except the 4½ per

---

[1] C.O. 314:1, Board of Trade Report on Petition of Captain John Walton, 9 Sept. 1715. [2] *A.P.C.* ii, No. (1152), p. 656.

[3] C.O. 316:1, Minutes of Council, 1 Feb. 1774. The earliest assembly minutes extant are in the same volume, commencing 24 Feb. 1775.

[4] See George Suckling, *An Historical Account of the Virgin Islands*, London, 1780, pp. 21-33.

cent, but it was agreed to appoint an agent.[1] The assembly's nomination of Sir William Meredith was disapproved on the ground that "there would be an Impropriety in appointing a Gentleman in his high rank,"[2] and it was decided, thereupon, to appoint John Pownall, Under-Secretary of State in the American Department, and Secretary to the Board of Trade. The act was not passed until the following October, but in the meantime a letter was written to Pownall by a committee of both Houses appointed for that purpose to acquaint him that he had been chosen agent, stating their reason that "The Condition of the Virgin Islands, at present without laws or police, requires the greatest expedition of the publick business thereof."[3]

The act provided for the continuance of the agent until a successor was appointed, but if the account of George Suckling is to be believed[4] the failure of the legislature to raise any money for the expenses of administration resulted in the termination of the agency at the close of the first year; and it is probable

[1] Before the establishment of the assembly, William Payne Georges, agent for St. Christopher, was acting as agent for the Virgin Islands. C.O. 316:1, Minutes of Council, 20 Sept. 1774.

[2] Meredith was Controller of the Household. The discussion is in C.O. 186:5, Virgin Islands, Journals of Assembly, pp. 23-4.

[3] The act opened with the blunt declaration "Nothing is clearer than the Necessity of appointing a fit Person in London to negotiate the Public business of these Islands, from time to time, to promote the good of the People and secure their rights." C.O. 315:1, Act dated 30 Oct. 1776.

[4] *Op. cit.*, pp. 69-70. Suckling was appointed chief justice of the Virgin Islands in 1776. The value of his work is greatly diminished by his obvious bias; but it is interesting that he lays great stress on the intrigues of a London group who aimed at securing a separate government for the islands.

that the office was not revived until in 1783 a new agent was appointed, Henry Rawlinson, of Liverpool. Henceforth the agency continued uninterrupted until the middle of the nineteenth century.

The Ceded Islands.—In the meantime, however, other agencies had appeared. The history of the West Indies throughout the seventeenth and eighteenth centuries was intimately bound up with questions of sea power. It had been seen repeatedly that if, as time went on, Jamaica and Barbados proved themselves strong enough to be immune from foreign conquest, the Leeward Island group, in extent and population smaller, and in their position placed right athwart the French colonies, were subject to constant fear of attack, repeatedly realised. And the Virgin Islands and the Bahamas were in like manner open to hostile ravaging. Periods of war, therefore, were inevitably accompanied by dangers from the enemy, only to be avoided by the maintenance of strong squadrons and the carrying out of counter-attacks on the French islands.

In the Seven Years' War the balance of success fell to the English. Guadaloupe was captured in 1759, Martinique in 1761, and then the neutral islands, Grenada, St. Lucia, and St. Vincent. The peace of 1763 restored to France Martinique, Guadaloupe, and St. Lucia, but gave to England Grenada, St. Vincent, Dominica, and Tobago. During the war all the islands conquered by the English were placed under military rule, but at the conclusion of peace a more definite settlement took place.[1] Of the islands ceded

[1] During the occupation of Guadaloupe Robert Deshayes was sent to England as agent. B.M. Add. MS. 32911, f. 168 (Newcastle Papers), Memorial of Robert Deshayes, 8 Sept. 1760.

to England, Grenada had been for some time planted with sugar by the French, and in the other islands, although nominally they had been after the Peace of Aix-la-Chapelle " neutral," and in the hands of the Caribs, French settlers had, in fact, acquired estates. The islands, moreover, were fertile, and capable of rapid development. When the lands were put up for sale, purchasers both in England and in the islands were easily obtained, and within a few years the new islands were ready to take their place commercially amongst the other English sugar colonies. And as early as 1773 a group of London " Merchants trading to Dominica " was taking public action regarding the importation of coffee, and, together with planters of the island, regarding the duty on negroes.[1] The rapidity of economic development was paralleled by their constitutional progress. Almost immediately after the peace civil rule was established, Grenada being appointed the seat of a general government of the ceded islands. Very soon, however, the other islands were freed from her control; representative institutions were granted, and within six years assemblies had met in all the islands.

As in the Virgin Islands a few years later, the meeting of the assemblies was quickly followed by the passage of agency acts. In 1767 Grenada appointed Richard Maitland agent by a colonial act modelled closely on those of Antigua. In the same year St. Vincent passed a similar act and in 1770 Tobago.[2] Of all the islands, only in Dominica was there any echo of the controversies over appointment which had been so marked a feature of the earlier history of the agencies. There,

[1] Merchants' Minutes, vol. i, meetings of 1 and 11 June 1773.
[2] C.O. 324:60, pp. 127-131, 138-41, 204-10.

the first proposal to appoint an agent appears to have been made in 1769, when the assembly passed a resolution requesting a conference with the President and council over the choice of an agent. The project, however, fell through, because the council objected to the assembly's nominee, a prominent planter of the island, Sir George Colebrooke, and also apparently raised protest against an assumption by the assembly of the sole right of issuing instructions.[1] Next year another attempt to pass the bill was made, the assembly once more claiming that directions to the agent were a matter for its members alone, " who are the representatives of the people of the Colony for whose benefit solely he is appointed."[2] This was in September. Three months later the assembly reiterated their assertion

> it is the unanimous Opinion of this House, that as representatives of the People, they think it absolutely necessary, their having a power of remonstrating through the Agent . . . Independent of any part of the Legislature whatsoever.[3]

The assembly, however, was compelled to give way, and in 1771 an agency bill similar in its main features to those of other islands was passed.[4] In none of the islands after this date do the acts of appointment appear to have caused difficulty between council and assembly. In St. Vincent in 1778–9 there was

[1] C.O. 74:3, Journals of Assembly, pp. 7, 15, 55, 59, 11 and 12 July, 23 and 28 Aug. 1769.
[2] C.O. 74:4, Minutes of Council, p. 6, 25 Sept. 1770. There is a gap in the Assembly Journals from 17 July 1770 to 29 July 1771.
[3] C.O. 74:4, Minutes of Council, p. 23, 13 Dec. 1776.
[4] C.O. 324:60. Proceedings of both Council and Assembly are wanting between Dec. 1770 and April 1771.

THE NEW AGENCIES

an interruption of the agency owing to internal disputes, but the difficulty did not arise from a discussion as to the agent.[1] Everywhere the need for an agent was recognised, and in Tobago so eager were the colonists for representation that after the return of the island to France in 1783 the agency was interrupted only until 1794,[2] the year after its reconquest by the English.

The appearance of the new agencies after the middle of the century had no perceptible effect on the general constitution of the office. Before this time, the method of the agents' appointment had become so far assimilated for the older islands that a definite conception was in existence as to it, and this idea, partly by correspondence between colonies and partly through the intercourse of agents at home, was available for application when new appointments were made. On all sides there were forces working to give to the office of agent recognised characteristics, and the measure of their success is well illustrated by the way in which newer colonies inherited from those whose agencies were nearly a century older the traditions formed by their experience.

[1] C.O. 260:5 and 6 *passim*. Agents imperfectly accredited acted on behalf of council and assembly during the disputes.

[2] An agency act was passed on 14 February 1794. C.O. 287:2.

CHAPTER VI

THE FUNCTIONS OF THE AGENTS

IN the work of the agents, as in the method of their appointment, the period of development extended from the seventeenth century over the first half of the eighteenth. The representatives of the islands in the early days, before the practice of maintaining agents had become general, were sent over to England or received commissions in England to transact the business of the island only when some matter of special urgency was in question. And, as was natural in such circumstances, not only did the work of the agents appointed by one colony differ from that of agents of another, but successive agencies of the same island often dealt with concerns entirely diverse in character.

Nevertheless some generalisation is possible. Barbados was mainly interested in matters relating to trade, the $4\frac{1}{2}$ per cent. duty, the working of the Navigation Acts, the supply of labour, the imposition of taxes on sugar. The Leeward Islands, on the other hand, showed most conspicuous care for the possibilities of defence: with them the desire to obtain white settlers, even if need be convicts, was dictated, not by the necessities of the estates, but the insufficiency of defence against foreign aggression; and among their most frequent solicitations were those for a supply of military stores and for the reparation of forts: it was as a result of French attack that even the application for a separate government arose. Lastly, in Jamaica, while there was comparatively little anxiety shown to secure aid and privileges from the home government, there was, deepened by the experience of the Earl of Carlisle's rule, a strong desire to prevent any unfavourable interference in the concerns of the island.

Very great stress, however, must not be laid upon this measure of uniformity in the solicitations of the agents. In all the islands the directions to their representatives at home were occasioned by the exigencies of the moment, and little general conception existed until the firm establishment of the office in the middle of the eighteenth century. By that time generations of experience in the solicitation of affairs led to a great measure of similarity in the work of all the agents in England. When the later agencies came into existence a clear idea was prevalent as to the functions of the agent, so that the framers of the first agency act of the Bahama Islands in 1785 were able with confidence to confer on their agent " all such powers and Authorities as are usually vested in any person or Persons, acting as Agent for any British Colony."[1]

Over a hundred years before the first agency act of the Bahama Islands, attempts were being made to build up with very little precedent[2] a permanent

[1] C.O. 25:6, 26 April 1785.
[2] The only possible precedent was the work done by Colonel Francis Moryson on behalf of Virginia in the years immediately following the Restoration. The wording of Moryson's petition of 1665 suggests that he was permanently retained in the service of the island, but his payment was irregular, varying according to the functions he was called upon from time to time to fulfil. C.O. 1:19, No. 46, 10 April 1665.

116 COLONIAL AGENTS OF WEST INDIES

agency for Barbados : Thomas Povey, working for the appointment of himself, and the absentee planters of Barbados on behalf of their friend and nominee Edward Thornburgh. Both tried in their recommendations as to the office to prove the desirability of the appointment and so indicated their conception of the duties of an agent. In Povey's mind the predominant thought was the defence of the Governor's interests : the agent was to " stand sentrie and bee watchfull " so that he could stir up the Governor's friends at home, if any danger threatened his position ; and, although he proposed that their functions should be extended to the concerns of the whole island, this appears as an afterthought caused by his knowledge of Lord Willoughby's wishes.[1] The Gentlemen Planters, on the other hand, thought chiefly of the assembly, of those whose interests, like their own, were bound up in the sugar trade and the prosperity of the plantations ; yet their idea was largely the same, to " give notice . . . what is in Agitation relating to Barbados."[2]

Standing Sentry.—The attitude to the agents' functions taken by Povey and the Gentlemen Planters was not without justification in the time in which they were working. There was considerable difficulty in securing information as to the intentions of the government. In 1671 the London sugar refiners had proceeded so far with their intrigues regarding the

[1] Povey to William Lord Willoughby, 10 March 1672/3, Egerton MS. 2395, ff. 487-9. *Vide infra*, Appendix III, pp. 257-8, where the greater part of the letter is printed.

[2] The Gentlemen Planters to the Deputy-Governor, Council and Assembly of Barbados, 14 Dec. 1670. C.O. 31:2, pp. 15-17. Subsequent communications between Barbados and the Gentlemen Planters were conducted by the assembly alone.

THE FUNCTIONS OF THE AGENTS 117

import duty on sugars before the Barbados planters heard of it that it was nearly too late to avert the danger.[1] Two years later Thornburgh described to the assembly at Barbados the care he had been taking of their concerns at Westminster. He had been, by order of the Gentlemen Planters, in daily attendance on Parliament in order to "give notice to them, if any thinge were in Agitation relateing to you^r Interest," and he heard that "Sir Robert Howard[2] had Demanded a Coppy of the old Excise Bill from the Clerke of the Parliament." Whereupon he concluded that there were prospects of a revision of import duties, and he and the planters summoned a meeting with the sugar refiners and the merchants and agreed to oppose any additional imposition on sugars with all their power. As the matter turned out, the Parliament of 1673 had other affairs to deal with than those concerning the sugar trade, and the question was never debated. The work of Thornburgh, however, was not useless. While he was attending at Westminster he heard of a new difficulty: the merchants trading to Virginia complained that the New England ships carried tobacco and other colonial products to New England and thence to foreign countries, thus evading the restrictions of the Navigation acts. As soon as news of this complaint was obtained representations were made that no such illicit trading took place in plantation sugar. To prevent the rumoured threat of "an Imposition upon all tobaccoes & sugars

---

[1] Gentlemen Planters to Assembly of Barbados, London, 1 May 1671. C.O. 31:2, pp. 45-9.

[2] *Vide sub nom. D.N.B.* He was secretary to the Commissioners of the Treasury, and, probably a little later than this date, Auditor of the Exchequer.

shippt from any of his ma^{ties} Plantations for New England," an organised stirring up of interest was undertaken; several " Parliament men " were approached to persuade them " how unpracticable it was for them, to lay a tax on those that had noe members in their house"; and, although the agitation ended in failure, a step forward had been taken in building up a system of constant watchfulness.[1]

As time went on, the development of the press and the growth of a closely organised West India interest with many friends in the House of Commons made the task of obtaining news of any threatened danger far more easy. Yet the need for someone to " stand sentrie " did not cease. There were many interests in existence in London which worked in opposition to those of the islands. In the seventeenth century the competition of the Portugal merchants had been a serious matter, made more dangerous by their wish to place Portugal and plantation sugars on the same footing in the English market : then throughout the period of West Indian monopoly there were the sugar refiners, always eager for a plentiful supply of cheap sugar, constantly intriguing for importation from foreign sources : and, in the latter half of the eighteenth century, there arose, finally to be successful in breaking the monopoly of the islands, the danger of competition from the East Indies. There was, further, danger from the North American Colonies. Very early in the eighteenth century the existence of illicit trading, forbidden by the Navigation acts, between the continental colonies and the French West Indies, was noticed by

[1] Thornburgh to Assembly of Barbados, 1 April 1673. C.O. 31:2, pp. 123-4. The act, 25 Car. II, c. 7, sect. 11, laid duties on interplantation trade.

THE FUNCTIONS OF THE AGENTS

the colonists; and to secure the safety of the islands in opposition to any privileges which the adherents of the northern colonies might obtain from the government provided another necessity for watchfulness on the agents' part. Moreover, there was a source of anxiety in the Royal African Company. The planters needed cheap labour, supplied in large quantities; if the regulation of the African trade were on too narrow a basis, it might result, together with a great increase of profit to the participants, in a shortage of negroes in the islands, and so any alteration in the form of the company demanded instant care from the representatives of the islands in England. And lastly, in addition to these broad issues there was the possibility of less fundamental changes equally the concern of the islands: acts passed in one colony might be detrimental to another, or measures taken for the defence or in the interests of one colony might expose another to attack.

Against all these dangers the agents had to guard. In October 1730, when the assembly of Jamaica drew up instructions to their proposed agents, great importance was attached to this aspect of the agent's duties. He was to be directed:

> That on all occasions he be attentive to the interest of this island; and in case any thing be offered in parliament or elsewhere, which may be for the advantage of the island, in its trade or otherwise; that he use his utmost interest to promote it, and, if to the prejudice of the island, that he oppose it:
> That he, from time to time, give the earliest accounts of all things that may be intended to the prejudice of the island; and,
> That he oppose the passing of any laws, from any other of his majesty's colonies, that tend to burden or to the laying

any duties on any of the commodities or produce of this island, or that is otherwise prejudicial to the trade.[1]

And forty years later when in the Barbados assembly there was a debate as to the salary to be paid to the island agent, the same view was expressed. Quite close to them, a member of the House said, were " New and Rich settlements " in the interests of which Barbados might " be loaded above our strength." The Northern Colonies might have to be appeased, and indulgencies granted to them at the expense of the sugar colonies, or all alike might suffer from " unusual and Unconstitutional Taxes . . . laid upon the Inhabitants of America in General " : in all such circumstances instant remonstrances would be necessary, which could only be made by an efficient agent in London.[2]

On numerous occasions the agents proved of service in this respect. In 1744 the agents, John Sharpe, of Jamaica and Barbados, and Samuel Martin, of Antigua, Nevis, and Montserrat, combined with the absentee planters and the London merchants to defeat a tax on sugar.[3] And again towards the close of the century, in 1780 and 1781, there was a prolonged struggle between the sugar refiners on the one hand, and the planters and merchants and the agents on the other,

[1] *Journals*, ii, pp. 739-40, 23 Oct. 1730.
[2] C.O. 31:36, pp. 120-1, Journals of the Assembly, 3 June 1772.
[3] " It is my duty to inform you of the Particular Steps which I have taken in Conjunction with the other Agents and with the Merchants and Planters here, to Ward off the Additional Duty which was Designed to be laid upon you. . . ." Samuel Martin to Council and Assembly of Montserrat, London, 24 Feb. 1743/4, C.O. 177:5. Minutes of Council in Assembly, 26 May 1744. See also Letter-book of Messrs. Lascelles and Maxwell, Sept. 1743 – Jan. 1745/6 *passim*. *Vide infra*, Appendix III, pp. 282-4.

THE FUNCTIONS OF THE AGENTS

as to the importation of prize sugar.[1] And still later protests were raised as to other threats to the West Indian monopoly of British markets. So also in 1737, John Yeamans received the thanks of the legislature of Antigua for " so signal a mark of His Vigilance and regard to the publick safety of this His Country " when he had, on hearing of " the General Consternation of the people from the Intended Insurrection of the Negroes," made immediate application for an increase in the military forces stationed in the Leeward Islands.[2] And in 1768 Richard Maitland, lately appointed agent for Grenada and the Grenadines, opposed the application of Dominica for separation of government. He had received no instructions on the matter, " Yet as Your Agent, I thought it my Duty to appear against any plan to Dismember the Government." [3]

Securing Privileges.—In the second quarter of the eighteenth century, when the power of the West India interest was at its height, the work of the agents was extended to cover acts of aggression, gaining for the islands increase of privileges from the home government. The gains related mainly to the sugar trade. Under the system of the Navigation acts the islands both benefited and lost. They were given a free control of the English and North American markets; their access to foreign markets was restrained. To gain the full advantage of the first and to mitigate the losses of the second was their ideal. And so in this period of their power they set themselves to secure the

---

[1] *Vide infra*, Appendix III, pp. 285–6.

[2] C.O. 9:12, Journals of Assembly, 31 March 1737.

[3] C.O. 104:4, Journals of Assembly, 12 March 1768. The letter is printed in Appendix III, *infra*, pp. 275–6.

suppression of the illicit trade of the North American mainland, which threatened their profitable monopoly; and when this was done to free themselves from the restrictions on their own foreign intercourse. They achieved the first in 1733, the other six years later. The victory of the West India interest in 1733 in the question of illicit trade between the North American colonies and the French islands was the termination of a long contest, but the agents played no very great part. Barbados and Jamaica, through the lack of unanimity in their legislatures, had no official agents to take action on this business,[1] and the solicitation was entrusted to men of less regularised position.[2] John Yeamans, however, agent for Antigua and Montserrat, was already showing the zeal that characterised his whole period of office, and in the last two years of the agitation took a prominent share. After the success in 1733 Yeamans proceeded with equal vigour to gain new favours. By this time Barbados and Jamaica had settled the difficulties as to appointment and were represented once more by official agents in London: and all the agents together, strengthened by the absentee planters in London, joined in solicitations to gain their ends.

[1] *Vide supra*, pp. 88, 91, and *infra*, Appendix II, p. 250–1. Peter Le Heup and Samuel Foster, debarred from appointment as colonial agents of Barbados by the attitude of the Council, carried on the solicitations to England as unofficial representatives of the island. See Pitman, *op. cit.*, pp. 249–51. These agents together with John Yeamans were regularly appointed in 1732. C.O. 31:20, Journals of Assembly, 18 Nov. 1732.

[2] Jamaica specially empowered not only Charles Delafaye, the assembly agent, but also Richard Harris and other planters and merchants: their appearance at the Board of Trade is noted in C.O. 391:4, pp. 184–5. See also report of proceedings in the assembly published in the *Mercury*, 15 Nov. 1732. B.M. Add. MS. 22676, pp. 93–4.

THE FUNCTIONS OF THE AGENTS 123

The next achievement was one which had been sought by the islands already for some years, the right of exporting sugar direct to foreign ports. As the decade passed on, the early part of which had been signalised by the victory over the Northern Colonies, the reports made by Yeamans to the legislatures of the islands began to take a hopeful tone. In 1738 he wrote to Montserrat that he had

> waited upon Mr Walpole, and begg'd his Countenance to an Application for the Continuance of our Act (*i.e.* the Sugar Act of 1733) And a farther Bounty or Allowance of two shillings p hundred to be added to the six allready given on all wrought Sugars exported from hence ; and also that We may have the Liberty of Exporting Our sugars directly from South America to Foreign Marketts.[1]

The character of the reply sent by the legislature of Montserrat shows that for the vigour of the advance being made on behalf of the islands the West India interest at home was largely responsible. They were " extremely Glad, that there is a fair Prospect of the Continuance of Our Act," and hoped that some additional bounty or allowance would be granted.

> And as to exporting our Sugars directly from hence to foreign Marketts, it is certain ; that if We were Allowed so to do, it wou'd be only puting us on an equal footing with our Neighbours the French.[2]

When further time had passed, indeed, it was not found possible to secure all the desires advanced by the West India interest. The negotiations that led

[1] Passage quoted from recent letter from agent in one from President of Council and Speaker of Assembly. The original letter was not entered in the Journals. C.O. 177:2, Journals of Assembly, 27 May 1738.   [2] *Ibid.*

to the War of Jenkins' Ear, dictated as they were by a consideration of the interests of trade, made the time unfavourable for too great demands on the good favour of the administration.[1] The renewal of the Sugar Act was obtained, but without any revision of the clauses; and the idea of a bounty had to be abandoned, as such grants were not " popular Methods in Parliament or very practicable at the Treasury." And although, despite strong opposition, the bill "for the direct exportation of sugar to foreign Marketts" was carried, there were more restrictions in it than the agents and their friends had expected: these, Yeamans said, it was hoped would be removed at another opportunity. And he finished his letter of July 1739 with the hopeful assurance " The next Session I believe we shall go on again to work in Order to obtain some farther Advantage for the Sugar Colonies."[2] Before the end of 1739 the outbreak of war transferred the interests of the islands on other matters, to defence and supplies, as always in such times. The interval of peace after 1748 saw a renewal of the dispute with the North American colonies, and for three years representations and counter-representations were made before the Board of Trade.[3] But little success was obtained, and the outbreak of the Seven Years' War soon once more turned away the islands' concern.

The close of the war in 1763 marks the beginning of the decline of the West India interest. Gradually from this time the representatives of the islands had perforce to abandon their attitude of aggression and concern themselves once more with the prevention

---

[1] C.O. 177:2, Journals of Assembly of Montserrat, 27 July 1738.
[2] C.O. 177:3, Journals of Assembly of Montserrat, 18 Oct. 1739.
[3] Cf. Pitman, op. cit., pp. 298-301.

THE FUNCTIONS OF THE AGENTS

of measures prejudicial to the islands. In the last quarter of the century the change was complete: for the loss of the mainland colonies combined with new theories of trade and new motives of philanthropy to destroy the influence of the West India interest. In the fight against the abolition of the slave trade the agents once more were striving to prevent damage to the interests of the islands: in 1788, when the question of abolition was moved in the House of Commons, petitions from the agents were sent together with those from the various mercantile interests of the kingdom.[1] By this time it is clear that the position of the West India interest was no more secure than when, over a hundred years before, the Gentlemen Planters of Barbados gathered together their resources to defeat the attempts of the necessitous court to wring money out of the sugar trade.

Instructions from the Islands.—The early agents in the seventeenth century, besides the duty " of standing sentrie," acted in the main in answer to definite instructions from the islands. In 1671 those empowered for the service of Barbados were charged to present addresses regarding the use of the revenues derived from the $4\frac{1}{2}$ per cent. duty, the trade to Scotland, especially in " Christian servants," the summons of persons in England to answer complaints against them, the disbanding of a regiment lately arrived, the desirability of a direct trade to friendly

---

[1] *e.g.* Petition of Charles Spooner, agent for Grenada and the Grenadines, on behalf of all the islands ceded in 1763: *Journals of the House of Commons,* vol. xliv, pp. 356 (*b*)-358 (*a*), 12 May 1789. Of John Burton and William Hutchinson, agents for Antigua: *ibid.,* p. 380 (*a*), 20 May 1789. Of Stephen Fuller, agent for Jamaica: *ibid.,* p. 399 (*a*) and (*b*), 21 May 1789.

powers.¹ So also with the agents of the Leeward Islands : Crispe and Jory in the years 1679 to 1681 acted as agents for all the islands with regard to the proposed Treaty of Neutrality with the French.² Christopher Jeaffreson, when agent for St. Christopher in 1682 and the following years, was commissioned to secure a supply of convicts to settle in the island and the grant of stores of war, both with the object of strengthening the power of the island in defence.³ Jory, appointed once more in 1705, and another merchant, Richard Cary, appointed the previous year, were empowered by the General Legislature of all the Islands to solicit the confirmation of the general laws. They were to see that the laws " wth all convenient speed, be laid before ye Lords Commissioners of Trade & ye plantations," and that then " all possible Application be made for his Majesties Royal Assent," and they were to maintain a correspondence with each island as to the issue of their labours.⁴ So also William Barnes, of Antigua, was sent home in 1683/4 to secure the passing of the acts of Antigua,⁵ and Ralph

¹ C.O. 31:2, p. 14, Journals of Assembly.
² *Vide supra*, pp. 62–3.
³ Jeaffreson MS., letters dated London ffebruary ye 1st 1682/3, May the 16th 1683 *et passim* (J. C. Jeaffreson, *op. cit.*, ii, pp. 29–31, 58–9), *cf*. C.S.P. vi, Nos. 800, 890, pp. 336–7, 370, *et passim*.
⁴ C.O. 155:3, Minutes of General Council in Nevis, 25 June 1705. The minutes contain at their close a list of instructions to the standing agents of the islands, and a letter to Colonel Jory, chosen to act on behalf of the General Legislature. This letter is printed in Appendix III, *infra*, pp. 274–5. Reference to the earlier appointment of Richard Cary is given in a letter dated 28 May 1705 from Colonel Codrington, " now one of the Gen^{ell} Councill," to the General Assembly then sitting. C.O. 155:3, Minutes of General Assembly in Nevis, 25 June 1705.   ⁵ *Vide supra*, pp. 67–8.

THE FUNCTIONS OF THE AGENTS

Knight by the legislature of Jamaica in 1688 to perform the same functions in connection with that island.[1] Lastly, in the early years of the eighteenth century, it was planned that specially commissioned agents for the Leeward Islands should be sent home to solicit for reparation of the losses incurred in the Spanish Succession War, an application later entrusted to the permanent agents.[2]

The Confirmation of Laws.—As time went on, some of these special activities for which the early agents had been commissioned tended to become stereotyped. The most important was that of the solicitation for the passing of laws.[3] The earliest notice of any special agency connected with this business was the mission of William Barnes from Antigua, and numerous entries in the minutes and journals of the late seventeenth century show the zeal in this matter of the Antigua assembly. In 1693 there was a prolonged exchange of resolutions between the assembly and the Governor-General in council with respect to the sending home of laws for confirmation. "We may," the assembly complained, "for ever be making Lawes, and yett know not what we have to trust to."[4] It

[1] *Vide supra*, p. 75.

[2] C.O. 155:4, Minutes of Council of Montserrat, 22 Jan. 1712/13; *cf.* C.O. 155:5, Journal of Assembly of St. Christopher, 6 Aug. 1713. In 1743 Samuel Martin, agent for Montserrat, was instructed to revive the application. C.O. 177:5, Minutes of Council in Assembly, 28 May 1743.

[3] The endorsements on the colonial acts preserved amongst the C.O. papers show that the acts were sometimes sent home by the Governors as enclosures in their letters, and sometimes to the agents, who presented them to the Council Office or the Board of Trade (*i.e.* " Plantation Office ").

[4] C.O. 155:2, p. 34, Minutes of Council and Assembly of Antigua, 5 July 1693.

was a natural outcome of this attitude that, in comparison with the other West Indian agency acts passed in the seventeenth century, the act of Antigua of 1698 is distinguished by the stress laid on the confirmation of laws, the preamble giving it the first place in the functions of the agent.

In Jamaica, despite the embassy of Ralph Knight in 1688, the importance of this function was not recognised until a later date. The act of 1693, like that of Barbados two years earlier, specified no one branch of the agent's activities. During the long agency struggle of 1704 to 1731/2, however, the action of absentee planters and merchants trading to the island in soliciting for and against laws showed the urgency of official representation, and special mention of this function was in consequence included in the acts of appointment.[1] In December 1713 a resolution was passed condemning the officiousness of "some persons, who have estates in this island, appearing and soliciting in Great Britain against laws passed in this island."[2] As a result in the next agency bill the title specified "the passing of laws" as the main purpose in raising the money,[3] and the act of 1731/2 made this feature permanent.

Of the other islands Barbados retained its early form, merely referring generally to "affairs ... for the good of this Place"; Nevis, St. Christopher, and amongst the islands whose agencies appeared later, the Bahamas and Virgin Islands, adopted somewhat similar terms; while Montserrat, after some experiments, followed the example of Antigua, the wording

---

[1] *Cf.* Act of 1731, printed in Appendix III, *infra*, pp. 269-71.
[2] *Journals*, ii, pp. 81-9, 4-11 Nov. 1712, and p. 107, 5 Dec. 1713.
[3] *Ibid.*, p. 106, 1 Dec. 1713.

THE FUNCTIONS OF THE AGENTS

of whose acts was closely imitated also by the islands ceded in 1763. Quite early in the eighteenth century, however, the difference had become purely formal, for all the agents fulfilled the same functions in relation to the laws. In the years 1722 to 1724, when Nevine, appointed agent by Antigua, St. Christopher, and Montserrat, was busying himself in connection with the confirmation of their laws,[1] the agents for Barbados were also appearing at the Board of Trade regarding acts of that island;[2] while a little later when the assembly of Jamaica, in despair of securing an official agent, nominated representatives of its own, these also negotiated the passing of laws before the Board.[3]

Defence.—Next to the solicitations regarding laws, the most frequent of the agents' activities was in respect of matters of defence. In time of war the trade passing to and fro between England and the island required convoys; the islands themselves frequently wished for a squadron of men of war, and stores and supplies of all sorts were required. While the earliest agent for the Leeward Islands, Ferdinando Gorges, lost the favour of St. Christopher's Island by his negligence in this matter of defence,[4] at almost the same time the representatives of Barbados incurred the displeasure of their island by the ill-informed zeal with which they besought the Lords of Trade for a grant of pikes

---

[1] *Vide* his letters of the Council and Assembly of St. Christopher. C.O. 155:6, Minutes of Council of St. Christopher, Feb. 1722, 7 Nov. 1722, 17 April 1724. He sent letters practically identical in wording to all four islands.
[2] *e.g.* C.O. 391:32, pp. 88–9, 115–6 *et passim.*
[3] *e.g.* C.O. 391:39, p. 266, 13 Oct. 1730.
[4] *Vide supra*, p. 64.

to arm the troops.[1] Throughout the eighteenth century the outbreak of war found the agents, aided by the London merchants, attending at the Board of Trade regarding the safety of the islands, and frequently instructions as to these matters were sent to the agents by the legislatures. In 1705 the instructions sent by the General Council and Assembly of the Leeward Islands to the agent at home gave a prominent place to the safety of the island from attack. The French had " seldom Less than Twenty Privateers out at a Time, & possibly ye best Saylors in all ye world," and so " Two or three or more nimble Frigots " were to be requested as a security for trade ; while at the same time it was desired that a depot for stores should be erected in one of the Leeward Islands

> to supply ye s^d Men of War, That they may not be Obliged to go for Barbados to fetch Stores from thence, & in ye mean Time Leave ye Islands defenceless & open to ye Enemies Insults.[2]

So also the instructions drawn up in Jamaica twenty-five years later : two out of the six items were devoted respectively to the protection of the island in time of war, and the safeguarding of trade at all times.[3] The outbreak of the Wars of Jenkins' Ear and the Austrian Succession were responsible for the numerous references that occur in the correspondence of John Yeamans to the supply of stores of war required for the Leeward Islands ; " above all things," wrote the President and Speaker of Montserrat in 1740, " be

---

[1] *Vide supra*, pp. 54–5.
[2] C.O. 155:3, Minutes of General Council held in Nevis, 25 June 1705.
[3] *Journals*, ii, pp. 739–40, 23 Oct. 1730.

THE FUNCTIONS OF THE AGENTS 131

Assiduous in applying for a squadron of Ships of War."[1] The French Revolutionary War half a century later produced similar applications, in which, by that time, the London merchants took the predominant part.

Miscellaneous Duties.—The other duties confided to the agent were multifarious in character. In the middle of the eighteenth century the agents were required to oppose the absentee planters of Antigua and Jamaica, who made complaint of the placing of additional obligations upon their estates under the terms of the deficiency acts. Regular agents were in existence for both the colonies concerned, and these were heard repeatedly before the Board of Trade and committees of the Privy Council in opposition to the counsel employed by the absentees.[2] Instructions regarding the islands' trade were also from time to time entrusted to the agents' care, as in 1773 when the establishment of a free port in Barbados was asked for by the island,[3] and, a few years later, when like privileges were desired for the island of Jamaica.[4] Details in connection with trade were generally left in the hands of the London merchants with whom the agents were closely associated.[5]

---

[1] Journals of Assembly, C.O. 177:3, 19 April 1740.

[2] An account of the contest is given in Pitman, *op. cit.*, pp. 35–9, especially note 82. The final hearings of the agent for Jamaica before the Board of Trade is under date 22 April and 5 May 1752, C.O. 391:59. A revival of the dispute in connection with Jamaica took place in 1764. C.O. 391:71, 17 Jan., 30 Jan., 3 March, 6 March 1764. The Counsel for the absentees was Ferdinand Paris.

[3] C.O. 31:36, Journals of Assembly, 31 Aug. 1773.

[4] *Journals*, ix, pp. 184, 262, 13 Dec. 1792 and 4 Dec. 1793.

[5] *Vide infra*, pp. 206–7.

The instructions also dealt with difficulties arising from differences of interest between the various islands, as when in 1742 Samuel Martin, agent for Montserrat, was directed to guard against the attempts anticipated from Antigua to establish in that island the forces stationed in Montserrat;[1] or twelve years later when John Sharpe in his capacity as agent for Antigua was informed that opposition should be made to the confirmation of an act recently passed in Jamaica, whose tendencies it was feared would be to depopulate the other islands.[2] Upon still other occasions accusations against the Governor were ordered to be pressed or refuted, as in 1739 when the island agent defended the Governor of Antigua against the complaints of a former secretary of the island, Wavell Smith,[3] in 1796 when the agent for Jamaica was instructed to deal with alleged libel against the Earl of Balcarres,[4] and in 1781 when representations were required in opposition to Governor Cunninghame of Barbados.[5] There was little limit to the scope of the agents' instructions; but even John Yeamans became rather restive when he had tried in vain for some years to secure a clergyman of " good sober character " for one of the three parishes of Montserrat, and begged that he " be excus'd from any thing of this sort for the future."[6]

Consultation by Home Government.—One of the main factors in producing the large measure of uniformity

[1] Letter from Speaker of Assembly to Samuel Martin, 4 Sept. 1742, C.O. 177:3, Journals of Assembly, 4 Sept. 1742.
[2] C.O. 9:20, Journals of Assembly, 26 April 1754.
[3] *A.P.C.* iii, No. (374), pp. 495–501, and No. (447), p. 615.
[4] *Journals*, ix, p. 613, 9 Dec. 1796.
[5] C.O. 31:41, Journals of Assembly, 18 April 1781, pp. 79–83, etc.
[6] Letter dated 1 Jan. 1739/40. C.O. 177:3, Journals of Assembly, 5 June 1750.

THE FUNCTIONS OF THE AGENTS

in the functions of the agents during the course of the eighteenth century was the attitude taken by the home government. To the practice of consulting planters and merchants, adopted by the various authorities responsible for plantation affairs, Edward Long in his *History of Jamaica*[1] appears to ascribe the rise of the agency; and, while this is not altogether true, there is no doubt that when the agencies were once established a very considerable share in their usefulness was due to such action. In 1678, indeed, the Lords of Trade asserted, uncompromisingly enough, their right to consult whomever they pleased, and not merely the accredited agent of the colony;[2] and throughout the eighteenth century the consultation of merchants and planters was continued. Nevertheless, the more official character of advice from the agent was put constantly into use. As early as 1665 it was this aspect of the agent's duties that suggested to Colonel Francis Moryson, of Virginia, that a salary should be allowed him out of the revenues of the colony,[3] and a century later the same attitude on the part of the government led to the appointment by royal warrant of agents for those colonies whose constitutional or financial position made impossible a colonial agency of the ordinary type.[4]

The action of the administration was natural under the system of control then prevailing. They were burdened with many responsibilities in relation to the colonies. Colonial governors required not only commissions but a series of instructions the wording of

---

[1] Edward Long, *History of Jamaica*, London, 1774, vol. i, p. 114.
[2] C.O. 391:2, pp. 205-6, 19 Jan. 1677/8.
[3] *Vide supra*, p. 115, n. 2.   [4] *Vide infra*, pp. 169, n. 2; 234, n. 1.

which was a matter of considerable importance. Minor officials such as the secretary and the provost-marshal also held their posts by virtue of royal appointment, as did members of council. In all those matters the opinion of the agent was asked, as well as from time to time that of the principal absentees or merchants, as to the conditions in the island, the wishes of the inhabitants, or the suitability of an applicant for office. In 1680 the assembly of Barbados wrote to their agents Colleton and Drax that they trusted to them to see that suitable persons " out of the freeholders, of the best Interest; Judgement, & Integrity," were appointed as councillors.[1] And constantly in the eighteenth century the Board of Trade summoned the agents of the islands to ask their opinion as to the councillors proposed by the Governor or by merchants and planters at home,[2] or simply to draw up a list of the most suitable persons.

On other points also, information was sought from the agents. Some were in connection with constitutional difficulties relating to the colonies, such as when in October 1697 the Barbados agents were asked as to " the Law about the Decision of controverted Elections."[3] And, again, in October 1704 the Barbados agents were required to furnish an explanation of the existence of an alleged quorum of 15 members of the assembly.[4] Others related to the conditions

---

[1] Letter dated 15 April 1680, C.O. 31:2, Journals of Assembly, pp. 382–6.

[2] *e.g.* in 1708, *Journal of the Commissioners for Trade and Plantations*, pp. 421, 537, 547–8, 553–4.

[3] C.O. 391:10, p. 299, 7 Oct. 1697.

[4] *Journal of the Commissioners for Trade and Plantations*, Minutes of 17 and 19 Oct. 1704, pp. 47, 48.

THE FUNCTIONS OF THE AGENTS 135

of the islands, as in June 1697 when the Barbados agents were requested to furnish information as to any " alterations " that had occurred " between the English and French in the Island of Barbadoes or any of the other Islands thereon depending and more especially in or with relation to Sta Lucia."[1] And again, in January 1698/9 when inquiry was made from the agents as to whether any ships sailed from London to Tobago or whether there were any plans in progress for planting the island under the protection of the Duke of Courland;[2] or similarly in 1755 when the agents for the Leeward Islands and the principal merchants trading thereto were asked to state their views as to the establishment of civil government in the Virgin Islands.[3]

In the history of the functions of the agents of the various islands, the eighteenth century saw an even greater measure of assimilation than in that of appointment. In England the agents worked to a large extent together, and from the point of view of the home government their duties were regarded as identical; and so, gradually, they acquired a regularised position, and the traditions of their office provided sufficient indications to them of a great part of their functions. Their work was indeed many-sided, to represent the interest of the islands on all occasions, and the measure of their zeal was to a very great extent the determining factor in regulating the volume of business transacted by them. But for an industrious agent there was no lack of opportunity. The passing of laws and the

[1] C.O. 391:10, pp. 137-8, 30 June 1697. The reply of the agents is in C.O. 20:3, No. 36, 10 July 1697.
[2] C.O. 391:11, p. 337, 16 Jan. 1698/9.
[3] C.O. 391:62, 14 Jan. 1755. The agents attended on 16 January.

safety of the islands in time of war were in themselves sufficiently onerous responsibilities, but to these were added the duty, capable of very elastic interpretation, of preventing anything to the detriment of the island's prosperity, whether it came from a mercantile interest, from those concerned in another colony, or, soon to become most important of all, those whose principles impelled them to override all arguments of rights of property. Lastly, there were frequent demands of service from the island authorities or from the administration at home. The only limitation of function appears to have been that the agents' instructions came from the legislature of the island, and wherever the legislature saw or might see its interests involved the agents' duty was to obey or if possible to anticipate its behests.

CHAPTER VII

CONTROL BY THE ISLANDS

THE great distance of the islands from the mother country, while it contributed largely to the recognition of the need for an agent, made exceedingly difficult the problem of control. The colony had, indeed, but a very insufficient check on the agent's actions: he might be inattentive to business, or he might be influenced in its discharge by interested persons in England, and in either case it was not easy to discover his misdeeds. These difficulties considerably hampered the development of the agency in Barbados and the Leeward Islands. As early as 1679 the island of St. Christopher was deterred from choosing an agent by " the bad successes they have had in the persons formerly employed ":[1] and the prejudice was by no means unjustified, for in 1705 an attempt was still being made to recover from Joseph Crispe the funds entrusted to him for solicitations connected with the proposed Treaty of Neutrality of 1678.[2] Barbados also had from the earliest years of the agent's history found it hard

[1] Jeaffreson MS., letter dated St. Christopher's Island, July y⁰ 10th 1679 (J. C. Jeaffreson, *op. cit.*, i, p. 239).
[2] Acts were passed by the General Legislature of all the Islands in 1692 and 1705 with a view to secure the return of these funds. *Acts of Assembly passed in the Charibbee Leeward Islands, From 1690 to 1705*, London, 1740, pp. 3, 24.

to exercise adequate control : in 1672 the power of the Gentlemen Planters in England virtually succeeded in depriving the assembly even of the right of appointment, while five years later the independent action of Colleton and Thornburgh caused dissatisfaction to all parties in the island.

Private Sources of Information.—In increasing measure, however, during the late seventeenth and early eighteenth centuries unofficial sources of information regarding the actions of the agents were becoming of use. Frequently the agent himself was a planter of the island by which he was appointed, or a merchant concerned in its trade, and had therefore to maintain a correspondence in his own interests with the resident planters and merchants. Thus Christopher Jeaffreson when acting as agent in London wrote not only to the Deputy-Governor of St. Christopher, but to various of the principal planters.[1] Nor was this all : as the method of trade between the islands and the merchants at home approximated more and more to the system prevailing in the latter part of the eighteenth century, all the principal planters in the islands were, on matters connected with their estates, constantly in communication with the London merchants, to whom they consigned their products, and from whom they received the credit essential to the prosperity of their plantations. The scope of the merchants' letters was in no way confined to the details of business, and the accounts given of their dealings with the agents added considerably to the information possessed in the island regarding his work. To this source Sir John St. Leger

[1] *e.g.* Letters to Captain James Phipps. J. C. Jeaffreson, *op. cit.*, ii, *passim*.

appealed in 1713 when he discovered the unfavourable attitude which was taken towards him in Antigua. " I can refer myself," he wrote to the Speaker of the assembly in July, " to the Merchants and your friends here, whether . . . I was not both diligent and serviceable ";[1] and again a few months later " There are now a great number of your Friends in England, to whom I appeal and from whose Character of me, I expect my Establishment or Dismiss."[2] And, in this unofficial manner, in October 1744 a merchant trading to Barbados described to a planter of that island his negotiations with the agent, John Sharpe, regarding the ejection of the French from St. Lucia,[3] and the steps contemplated by the agent in connection with certain accusations against the Governor.[4]

In the first half of the eighteenth century another result of the changing system of trade was of some importance in relation to the agency. During the whole of this period the Leeward Islands continued the use of sugar to supplement their scanty metal currency,[5] and the stocks raised in taxation had in the same way as those of private planters to be consigned

[1] C.O. 9:3, Minutes of Council in Assembly, 27 July 1713.

[2] *Ibid.*, 15 Dec. 1713.

[3] Letter dated 16 Oct. 1744 to Thomas Applewhaite. Letter-book of Messrs. Lascelles and Maxwell, Sept. 1743 – Jan. 1745/6, p. 215.

[4] Letter dated 15 Jan. 1745/6 to Thomas Applewhaite, *ibid.*, p. 3. As the century passed the importance of the intercourse between the agents and the planters and merchants in England steadily increased. *Vide infra*, Chapters IX and X, *passim*.

[5] The Nevis agency act of 1751 provided that the agent's salary should be sent to England in " Sugar, or Merchandise of the Growth and Produce of the Island, or . . . Bills of Exchange." C.O. 324:60, pp. 61–2. *Cf.* Act of St. Vincent dated 11 July 1767, *ibid.*, pp. 138–9.

to a merchant at home. It was customary, therefore, at any rate in St. Christopher and Montserrat, for a merchant in London to be chosen to receive and dispose of the sugar[1]; and there was consequently in addition to the agent a merchant of semi-official status in frequent communication with the island. From him, from time to time, information was received as to the progress of the island's affairs.[2]

Machinery for Control.—There were, further, official means of control available to the colonists. The acts of appointment supplemented by resolutions of the legislature laid down in all the islands a channel for the issue of instructions to the agent. In Barbados and Jamaica, after the struggles for appointment and control in the early eighteenth century, a committee of both houses was named in the appointing act. In Antigua the Commander-in-Chief, Lieutenant-Governor, or President of the council, jointly with the Speaker of the assembly, were empowered to direct the agent on the question of the island's laws, the Speaker alone in the matter of " a Remonstrance or complaint of any Grievance." In Montserrat[3] and St. Christopher the wording of the acts evolved

---

[1] Some reservation is probably needed in the case of Antigua and Nevis. In Nevis in 1728, since it was impossible to dispose of " the Sugars belonging to the Publick of the Island " for cash it was decided to ship them to the agent, Colonel Butler, and draw bills upon him to their value. C.O. 186:1, Minutes of Council, 2 Sept. 1728.

[2] As in Montserrat when William Nevine was agent and William Gerrish dealt with the sugars belonging " to the public." C.O. 155:6, Minutes of Council of Montserrat, 23 June 1722, 8 Jan. 1723. *Cf.* C.O. 177:2, Journals of Assembly, 5 Feb. 1731/2.

[3] Montserrat, however, during the greater part of the century, commencing in 1737, imitated the form of the Antigua Acts. C.O. 176:4, Act dated 13 Aug. 1737.

in the early eighteenth century made no provision for instructions, nor did that of the acts of Nevis when appointment by act was later adopted by that island. In practice, however, in all the islands committees of correspondence were appointed by council and assembly. Of the islands whose agencies dated from the second half of the century, the Bahama and Virgin Islands nominated a committee of both Houses in their acts of appointment; Grenada, Tobago, and Dominica, although following closely the form of act usual in Antigua, added a provision regulating the choice of commissioners of correspondence if they should be thought necessary; while in St. Vincent, although in its early acts no reference was made to any machinery for instruction, in practice committees were empowered from time to time.[1]

The Jamaica Committee.—The authorities thus constituted had in each island certain peculiarities both of origin and functions. In Jamaica the committee was entrusted, ever since the act of 1693, with greater powers than in any other island. During the sessions of the assembly, it is true, it could act only in accordance with the directions of the two Houses, but in the intervals of assembly it was itself responsible, having power even to dismiss or appoint an agent. So important was the committee considered that the titles of the acts of appointment described the purpose of the act as to appoint, not only agents, but " commissioners of correspondency." The result of the importance of the committee was that there were, in the early years of the century, disputes as to its composition between council and

[1] Before the close of the century St. Vincent altered the form of its acts in accordance with those of the other ceded islands.

assembly.¹ Later, an obstructionist policy was adopted by the council, no member of the council's nominees appearing when the committee was summoned, thus making impossible a quorum.² Perhaps it was to defeat this action, or because there was rivalry for seats on the committee, that the numbers of the committee steadily rose in the second half of the eighteenth century, reaching its climax in 1794, when the agency act named as commissioners all the council and the assembly then serving, and the members of each " for the time being resident in the Island."³

There was, during the second half of the century, a contemporaneous development in the organisation of the committee. Copies of all their proceedings were from the earliest times directed to be entered in a " fair Book to be bought and kept for that purpose" ready to be laid before the legislature when required : a salaried clerk was allowed the committee to assist in their work.⁴ In 1767 it was further provided that the committee might be summoned to meet on the

¹ *e.g. Journals*, ii, p. 650, 18 July 1728.

² Edward Long, *History of Jamaica*, London, 1774, vol. i, pp. 116-18. Long was writing almost immediately after the event, and down to the year 1769 he was in Jamaica holding the position of judge of the vice-admiralty court. *Vide sub nom. D.N.B.* In both Jamaica and Barbados the presence of a member of the Council was necessary to form a quorum.

³ C.O. 139:48, No. 896, 20 Nov. 1794. Before this time two experiments had been made which were not repeated. The act of 1763 entrusted the whole management of the agency to commissioners appointed by Act. C.O. 139:22, 21 Dec. 1763. *Cf.* proposal of 1714 : *Journals*, ii, p. 132, 17 Feb. 1713/14. The act of 1767 provided that in case of persistent disagreement between the two sections of the committee they might " act separately." C.O. 139:23, No. 105, 10 Dec. 1767.

⁴ Act of 10 Aug. 1693, Plantation Register, i, pp. 249-53.

CONTROL BY THE ISLANDS 143

business of the agency at any time on the motion of any two of the members, and, moreover, that the meetings should always be held in " the Room, in which the present Assembly is now Convened in the Town of Saint Jago de la Vega, and no other . . . place."[1] Finally, in 1794 there was a further advance when it was stipulated that a room should be hired in St. Jago de la Vega for the meetings of the committee, where alone the commissioners or any two of them might open letters received from the agent.[2]

Committees in the other Islands.—In Barbados the committee of correspondence was not by the acts of appointment granted any such extensive functions as those delegated in Jamaica. In the earliest acts, indeed, there was no mention of any such committee;[3] but when occasion demanded a committee was appointed to write letters to the agents.[4] During the period 1699 to 1705, however, when the agency was in the hands of the assembly alone the disadvantages of this system were realised. It was discovered in 1701 that the letters and proceedings of the committee had " been dispersed into the hands of private persons, so that the same cannot now be found," and it was resolved that for the future all the business of the committee should be entered in a special book.[5] Three years later, a motion was agreed that the committee should be supplied with

[1] C.O. 139:23, No. 105, 10 Dec. 1767. The relevant portions of the act are printed in Appendix III, *infra*, pp. 271-2.
[2] C.O. 139:48, No. 89, 20 Nov. 1794.
[3] *i.e.* the acts of 1691 and 1695, C.O. 30:5, 1 Sept. 1691, and *The Laws of Barbados* . . . London, 1699, No. 408, p. 195, 18 Dec. 1695.
[4] *e.g.* C.O. 31:4, pp. 207-8, Minutes of Council, 4 Aug. 1691, and C.O. 31:3, p. 358, Journals of Assembly, 14 Nov. 1693.
[5] C.O. 31:6, p. 442, Journals of Assembly, 18 Nov. 1701.

minutes of assembly as often as they required them, either for sending to the agents or for their own information.¹ Only a few weeks after, the committee was further empowered to meet whenever they thought fit, and to have " a Clerk to write ffor them, and enter their proceedings in ffair books ready ffor the View of the house." ² The development had, indeed, before the passing of the act of 1705 reached nearly the same position as that of the committee operating in Jamaica. In 1705 no attempt was made to define the functions of the commissioners, the authority of the committee, presumably of the assembly alone, already in existence, being continued.³ The next year, however, a joint committee of the two Houses was named " to Correspond with the Agents, and transmitt to them such papers and Instructions as they shall from time to time be directed to transmitt " ; ⁴ and this remained with little change the form in succeeding acts. There were no developments in personnel similar to those that took place in Jamaica, the reason being no doubt the smaller scope of the committee's functions.⁵

Amongst the other islands only in the Bahama group ⁶ was there any approximation to the import-

¹ C.O. 31:7, Journals of Assembly, 6 Sept. 1704.
² *Ibid.*, 27 Sept. 1704.   ³ C.O. 30:6, pp. 481-4, 7 Aug. 1705.
⁴ C.O. 30:6, pp. 573-5, 29 Oct. 1706.
⁵ The committee was responsible for the drafting of letters to the agent, for they were not communicated to the Assembly until after their dispatch. C.O. 31:29, p. 17, Journals of Assembly, 22 Jan. 1755. But the letters were written in consequence of a resolution of the legislature.
⁶ In the Bahama acts of appointment the committee was named in the act, and letters to George Chalmers, agent in the last fifteen years of the century dated from the " Office of Correspondence." B.M. Add. MS. 22901, Letter-book of George Chalmers, 1797-1805, *e.g.* f. 296.

CONTROL BY THE ISLANDS

ance of the committee of correspondence in Jamaica. Even in the Virgin Islands, where the acts of appointment nominated joint committees of Council and Assembly, they were, like those of Barbados, concerned merely with the drafting and opening of letters, and in the other Leeward Islands and the islands ceded in 1763 the less formal method taken in the naming of the commissioners and the consequent limitation of their period of office militated against any conspicuous growth in organisation. The functions of the Committee were secretarial in character,[1] and there is little evidence of rivalry in its formation.

Constitutional Difficulties in the Leeward Islands.—In the Leeward Islands the same problems occurred in connection with control as marked the history of appointment. The position of a general government complicated the attempts to control the agents made by the legislatures of the individual islands. The main difficulty was in connection with the authority of the Governor-General. The act of Antigua passed in 1698, which established the channel for control in that island, named the Governor-General or deputy Governor or President of the council as one of the powers to give instructions to the agent on the subject of the island's laws. When, however, in 1737 the assembly of Montserrat drew up an agency bill avowedly in imitation of that of Antigua the Governor-

---

[1] *Cf.* President and Council of Montserrat to Assembly: " To be as serious with you as you please upon Account of your Letter, we don't know by what Authority a Committee can take upon them to give Directions to An Agent, & to make Promises in behalf of the Publick, even of Giving away money, when their orders were only to write a Letter of thanks." C.O. 177:3, Journals of Assembly, 28 Feb. 1739/40.

General condemned it, on the ground that the authority of the Deputy-Governor or President in sending home the laws should not be regarded as of equal validity with his own.[1] The Governor-General had some justification for his complaint, for in practice he was responsible for the correspondence on this matter,[2] and as a result, in the earlier part of the eighteenth century, he tended to monopolise the correspondence with the agent.[3] The meticulous accuracy of John Yeamans, however, during his agency led to a more careful observation of the rules laid down in the acts of appointment regarding the vehicle for instructions.[4]

In the early years of the eighteenth century there was the possibility of further complication in control by the meeting from time to time of the General Legislature of all the Islands. The temporary amalgamation of agencies of the Leeward Islands during the

[1] C.O. 177:2, Journals of Assembly, 9 Nov. 1736-8 March 1736/7.
[2] In Antigua this was the subject of controversy: see C.O. 155:2, Minutes of Council and Assembly of Antigua, p. 5, 3 Nov. 1692, when the Assembly suggested that acts should be sent home by the Speaker. See also *ibid.*, pp. 23, 31, 32-4, 99. In Montserrat the assembly received complaints from the Governor-General when no agent was appointed. C.O. 177:2, Journals of Assembly, 5 June 1736.
[3] *e.g.* Letter from Assembly of Antigua to the agent William Nevine, 27 Aug. 1717. C.O. 9:4, Journals of Assembly, 27 Aug. 1717. Also *ibid.*, 10 March 1719/20; *ibid.*, 24 March 1719/20; *cf.* C.O. 155:6, Montserrat, Minutes of Council in Assembly, 7 March 1721/2. Also C.O. 155:6, St. Christopher, Minutes of Council, 17 April and 19 Aug. 1724, and C.O. 241:3, St. Christopher, Journals of Assembly, 22 July 1735.
[4] *e.g.* Antigua. C.O. 9:6, Journals of Assembly, 2 and 17 Sept. 1728, 2, 17, and 27 Jan. 1728/9. C.O. 9:7, Journals of Assembly, 26 Feb. 1729/30 *et passim*. *Cf.* Montserrat, C.O. 177:3, Journals of Assembly, 14 April, 29 June, 18 Oct. 1739, 19 Feb. 1739/40.

CONTROL BY THE ISLANDS 147

last decade of the seventeenth century in a general agency of the whole group [1] led to a desire on the part of the General Legislature to establish a permanent hold upon the agents. The difficulties in obtaining a full session of the General Assembly prevented any action with regard to the agency in 1698; but in 1705 a serious attempt was made to exert a common control over the agents. The matter was first proposed in the General Council on 28th May. The assembly, in representing the necessity for an application for three cruisers to defend the islands, had suggested the drawing up of an address to Her Majesty. The council in reply said that it would be preferable to instruct the agents to make application,

> and that in Order to this wee thinke it will bee necessary that Montserrat should name an Agent, and that the Gent^n of St. Christophers should be put in mind to pay their Agent what's due to him, that applications may be Carried on Joyntly for the future, with diligence and vigour for the service of the whole Government.[2]

The suggestion was promptly taken up by the assembly, which resolved two days later that

> ye particular Agents of ye Islands be Required to consult together on all urgent matters, y^t may be offered for ye benefit of all ye Islands, meeting together once a Month for ye purpose y^t proper Applications be by y^m made.[3]

[1] During the general agency, control was exercised mainly by the individual legislatures of the islands: *vide* letter from the President of the Council and Speaker of the Assembly of Nevis dated 21 Oct. 1697. C.O. 155:2, Journals of Assembly of Nevis, p. 434, 21 Oct. 1697.
[2] C.O. 155:3, Minutes of General Council held in Nevis, 28 May 1705.
[3] C.O. 155:3, Minutes of General Assembly held in Nevis, 30 May 1705.

Instructions to the agents were thereupon drafted, and issued by the President of the General Council and the Speaker of the General Assembly on 25th June. The agents were to meet once a month, the expenses of their meeting being charged to the public of the islands, and each agent was to communicate to the rest anything of common interest that came to his knowledge, and to inform constantly by each packet boat the treasurer of his island as to " all occurrences that do happen." [1]

It is doubtful whether the meetings recommended were held. The instructions were received by Richard Cary and Joseph Jory, agents for Antigua and Nevis,[2] but they were already closely associated in their private and public interests, and it seems probable that the formal directions made little change. At a meeting of the General Legislature in February and March 1710/11 held in Antigua, the suggestion of a general agent was refused by the Assembly, the counter-proposal being made of the recommendation by the Governor-General to all the islands of some one person.[3] But the short and unpopular agency of Sir John St. Leger, the agent so chosen, prevented any precedent from being created from this expedient. Henceforth the agents, save in so far as they received

[1] C.O. 155:3, Minutes of General Assembly held in Nevis, 25 June 1705. Certain instructions were added regarding specific solicitations; in connection with the evils of trade between the French West Indies and the Northern colonies it was stated that it was left to the judgment of the agents whether the co-operation of the agents of Barbados and Jamaica should be asked.

[2] *Journal of Commissioners for Trade and Plantations*, pp. 180–1, 2 and 6 Nov. 1705.

[3] C.O. 9:2, Meeting of General Council and Assembly, 3 and 6 March 1710/11.

CONTROL BY THE ISLANDS 149

directions from the Governor-General, were subject to the control of their own island alone.[1]

The Agents' Correspondence.—In all the islands the authorities for control adopted methods to a great extent similar for securing the carrying out of their instructions. In the first place it was expected that the agent should correspond with some frequency with his island. Colonel Jory was desired by the General Legislature in 1705 that he would

> frequently Correspond wth ye Treasurer of each Island, That no one Island may be in ye Dark or Ignorant of what becomes of their General Laws.[2]

And if the failure to receive instructions was regarded by the agent, as in the case of Sir John St. Leger, as indicating lack of confidence in him,[3] the intermission of the agent's letters was interpreted by the islands as evidence of a neglect of business.[4] To guard against

---

[1] The absence of similar difficulty in the ceded islands was due to the early abolition of the General Legislature. *A.P.C.*, v, p. 7, 7 Sept. 1768. The agency acts of these islands provided for the co-operation of Governor-General, Deputy-Governor, and Speaker in instructions regarding the confirmation of laws.

[2] C.O. 155:3, Minutes of General Council held in Nevis, 25 June 1705.

[3] Antigua, C.O. 9:2, Journals of Assembly, 18 May 1713, and C.O. 9:3, Minutes of Council in Assembly, 27 July 1713. This was not always the explanation. Sometimes it was due to disagreements in the island. *Cf.* letter to agent in Bahama Islands, George Chalmers, printed in Appendix III, *infra*, pp. 276–7; and letter in similar effect four years later. B.M. Add. MS. 22901, f. 115. Letter dated Nassau, 5 Nov. 1800.

[4] The dismissal of Henry Wilmot from the agency of St. Christopher was said to be due to neglect of business evidenced in this way. *Vide infra*, Appendix III, p. 273.

this conclusion in 1722 William Nevine, agent for Montserrat, assured the Council and Assembly:

> (tho' I can't pretend to have been a punctual Correspondent) yet I have unexceptionable Witnesses that there has not been at any time the least Intermission of my Care of the Publick affairs of ye Island.[1]

The most successful agents, John Yeamans, John Sharpe, Stephen Fuller, George Walker, wrote constantly to their employers in the islands;[2] and examples occur where the desire to get rid of an agent was dictated by his slackness in correspondence.[3]

The test thus imposed was by no means worthless. While there were some matters, especially solicitations regarding laws[4] or questions of defence, in which it was possible for the agent to proceed to some extent by routine, there were numerous instances when affairs of the island came under his notice for which no instructions had been issued. Sometimes the urgency of

[1] C.O. 155:6, Montserrat Minutes of Council, 17 Nov. 1722.

[2] *Vide* letters from John Yeamans entered in full in the Journals of Assembly and Minutes of Council of Montserrat, C.O. 177:2 and 3 *passim*. Notices of the receipt of his letters also occur in the Journals and Minutes of Antigua, C.O. 9:9–16 *passim*. Similar notices in the Journals of Jamaica and Barbados indicate the constant correspondence of the other agents mentioned.

[3] *e.g.* on the termination of the agency of Samuel Martin for Nevis. C.O. 186:3, Minutes of Council and Assembly, 27 June 1749.

[4] Votes of censure were passed on William Nevine in Antigua and Montserrat for his neglect of business. C.O. 9:5, Journals of Assembly, 12 Feb. 1722/3, and C.O. 155:6, Minutes of Council of Montserrat, 26 March 1729. It appears from Nevine's letters entered in the Journals and Council Minutes and also from the notices of his action in the Board of Trade Journal that while he was sufficiently energetic in connection with the confirmation of laws, he transacted little other business for the islands. Hence the scarcity of his letters.

CONTROL BY THE ISLANDS

the business demanded that an answer should be given at once; then he must either refuse action altogether [1] or run the risk of his measures receiving disapprobation; but at other times the matter could lie by while he wrote to the island for directions.[2] Sometimes when he was in the midst of a solicitation ordered by the island, reference was necessary in connection with some point arising from it.[3] Thus for his own sake as well as to quiet the anxieties of the island a zealous agent would write frequently to his employers.

The Agents' Accounts.—The value of the agent's letters was not merely that they proved his continued discharge of his duty, it lay also in the information they contained of the method of his activities. A still more useful source of information on this point was the agent's accounts. By the close of the seventeenth century it had become the rule that the colonial agents should receive a fixed salary

---

[1] *e.g.* the agent for Antigua in 1705. "Mr. Cary attending . . . and being asked whether he had anything to offer in relation to the trade to St. Thomas, he said that he had no instructions from the Island of Antego to move upon that matter, and therefore had nothing to offer thereupon." *Journals of the Commissioners for Trade and Plantations*, p. 181, 2 Nov. 1705.

[2] *e.g.* the agent for Antigua in 1755. John Sharpe requested instructions regarding representation from the Hamburg merchants, and a petition from the agent for Montserrat regarding the regiment stationed in Antigua. C.O. 9:22, Journals of Assembly, 23 Sept. 1705.

[3] *e.g.* the agent for Antigua in 1738-9. John Yeamans wrote to the Governor-General for further powers in connection with his defence against Wavell Smith. C.O. 1:92, Journals of Assembly, 9 March 1737/8. And again in 1739 he reported in connection with the same matter that certain measures had been suggested to him, and he had said "he had no authority given him to do anything of that sort yet he would venture to recommend." C.O. 9:12, Journals of Assembly, 18 Dec. 1739.

independent of the volume of business passing through their hands.¹ But, in addition to this allowance, there were charges for disbursements paid by the agent in the transaction of the affairs of the island, and, of these, accounts were rendered from the earliest time of the agencies. Thus, in 1674, Edward Thornburgh sent to the assembly of Barbados detailed schedules of his expenditure on behalf of the island;² and so also, in 1683, the papers and accounts of Beeston and Littleton, agents for Jamaica, were laid by the Governor before the assembly.³ Later, when the custom of appointment by act had become established, more definite provision was made for the review of the agent's accounts. Thus the agency acts of Antigua from the year 1728 required that the agent's charges should " be first sworn to before the Lord Mayor of London for the time being and attested under the publick seal of the City of London." ⁴ In Jamaica the committee of correspondence was authorised to examine the accounts.⁵

The scrutiny to which the accounts were subjected

[1] Some of the early agents derived their payment from the charge of a percentage on the money received or expended in the course of their work. This was the case with the personal agents of the Governors-General of the Leeward Islands, and with the agents for Jamaica appointed in 1682. See Higham, " The Accounts of a Colonial Governor's Agent in the Seventeenth Century," *American Historical Review*, Jan. 1923, pp. 263–85. A proposal for the return to his system was made in Montserrat in 1736, C.O. 177:2, Journals of Assembly, 5 June 1736. The salaries granted to the agents varied between £80 and £400 sterling per annum.

[2] The accounts are entered in full in C.O. 31:2, Journals of Assembly, pp. 109–15, 13 Nov. 1674.

[3] C.O. 140:4, Minutes of Council, 5 Sept. 1683.

[4] C.O. 8:6, No. 3, 25 Jan. 1727/8.

[5] Plantation Register, i, pp. 249–53, 10 Aug. 1693.

CONTROL BY THE ISLANDS

was by no means a mere matter of form. As early as 1697 the Council and Assembly of Nevis protested against certain items in the accounts of the commissioners for the Leeward Islands appointed in 1690.[1] And twenty years later still stronger exception was taken by St. Christopher to the charges made by Stephen Duport in the service of the island.[2] Duport's accounts extended over a period of ten years, and they contained but little detail. One item was £215, "To expences unavoidable in a Constant attendance in the Offices," and another similar sum for coach hire: the Council commented that they "cannot think what Business has been recommended to him from us could engage him in such Charges & Coach hire & other Expences yearly." The assembly had a simple way of evading the difficulty. Apparently no undertaking had been given regarding salary, and in the accounts spaces had been left blank "to my Troubles and Attendance . . . left to the Equity of the Gentlemen of the Council and Assembly." The accounts were submitted to a committee of both Houses, and upon the suggestion of the assembly it was finally decided to pay Duport the balance of his disbursements, providing no remuneration at all for his services.[3] At about the same time Colonel Jory, of Nevis, had submitted his list of expenditure over a similar period, apparently in some considerable detail. A committee of the assembly was appointed to examine them, and a full report was made, comments being inserted on the various items charged, and, despite the favour

[1] C.O. 155:2, Journals of Assembly of Nevis, 21 Oct. 1697.
[2] C.O. 155:5, Journals of Assembly of St. Christopher, 16 July 1717.
[3] *Ibid.*, 6 March 1717/18.

with which he was generally regarded, it was recommended that a deduction should be made of £41.[1]

Reproof and Dismissal.—While the agent's letters and accounts gave opportunity for the gathering of information as to his services, and for the expression of disapproval where necessity arose,[2] little was to be gained unless some effective means existed for enforcing upon the agent the recognition of the authority of the colony. There were several ways in which such action might be taken. In the earlier years of the agency it was contemplated on more than one occasion that all payment should be refused to an agent whose activities were disapproved. Thus, in Barbados, in 1704, the assembly resolved that one of their agents, William Heysham, had not " Justly and ffaithfully acquitted himself of the Trust . . . reposed in him," and it was ordered that he should " have no advantage of any sallary or profitts for the said Agency."[3] So also in Antigua there appears to have been some disinclination to make payment to the unpopular agent Sir John St. Leger.[4] But in both cases the attitude was abandoned. Five years after the termination of Heysham's agency a report was made recommending the payment to him of over £300 due to him as agent.[5] And in the case of Sir John St. Leger it was agreed that his salary and disbursements should be paid up

---

[1] C.O. 155:5, Minutes of Council in Assembly of Nevis, 28 July 1718. An elaborate report of the committee on the accounts is there inserted.

[2] In 1757 an application from Joseph Pickering, agent for Barbados, for the repayment of £100 sterling advanced in England, was refused by the assembly. C.O. 31:29, Journals of Assembly, 25 Oct. 1757.

[3] C.O. 31:6, Journals of Assembly, 17 Nov. 1704.

[4] C.O. 9:12, Journals of Assembly, 5 July 1736.

[5] C.O. 31:6, p. 776, Journals of Assembly, 21 Feb. 1709/10.

to the date on which a successor was nominated in the assembly.¹ A more successful use of this weapon of control was made by the assembly of Antigua in 1744, when, fearful of incurring claims for salary from Samuel Martin on the ground of his action as deputy to Yeamans, a protest was made that no payment would be allowed after a certain date; and this decision was maintained when the time for settling the accounts arrived.²

The most obvious method of expressing disapproval, however, and the one in practice adopted, was the substitution of a new agent. The greater number of the agency acts held valid only for a limited period of time, and it was therefore easy to appoint a fresh agent when the existing one had been proved unsatisfactory. Thus in Antigua and Montserrat a new agent was chosen in the place of William Nevine. This was done also by Barbados in 1763 when George Walker was appointed to take the place of Joseph Pickering;³ and probably the same idea was operative at an earlier date in the agencies of Barbados and Jamaica, when the agents chosen varied frequently.

There was, indeed, on a few occasions in some of the islands a doubt as to the validity of this method. In Nevis in 1749 the assembly desired to appoint a

¹ C.O. 9:12, Journals of Assembly, 29 Sept. 1736.
² C.O. 9:16, Journals of Assembly, 8 May 1744 and 28 Feb. 1744/5. The value of the power of withholding payment of part or all of the agent's charges was diminished by the general delay in the payment of the agents. *Vide* letter of apology from Montserrat to John Yeamans in 1738, C.O. 177:2, Journals of Assembly, 12 Sept. 1738. Upon the death of John Sharpe in 1757 Jamaica owed him £2,534 5s. 8d. *Journals*, iv, p. 377. Delay in payment was sometimes due to the poverty of the island and sometimes to negligence on the part of the treasurer. ³ C.O. 30:11, Act of 4 June 1763.

new agent in the place of Samuel Martin, who was suspected of negligence. The agents of Nevis had, however, hitherto been appointed by resolution of the two Houses without limit of date, and the council held the view that he could not be discharged " till we have his answer to know whether he has resigned." [1] So a letter was written to the agent, and upon the appointment of his successor in 1751 an act was drawn up and it was specifically provided that the right of dismissal was reserved by the legislature.[2] A similar incident occurred in Grenada in 1776. An act had been proposed appointing Alexander Campbell agent in the place of Edward Montague. A petition was received setting forth

> That the said Edward Montague has accepted of the Office of Agent to these Islands in the Confidence that he would not be removed from the same while he acted in the service of the colony with zeal, fidelity and ability.

And the council desired to suspend the operation of the new act until Montague's defence had been heard. This was, however, refused by the assembly, who asserted uncompromisingly their right of dismissal, and the act was passed.[3]

Despite, however, these opportunities for control exercised from time to time in the islands there remained considerable possibility of independent action, prejudicial to the interests of the island. The one essential, therefore, to the smooth working of the agency was that Governor, council and assembly should feel confidence in the agent: hence no doubt

[1] C.O. 186:3, Minutes of Council, 27 June 1749.
[2] C.O. 324:60, pp. 61-2, 1 April 1751.
[3] C.O. 104:4, Journals of Assembly, 19, 26, and 31 Jan. 1776.

the circumstance that when one island had found an agent whom it could trust, as did Antigua in John Yeamans and Jamaica in John Sharpe, the other islands tended to nominate him as their agent as well. The agent was not entirely either a mere mouthpiece or a plenipotentiary. It remained to him to distinguish which of the work that came under his hand he could do with safety, trusting to his own judgment or the guidance of his friends, and which must be referred back to the island. Sometimes, as was inevitable, mistakes were made, but on the whole the islands were fortunate in securing representatives who were not only zealous in their service, but capable of forming suitable decisions when speedy action was necessary.

CHAPTER VIII

THE PERSONNEL OF THE AGENCY

To the colonists in the islands the choice of an agent was no easy matter. With the exception of the Governor, no one maintained direct official communications with the mother-country; and private intercourse was in large measure restricted to the merchants with whom the colonists were connected in business and to those planters who, although their estates lay in the islands, spent part or all of their lives in England. Many of the colonists, indeed, returned to England for short spaces of time looking after their private concerns and visiting their relatives; and on such occasions they would come into contact with their fellow-planters and West Indian merchants, and also, perhaps through them, with men holding official positions in the English Government. Such were the sources of information available in determining the choice of an agent.

Importance and Method of Choice.—The importance of a wise selection was early seen to be a matter of great moment to the islands. It was impossible to make absolutely secure the authority of the legislature over the agent, and the success of the islands' representations depended largely on the zeal with which they were defended. Further, there was the question of local factions. If the agent did not observe proper impartiality, danger to one section or another in the island was bound to ensue, and

THE PERSONNEL OF THE AGENCY 159

hence there arose in times of disturbance vigorous competition over the nomination of the agent. The struggles of the assembly in Jamaica and Barbados for a monopoly of appointment were based in part at any rate, as the council suspected, on a desire to secure for themselves, in case of internal difficulty, the support of the agent at home. And so also in Antigua and Montserrat, where there was little or none of the declaration of principle regarding appointment made in Barbados and Jamaica, there were nevertheless in the early eighteenth century repeated difficulties arising from the favour of rival candidates. In Jamaica the issue of the disagreements was the choice of the agent by a conference of the two Houses,[1] but in the other islands no such formal solution was made, and in practice the predominant share in the decision as to nomination fell under the control of the assembly.

In the first half of the eighteenth century there was in Barbados at any rate considerable discussion in the assembly over the choice of the agent. The possibility of difference of opinion was seen from the very beginning of the agency. It was evidenced in 1663 when the two parties in the assembly, the opposition still led by Thomas Modyford, put forward for election Thomas Povey and Philip Froude.[2] Then again, thirty years later, on the expiry of the first agency act of Barbados, six names were proposed in the assembly out of which two agents had to be appointed.[3] As years passed, the conflict lost much of the element of party feeling, but there were still several agents proposed in the assembly and votes taken as to whose

[1] e.g. *Journals*, iv, pp. 64–70.　　[2] *Vide supra*, p. 50.
[3] C.O. 31:2, p. 357, Journals of Assembly, 31 Oct. 1693.

services should be accepted. In the passage of the agency act of February 1725/6,[1] for example, the Journals show considerable difference of opinion in the assembly. When the blank bill had been introduced, a vote was first taken as to the number of agents that should be appointed, and, out of the members present, nine voted for three agents, two for one, and two for no appointment at all. Then the nomination was made, and nine members voted for Charles Worsley, John Huggins, and John Sharpe, the agents finally placed in office, while one desired the substitution of David Ramsay for John Huggins, and two maintained their vote for no agents at all.[2] Later the choice of agents was apparently made informally before the motion was discussed in the House, for the rule after the long agency of John Sharpe, terminating in 1756, was for the name of the agent to be proposed by one member and seconded by another and the vote immediately taken without further debate.

The Barbados act of 1756 was marked by an innovation with regard to the appointment of Barbados agents which became the rule for the following twenty-two years. Probably in anticipation of the death of Sharpe, soon in actual fact to take place, the chairman of the committee charged with preparing a new agent's bill suggested the addition of a new clause appointing an assistant agent.[3] The proposal was adopted; and Joseph Pickering was appointed assistant agent " without any Fee, Reward or Sallary for any assistance he may give," his function being to take on Sharpe's work for the rest of his year of office " in Case the said

[1] C.O. 30:9, No. 55, 15 Feb. 1725/6.
[2] C.O. 31:17, Journals of Assembly, 1 Feb. 1725/6.
[3] C.O. 31:29, pp. 38-9, Journals of Assembly, 16 March 1756.

THE PERSONNEL OF THE AGENCY

John Sharpe shall die, or not continue to Act."[1] Upon the death of Sharpe, Pickering became agent and remained in office until his supersession by George Walker in 1763. Upon the dismissal of Pickering, it is noteworthy that his assistant, Thurstan Blackman, also disappeared, Samuel Estwick, afterwards to be Walker's successor, being named in his place. The later difficulties over Estwick's appointment[2] suggest that the change was due to the alternations of parties in the island : and perhaps the retention of an assistant agent was an attempt to lengthen the control of the party in power. There is no evidence that the agent had any voice in the appointment of his assistant.

In the history of the agencies of the Leeward Islands there exists one example at least of the recommendation by an agent of his successor. This was in 1744, upon the resignation by John Yeamans of his position as agent for Antigua. During the six months preceding his retirement Yeamans, with the consent of the island, had been looking after his private affairs in Boston, leaving the agency in the hands of Samuel Martin, who had recently taken over from him the agency of Montserrat. When he finally decided to resign his office Yeamans recommended the appointment of Samuel Martin.[2] The suggestion was refused by the assembly

[1] C.O. 30:10, act dated 14 April 1756. There is little evidence of any action taken by an assistant agent during the period of office of the agent : in 1766, however, Samuel Estwick, then assistant agent for Barbados, sent a memorial to the Board of Trade. C.O. 391:73, p. 280, 31 July 1766.

[2] Antigua : C.O. 9:16, Minutes of Council, 21 March 1743/4; cf. Yeamans' recommendation to Montserrat in Aug. 1742, C.O. 177:3, Journals of Assembly, 28 Aug. 1742. In fact, Martin had been appointed agent for Montserrat by an act dated 4 May 1742, C.O. 176:4.

against the wishes of the council, partly, it is probable, for fear of creating a precedent which might lead to the loss of the free choice of an agent.[1]

In determining the appointment of an agent, possibly some allowance must be made for the offers of service from candidates for the agency, but of this, too, there is little evidence.[2] The more normal method of choice was undoubtedly the recommendation to the council and assembly by someone of influence in the island : not generally, as was done in the case of Philip Froude, by persons of standing in England, but, as Jeaffreson recommended George Gamiell, by members of the island legislature. After the early years of the eighteenth century little use was made of the advice of the Governor. Sir John Stanley and Sir John St. Leger, both relatives and nominees of Governors,[3] had given discredit to this method of choice, and although in 1729 the council of Montserrat attempted to withstand the suggestions of the assembly by saying they had " made a complement of the Nomination of an Agent to his Excellency," [4] nothing came of their scheme, and from this time the only known example is that of the recommendation of Richard Cumberland to the Bahama Islands by Governor Shirley.

Planters and Merchants. — Recommendations by

[1] The alleged reason was the desire to appoint Thomas Kerby the merchant to whom the island's sugars were consigned : he was asserted to be of " Considerable Possessions in this Island." C.O. 9:16, Journals of Assembly, 30 March 1744.

[2] See C.O. 177:3, Montserrat, Journals of Assembly, 28 Aug. 1742.

[3] Sir John Stanley of Sir Beville Grenville, Governor of Barbados 1703-6; Sir John St. Leger of Walter Douglas, Governor-General of the Leeward Islands, 1711-15.

[4] C.O. 155:7, Minutes of Council of Montserrat, 26 March 1729.

THE PERSONNEL OF THE AGENCY

members of council or assembly placed certain limits on the field for the choice of the agent. In particular, it contributed largely to the confinement of the office to absentee planters and merchants trading to the islands. This, however, was dictated also by other reasons. Before the establishment of the practice of maintaining permanent agents in England, the solicitation of the islands' interests had been undertaken partly by the merchants and planters at home and partly by occasional missions from the islands when matters of importance arose. In both cases the island's representative had been someone whose private interests were involved in its prosperity. And in 1670, when the Gentlemen Planters made their recommendation for the appointment of a solicitor at home, they said that they "Advise that he may be some one Concerned (in) Barbados otherwise he may have distinct Interest from you And be mischievous."[1] So Oldmixon, writing at the beginning of the eighteenth century, in expressing his doubts as to the value of the agents' services spoke of the difficulty of finding suitable people to fill the office :

> No prudent Man can think, that a Gentleman, who is not bred up in the Business, and has no Interest in the Island, can be fit to make an Agent.[2]

And yet Oldmixon, like Edward Long, over fifty years later, did not regard the appointment of a merchant as desirable. "For there is no kind of Affairs that makes a Man so busy, and keeps him in such continual Hurries as Factorage."[3]

[1] C.O. 31:2, pp. 15-17, Journals of Assembly, 14 Dec. 1670.
[2] Oldmixon, *op. cit.*, ii, p. 54.
[3] *Ibid.*; *cf.* Long, *op. cit.*, i, p. 119.

164 COLONIAL AGENTS OF WEST INDIES

The prejudice with which Long and Oldmixon regarded the claims of merchants to appointment was not maintained constantly through the period of the agency. At times, indeed, there were disagreements between the merchants and the planters in the islands as in the case of Barbados in 1671,[1] and in that of Jamaica in 1725, but these were by no means normal. The Leeward Islands' assemblies, indeed, upon occasion showed a definite leaning towards the appointment as agent of the merchant to whom the island's sugars were consigned, as when in Montserrat in 1729 the assembly nominated William Gerrish[2] and in Antigua in 1744 Thomas Kerby.[3] In the seventeenth century Jamaica and the Leeward Islands had shown their readiness to appoint merchants. For the commissioners appointed in 1690 by the General Legislature of the Leeward Islands were with the exception of Jeaffreson all merchants, as were the three agents appointed by the Jamaica act of 1693. In the history of the agencies in the eighteenth century many of the most prominent names are those of merchants, Richard Cary of Antigua,[4] Joseph Jory of Nevis,[5] Stephen Duport of St. Christopher,[6] Stephen Fuller of Jamaica,[7] Richard Maitland of Grenada, St. Vincent, and Tobago.[8]

More frequently, however, the agent was a planter, temporarily or permanently an absentee. Probably the most popular of the agents in the islands which

[1] *Vide supra*, p. 49.
[2] C.O. 155:7, Minutes of Council of Montserrat, 26 March 1729.
[3] C.O. 9:16, Journals of Assembly, 30 March 1744.
[4] Agent 1698–1708.   [5] Agent 1699–1726.
[6] Agent 1706–1716.   [7] Agent 1764–94.
[8] Agent for Grenada 1767–75, St. Vincent 1767–75, Tobago 1770–5.

THE PERSONNEL OF THE AGENCY

appointed them were those who took up the office upon their return to England after spending the early part of their life on the island sharing in its interests and responsibilities. In this category came John Yeamans, Samuel Martin, George Walker, all well known in the islands to which they belonged before they assumed the work of an agent. They approximated more closely to the agents *a latere* of the seventeenth century, a type which was continued down to the American Revolution in the service of the North American colonies.[1] George Walker, indeed, presented markedly a close resemblance to this type, for although his return to England was caused by the exigencies of his private affairs his stay was protracted by his desire to continue in the service of the island.

Members of Administration.—In spite, however, of the general preference for planters and merchants, to which the assembly adhered on the greater number of occasions when the choice of an agent was necessary, there were other factors to be considered. To be of the utmost possible service to the island the agent must not only be zealous in its interests but he must, as the Governor of the Bahama Islands reminded the assembly in 1760, have " a favourable Access to the Boards before which he is to Sollicit."[2] To achieve this end, and to ensure that the agent should give weight to the representations with which he was entrusted, certain of the North American colonies in the period immediately preceding their secession from the Empire secured the services of prominent members of Parliament. Thus at the

[1] *Cf.* the agency for Bermuda, Appendix I, *infra*, pp. 247-9.
[2] *Journals of the Lower House of Assembly of the Bahama Islands*, vol. ii, p. 40.

beginning of the troubles in America the services of Edmund Burke were obtained by New York. Some idea of the advantages to be derived from such an association led the council of Jamaica in 1715 to propose the appointment of Walpole as agent.

> They conceive if a solicitor (or, what the board would more desire, a patron, of the island) be to be appointed, he ought to be a person of a known reputation and character in Great Britain : If the honourable Robert Walpole, esquire, would be pleased to accept of it, it could not be doubted but his appearance in favour of any matter . . . would have its weight. . . .

By the conclusion of their recommendation the council showed their motives, not altogether unjustified at that time :

> they cannot conceive that either merchants, who have their particular interests, or any private gentleman of the island, who may have their particular affections, can be no proper persons at this juncture to be entrusted with the affairs of the public.[1]

The proposal of the council was rejected by the assembly, and no subsequent attempt appears to have been made on these lines. The salary, indeed, conferred upon the agents was not great, the highest for a West Indian colony being £500,[2] given by Barbados in the last years of the agency; and it was not easy to secure the services of men prominent in the political sphere.

[1] *Journals*, ii, pp. 172–3, 23 Dec. 1715.
[2] *i.e.* salary alone. In Jamaica, after 1802, a larger sum was voted for the agent, but this included the charges for his disbursements. The agents for the "new colonies" received larger grants also : but these again seem to have included expenses.

THE PERSONNEL OF THE AGENCY 167

Civil Servants.—The West Indian colonies were content with men of less lofty position, but a similar motive led to their frequent nomination of an official in the service of the Government. John Sharpe, one of the most successful of eighteenth century agents, was Solicitor to the Treasury, carrying on in connection with his work a frequent correspondence with the Duke of Newcastle and other prominent statesmen, and conducting at the same time a vigorous private practice, much of it among West Indian merchants and planters.[1] Charles Delafaye, agent for Jamaica, was a clerk in office of the Secretary of State for the Southern Department, becoming in course of time Under-Secretary of State. John Pownall, agent for the Virgin Islands, had at the time of his appointment just completed a long term of office as Secretary to the Board of Trade and Plantations;[2] and one of his successors at the Board, Richard Cumberland, held office as agent for the Bahama Islands. George Chalmers, a later agent for the Bahamas, was appointed after the reorganisation of colonial business in 1782–6 chief clerk to the Committee of the Privy Council known as the Board of Trade, having the main responsibility for the administrative work down to his death in 1825.[3] Among other agents in the employment of the government were Sir John Stanley,

---

[1] Letter-book of Messrs. Lascelles and Maxwell, Aug. 1752 – May 1754, p. 62, letter dated 9 Dec. 1752 to John Brathwaite.

[2] Solicitor and Clerk of the Reports 1745–53, Secretary to Board of Trade 1753–76, Under-Secretary of State in American Department 1769–76. Andrews, *Guide to . . . Public Record Office*, i, pp. 86–7, and *sub nom.* Thomas Pownall, *D.N.B.*

[3] *Vide sub nom. D.N.B.* The record of his services to the Board can be found in B.T. 5:1–34 (Public Record Office). See also B.M. Add. MSS. 22900–2.

commissioner of the Custom House, Thomas Beake, a clerk in the Council Office, Lovel Stanhope, Law Clerk to the Secretaries of State, William Bridges, Peter Leheup, and Henry Wilmot.[1]

Of this group of agents John Sharpe was one of the most prominent owing to his extensive practice as a solicitor; but two others were even then better known generally, and in their case recognition has been to some extent permanent. These were George Chalmers and Richard Cumberland. In both cases their fame rests, mainly, not on their work as agents or in their official duties at the successive Boards of Trade, but on their published writings. Chalmers is best remembered through his *Collection of Treaties between Great Britain and other Powers*,[2] and as a contemporary authority of some weight on the constitution of the American colonies and the history of their revolt.[3] Cumberland's work is less evidently related to colonial affairs, yet he also gained some of his inspiration from his official duties. When he first entered the Board of Trade as private secretary to Lord Halifax he was given to study some " folio books of formidable contents " from which he was expected to gain information necessary for his work. For that purpose they were of little use: but the study was not wasted. They " furnished here and there some plots for tragedies, dumb shows and dances," and their

[1] Chamberlayne, *Angliae Notitia*, 1669–1755, and the *Royal Kalendar*, 1767–1845, give the names of civil servants and also of agents. The entries are not always accurate.

[2] 2 vols., London, 1790.

[3] Among his works are *Political Annals of the present United Colonies from their settlement to the Peace of Paris of* 1763, London, 1780; and *An Introduction to the History of the Revolt of the American Colonies* . . . 2 vols., Boston, 1845.

THE PERSONNEL OF THE AGENCY 169

influence can be found in several of the numerous dramatic works to which Cumberland gave the greater part of his time.[1]

Cumberland, indeed, found his official position of considerable value: it left him plenty of leisure for his literary activities, and not only provided him first with a regular income and then with a pension, but enabled him to obtain several profitable agencies. In 1759 he secured " through the patronage of Lord Halifax, a small establishment as Crown-Agent for the province of Nova-Scotia,"[2] a post which he retained for forty-three years: to this he added the colonial agency for the Bahamas in 1760 and in 1764 the agency for Quebec.[3]

Insistence on Personal Knowledge.—The appointment of Cumberland for the Bahamas was due to the influence of William Shirley, who in 1758 became Governor of those islands. As a rule the colonies were hampered in the choice of men likely thus to be effectual in their solicitations, by the difficulty of obtaining anyone sufficiently well known to them. The assemblies, in particular, adhered closely to the principle that the agent must be someone of whom they had knowledge. In 1750, when the council of Nevis suggested the appointment of Henry Willmot, the assembly refused: they did not know him, and they preferred not to make the appointment " untill we are better acquainted with his Character."[4] Some

[1] Cumberland was Secretary to Lord Halifax 1754–65, Solicitor and Clerk of the Reports 1765–76, Secretary to the Board 1776–82. Andrews, *op. cit.*, i, pp. 86–7. Cumberland, *Memoirs*, vol. i, p. 137.

[2] *Memoirs*, vol. i, p. 205. The office was purely financial. The appointment was by royal warrant. T. 28: 1, p. 14.

[3] For the character of this agency, *vide infra*, p. 234, n. 1.

[4] C.O. 155:8, Minutes of Council of Nevis, 30 March 1750.

years earlier, in 1713, the council of Antigua proposed as agent the Secretary of the Board of Trade, William Popple, recommending him as

> a Gen^t extreamly well Qualified for such an office and one who could more Immediately further any Applications we may have occasion to make either to her Majesty or the Board of Trade.

But the assembly of Antigua refused: they were anxious for the appointment of their own nominee, and they dismissed the council's suggestion with the statement that they were " strangers to Mr. Popple and his Qualifications."[1] Probably John Sharpe became known to the Barbados assembly through his private practice; and with Charles Delafaye it is certain that earlier agents came into contact in connection with their work. The importance attached to adequate knowledge of the agents prevented the frequent appointment of agents of this type, and this was made more difficult by the prohibition issued by the Board of Trade in 1724 forbidding the clerks of the Board to serve as agents.[2] It is not difficult to understand, however, how valuable it must have been to the colonists, anxious to get their laws confirmed or their grievances redressed, to have some one employed by them as agent who could promote quick attention to their concerns.

The measure to which the islands' choice of agent was confined to planters and merchants and then connected with them did not preclude the appointment of persons of influence in English politics.

[1] C.O. 9:3, Minutes of Council and Assembly, 23 Dec. 1713.
[2] C.O. 391:34, p. 110, 30 April 1724.

THE PERSONNEL OF THE AGENCY

With the exception only of Henry Rawlinson, of Liverpool, agent for the Virgin Islands,[1] all the agents were resident in or near London; and they were, moreover, men of some standing, wealthy West Indian merchants, absentee planters, already before the middle of the eighteenth century a class well known for its wealth and influence, or government officials, working in close touch with planters and merchants. The circle thus formed constituted no small factor to confront the statesmen of the time.

The Agents in Parliament.—Amongst the tale of agents, if there are several civil servants there are also a number of members of the Commons. Amongst them all, one of the early agents of Jamaica, Sir Gilbert Heathcote,[2] alone seems to have represented the City to which so many of them belonged, but in the country districts, especially in Cornwall, seats were more frequently obtained. Thus in the Parliament of 1705, two Barbados agents, William Bridges[3] and William Heysham,[4] were present, and further, in addition to Sir Gilbert Heathcote, Sir Bartholomew Gracedieu,[5] also one of the Jamaica agents. Ten years later, another Barbados agent, Joseph Micklethwaite,[6] obtained a seat in Parliament, as also at later dates Charles

---

[1] C.O. 315:1, Act dated 8 Feb. 1783.

[2] Arthur Beaven Beaven, *The Aldermen of London*, London, 1913, vol. ii, p. 195, etc.

[3] M.P. for Liskeard Borough, Cornwall, *Return of Members of Parliament*, 1705-1874, London, 1878, pp. 1, 9, 19, 20.

[4] M.P. for Lancaster Borough, Lancaster, *ibid.*, pp. 3, 11, 21, 31, 41.

[5] M.P. for St. Ives Borough, Cornwall (1705), *ibid.*, p. 2.

[6] M.P. for Arundel Borough, Southampton (1714-15), *ibid.*, pp. 44, 56.

Worsley,[1] John Sharpe,[2] Samuel Martin,[3] Lovel Stanhope,[4] and Samuel Estwick.[5]

Nevertheless, the strength of the agents' position did not lie in their presence in the House of Commons. There is little evidence, indeed, that as members they were able to do any conspicuous service to their colony. Nor was the possibility of such advantages a powerful factor in the minds of the colonists. A member of the Barbados assembly in 1772, when he had made reference to the agencies of Burke and Barré[6] for the islands' rivals on the continent, was in no way rendered discontented with the position of the Barbados agent, George Walker. Although, as he said, " in a Knowledge of all the Great and General Affairs of our Mother Country " these powerful agents of the North American colonies might excel,

> Yet in the particular Concerns of the Colonies and the proper Interests of America I will venture to say the present Agent of Barbados is Second in Understanding to none . . .[7]

Viewing the period of the West Indian agencies as a whole, the choice of the islands, it is obvious, fell first on those at home with whom their interests were connected. If from time to time the desirability of expert aid was so far recognised that some govern-

---

[1] M.P. for Newton Borough, Southampton (1722), *ibid.*, p. 55.

[2] M.P. for Callington Borough, Cornwall (1754), *ibid.*, p. 110.

[3] M.P. for Camelford Borough, Cornwall (1754 and 1761), *ibid.*, pp. 98, 110, 124.

[4] M.P. for Winchester City, Southampton (1780), *ibid.*, pp. 155, 168.

[5] M.P. for Westbury Borough, Wiltshire (1790), *ibid.*, p. 196.

[6] No evidence has been found to justify this assertion that Barré was a colonial agent.

[7] C.O. 31:36, p. 124, Journals of Assembly, 3 June 1772.

ment official was appointed agent, this occurred in by no means the majority of cases. The islands wanted someone whom they knew, of whose integrity they had evidence in the personal experience of the planters, and for any additional support which this policy might make necessary they looked, not in vain, to the great influence of that great community at home whose prosperity like their own was bound up in the safety and progress of the plantations.

CHAPTER IX

AGENTS, PLANTERS, AND MERCHANTS, 1660–1760

THE history of the West Indies in the eighteenth century is one of apparent prosperity masking the evidences of decline. As early as 1689 an agent of Jamaica and Barbados, the author of *The Groans of the Plantations*,[1] indicated the source from which the safety of the islands was threatened. In the minds of the colonists for whom he spoke the 4½ per cent. duty, the imposition on sugars imported into England, the prohibition of direct trade to European ports, the high price of negroes due to the cupidity of the African merchants, the trade carried on by the North American colonies with the French West Indies, these causes combining with the depreciation of the soil were responsible for the state of the islands, sinking slowly to decay. The pamphleteers of the eighteenth century bear witness to the fact that the suppression of the slave trade and the abolition of slavery were not alone responsible for the disappearance of the early prosperity of the West Indian Islands.[2] Whether the predominant factors were those asserted by West

[1] Edward Littleton, agent for Barbados 1691–8.
[2] This is fully realised by a mid-nineteenth century historian of the West Indies, John Davy. See *The West Indies before and after Emancipation*, London, 1854, pp. 6–8.

Indian planters, or, as was replied by the North American colonists, the extravagance of the planters themselves, it is certain that before the close of the eighteenth century the condition of the West Indian islands had deteriorated markedly from that prevailing a century before. In 1799 so great was the depression in the West Indian trade that the merchants of London, "many of them ... in advance for their Principals (i.e. the planters) far beyond the value of the Consignments they ... hold" were compelled to request a loan from the Bank of England to enable them to subsist,[1] while on the islands numerous estates fell into the hands of merchants and other mortgagees in London.[2]

Amongst the causes for the decline was unquestionably the prevalence of absenteeism, and this has an additional significance as it was of vital importance to the work of the agent at home. There had been absentees in England as far back as the Interregnum, and this number rapidly increased in the eighteenth century, until in 1798 the Younger Pitt estimated the value of incomes derived from the West Indies at £4,000,000, as opposed to £1,000,000 from the rest

---

[1] Details of this transaction exist in the Minute Book of a Sub-Committee of the Society of West India Merchants appointed to deal with the matter: it is now in the possession of the West India Committee. *Vide infra*, Appendix IV, p. 299. Deterioration continued still more rapidly after 1799. See *Report from the select Committee appointed to take into Consideration the . . . West India Colonies*, Parl. Pap. 1807 (65), iii, 1.

[2] See Davy, *op. cit.*, p. 6. In the latter part of the eighteenth century general meetings of those interested in the West India Islands included not only planters and merchants but "Mortgagees, Annuitants and other Creditors," *e.g.* meetings of 9 and 24 April 1789, Standing Committee's Minutes, vol. ii.

of the world.¹ The owners of this vast fortune, living in England as men of wealth and position, were able to exert considerable influence on British politics. By their riches, complained a pamphleteer in 1754, they were able

> to support contests in some of the richest and most populous cities in this country. No less than three brothers from one of our Sugar-islands . . . having offered themselves one for London, one for Bristol, and one for Salisbury ; and a fourth . . . intended for a Wiltshire borough . . .²

Throughout the period of the agents' activities, it was in association with such absentees and the merchants allied with them that they carried on their work. Together they formed the West India interest, a formidable force in the politics of the time.

The history of the West India interest, continuing unbroken to the present day, is one of increasing complexity of organisation. In the early days, in the Interregnum and Restoration periods, there was little permanent alliance. During the century following the return of Charles II the gradual development of organisation can be traced, never ceasing to change and adapt itself to new conditions, and reaching immediately after the close of this period to a form recognisably similar to that which was to prove permanent.

[1] J. Holland Rose, *William Pitt and the Great War*, London, 1911, p. 370. *Cf.* H. W. V. Temperley, *The Relations of England with Spanish America, 1720-1744*, Amer. Hist. Assoc. Rep. for the year 1911, vol. i, pp. 229-237.

[2] *Short Account of the Interest and Conduct of the Jamaica Planters In an Address to the Merchants, Traders, and Liverymen of the City of London*, London, 1754, p. 3. In 1754 William Beckford sat as one of the Members for London, Richard Beckford for Bristol, and Julius Beckford for Salisbury.

AGENTS, PLANTERS, AND MERCHANTS 177

Dinners and Token-feasts.—Of the conditions prevailing in the early times of immature development the evidence is in the nature of things incomplete, dependent on the preservation and accessibility of descriptions written by those who took part in them. But deficient as these are, they provide a fairly complete picture of the progressive growth of the times. Generally speaking, the meetings of planters or merchants in the seventeenth century were predominantly social in character. In some cases the social aspect is the only one apparent, such measure of political significance as attaches to them being derived solely from the fact that the main interests of the persons concerned lay in the islands. A custom prevailed amongst the planters on the islands, as yet but lately settled there, of organising at home in England amongst their relatives and friends what were known as " token " feasts. A planter returning to England, as did Christopher Jeaffreson in 1682, brought with him money from his friends in the island to pay the expenses of a meeting at home at which the drinking of their health would be the chief feature. Thus Jeaffreson wrote to his relative Captain James Phipps, of St. Christopher, in 1682 :

> We spent your tokens at the Sun Tavern behinde the Exchange ; where were present Mr Jackson and his lady, Mr Constantine Phipps, Mr Thomas Phipps Phipps and his lady, and kinswoman, one Mr Langford (an acquaintance of our brother Constantine) and his lady and kinswoman. . . . We drank your health, and were freely merry.[1]

Again, a few days later Jeaffreson was present at another similar meeting at the Swan Tavern only a few yards

---

[1] J. C. Jeaffreson, *op. cit.*, i, pp. 314–15. Letter dated London, 15 November 1682, to Captain James Phipps.

from the Sun, this time the object being to remember " our friends in Saint Christopher's." [1]

Sometimes the meetings had more distinctly a political aspect. Early in 1683 Jeaffreson was present at a meeting of merchants connected with the islands, where much bitter talk took place over the failure of the planters to pay their debts.[2] The object of this gathering is not known, but more definite evidence exists as to meetings held repeatedly in the seventeenth and eighteenth centuries by the merchants to do honour to Governors or others in whose power lay much influence on the fortunes of the islands. The first of these recorded was in 1659 given for one Mr. Gookin, as to whom there was " some discourse at Whitehall " relating to his substitution for Daniel Searle in the government of Barbados. The meeting took the form of " an invitačon to ye Cardinalls Capp." All those interested in the island, irrespective of their party sympathies, seem to have been asked, and the issue of the meeting—that Mr. Gookin should receive the support of the merchants only when it should " appear what the Parliam^t or the Councill of State should resolve " as to the position of Daniel Searle—suggests an amicable agreement between all parties represented.[3]

In the mid-eighteenth century one of the most usual resorts was Pontack's in Abchurch Lane. Here, in

---

[1] J. C. Jeaffreson, *op. cit.*, i, p. 325.

[2] Jeaffreson MS., letter dated London March ye 17th 1682/3 (J. C. Jeaffreson, *op. cit.*, ii, pp. 48-9).

[3] The agreement was nullified by the death of the proposed Governor. B.M. Add. MS. 11411, ff. 90-4, letter dated 20 Oct. 1659 from Thomas Povey to Governor Searle. Such meetings were by no means peculiar to those concerned in the West Indies, *cf.* letter

AGENTS, PLANTERS, AND MERCHANTS 179

1745, thirty West Indian merchants entertained Captain Knowles, whose care in the defence of the islands had gained their gratitude;[1] and again a year later Captain Holborne received a similar entertainment.[2] Dinners given to Governors were of more political importance: such as in 1750 to Governor Mathew, of the Leeward Islands,[3] and in 1753 to Governor Grenville, of Barbados.[4] The presence of the agents at such meetings was regarded as an aspect of their official duties. And this attitude was anticipated by Povey at the entertainment given to Mr. Gookin at the Cardinal's Cap, for he stated in a letter to Governor Searle that he attended in order to "bee knowing of everie point and Circumstance wch might relate to you, or Mr Gookin, or to ye Governm^t."

More official relations were not wanting even in the seventeenth century. The policy of the Lords of Trade continued by the Board of Trade and Plantations tended directly to foster the co-operation of

from Povey to the Governor of Nova Scotia: "Having had the honour to bee invited unto a Society which very much affects yor Person, and yor Interests ..." B.M. Add. MS. 11411, f. 97. Letter dated 20 May 1658 to Colonel Temple.

[1] Letter-book of Messrs. Lascelles & Maxwell, Sept. 1743 – Jan. 1745/6, p. 294, letter dated 24th Sept. 1745.

[2] Letter-book of Messrs. Lascelles & Maxwell, Feb. 1745/6 – Aug. 1748, letter dated 29 Aug. 1746.

[3] Henry Wilmot, agent for Montserrat, entered as an item of his accounts for disbursements under date 24 July 1750, "Paid my Ordinary at Pontacks when the Merchants entertained General Mathew ... £2 2. 0." C.O. 177:7, Journals of Assembly, 21 Nov. 1753. At a similar entertainment given on 28 March 1752 to the honour of Governor Thomas, Wilmot paid nothing, "the agents being treated." *Ibid.*

[4] Letter-book of Messrs. Lascelles & Maxwell, 20 Aug. 1752–16 May 1754, p. 163, letter dated 29 June 1753.

the agents with other persons connected with the islands. Thus in 1696 agents of Barbados were summoned together with the merchants to discuss the question of convoys.[1] And nearly twenty years earlier Sir John Griffith, described as agent for Jamaica, was summoned to attend the Lords of Trade together with Sir Thomas Lynch and Captain Molesworth.[2] So also in 1694 Gilbert Heathcote, lately appointed agent for Jamaica, was requested to discuss with the merchants the question of transporting troops to the island,[3] and again a few days later agents and merchants were summoned together to receive information regarding the transmission of mails.[4]

Coffee-house Meetings.—The frequent association of the Jamaica agents and the merchants trading to the island in the last years of the seventeenth century has perhaps a special significance. The agents, appointed in 1693, were themselves merchants. As yet the settlement of Jamaica had not proceeded far enough to permit of the presence in England of large numbers of absentee planters, and so, as it had been earlier in connection with Barbados, the merchants were the most frequent representatives of the interests of the island. But, more than this, the close interconnection of the merchants in the affairs of Jamaica coincided, perhaps not quite fortuitously, with the establishment in England of the first permanent institution connected with any West Indian island. This was a coffee-house, situated, like the Sun and Swan Taverns frequented

---

[1] C.O. 391:9, p. 309, 28 Dec. 1696.
[2] C.O. 391:1, pp. 288–9, 31 Jan. 1676/7.
[3] C.O. 391:7, pp. 326–7, 17 Aug. 1694.
[4] C.O. 391:7, p. 330, 28 Aug. 1694.

by Jeaffreson, in the immediate neighbourhood of the Royal Exchange.

The closing years of the seventeenth century saw the growth of the practice of frequenting coffee-houses which was so marked a feature of the forthcoming period. Round the Exchange, at this time, near enough to be used constantly by those who were present at the hours for the Concourse of Merchants,[1] there grew up a group of coffee-houses, some the resorts of merchants of different interests and some whose name indicates, in their early years at any rate, a connection with some particular trade. Amongst the latter was the Jamaica Coffee House in St. Michael's Alley, at one time known as the Jamaica and Guinea Coffee House, which came into existence in the year 1674. Within a short time it was well known as the meeting-place of those concerned in Jamaica. A notice inserted in the public press in 1750 refers to it as having been used for sixty years past as the place to which letters should be left for transmission to Jamaica. Here, it was stated by thirty-eight commanders of ships in the Jamaica trade, " all business is done . . . and . . . we are to be met with every Day at proper Hours."[2]

In the early eighteenth century the Jamaica Coffee House was used for more political purposes, and as the number of absentee planters grew it became the common resort for them as well as for the merchants. In 1707 a representation from Sir Gilbert Heathcote, Sir Bartholomew Gracedieu, and other merchants

---

[1] An interesting account of the meetings of merchants at the Exchange is given by Addison in the *Spectator*, No. 69, 19 May 1711.

[2] *The General Advertiser*, Tuesday, 18 Dec. 1750. Notice headed " To all persons Concerned with Jamaica Trade."

trading to Jamaica, relating to convoys, was dated at the Jamaica Coffee House.[1] In 1715 Richard Harris, of Jamaica, stated that a memorial from himself and other merchants was "left at the Jamaica Coffee House, to be subscribed by such others as concurr'd therein."[2] The letters of James Knight, like Richard Harris an unofficial agent for Jamaica, show that the Coffee House was used as a regular place of call for those interested in the islands. There he dated his letters to William Beckford, then in Jamaica, and received letters from him in return.[3] Too great stress, however, must not be placed on the political aspect of the intercourse of those concerned in the island of Jamaica. The main tenor of transactions at the coffee-houses was undoubtedly commercial in character, and their value as an assistance to the agent in his work was mainly the opportunity they gave him for private consultation with other merchants or planters.

The Committee for Barbados.—The ultimate development of a definite organisation of the West India interest was not on the lines of the Jamaica Coffee House meetings, but rather in accordance with the precedents created at the beginning of the history of the Barbados agency by the Committee for the Concern of Barbados. The Committee formed on 28th January 1670/1 comprised the Governor of Barbados, William Lord Willoughby, then in England, and twelve other members, the greater number of them absentee planters well known already in the solicitations of the island at home, and the others merchants. In spite of the presence of mer-

---

[1] C.O. 138:12, pp. 92–3, 16 May 1707.
[2] C.O. 391:24, pp. 435–6, 22 Feb. 1714/15.
[3] *e.g.* B.M. Add. MS. 12431, ff. 117–19, 120–1.

AGENTS, PLANTERS, AND MERCHANTS

chants, the predominant element in the Committee were the planters, and with the exception of Mr. Jacob Lucie, chosen treasurer for the organisation, none of the merchants took part in the business that followed.[1] The Committee was required to meet once a week [2] at a tavern already connected with meetings of the West India interest, the Cardinal's Cap in Cornhill. The Committee was empowered " to Imploy such person or persons as they shall see Convenient," and in accordance with this at the first meeting on 3rd February 1670 Edward Thornburgh was appointed " to attend the Committee," the beginning of his service as agent for Barbados.[3]

The organisation of the Committee for the Concern of Barbados, although it appears to have ceased in June 1672 and left little trace for future generations, yet has considerable importance. It shows in the first place a relation between the agent and the planters

[1] No doubt because of the disagreements between the resident planters and the merchants caused, as in the case of St. Christopher ten years later, by the laws passed in the island concerning debts. C.O. 31:2, pp. 15–17, Journals of Assembly.

[2] The Committee did not strictly observe this rule. The following meetings are recorded:

(i) 28 Jan. 1670/1
(ii) 3 Feb. 1670/1
(iii) 9 Feb. 1670/1
(iv) 14 Feb. 1670/1
(v) 28 Feb. 1670/1
(vi) 23 March 1670/1
(vii) 27 April 1671
(viii) 1 May 1671
(ix) 8 June 1671
(x) 15 June 1671
(xi) 1 Sept. 1671
(xii) 7 Sept. 1671
(xiii) 22 Nov. 1671
(xiv) 7 Feb. 1671/2
(xv) 19 Feb. 1671/2
(xvi) 22 March 1671/2
(xvii) 7 June 1672

Extracts from the minutes are printed in Appendix III, *infra*, pp. 260–2.

[3] C.O. 31:2, pp. 37–9.

never exactly repeated. In the spring of 1671 the agent was urged to apply himself "from time to time to the rest of our fellow planters Resident in and about the Citty of London for their good Advice & Direction,"[1] and again the same terms were used upon the appointment of a new agent in the following December.[2] So long as the Committee was in operation it had a large measure of responsibility for the government of the agency in England. In later times the agents worked in unison with a society which bears in its constitution marked resemblance to this Committee; but in the nineteenth century, when for the first time since this period the relative positions of agent and planters and merchants were once more defined, the agent was not in the same way subordinated to the group with which he acted.

Inter-Colonial Relations. — The Committee for Barbados contrasts in another important point with later organisations: it was confined to one island only, Barbados, in 1671 by far the most advanced commercially of all the islands. The distinction is vital in the history of the West India interest in London. In the seventeenth century there was but little cooperation between agents and planters of the various islands. Nor was this unnatural, for as yet there was only very slight identity of interest. Barbados and the Leeward Islands had only just borne witness to their divergency by the successful solicitations on behalf of the Leeward Islands for separation of government. Further, even when there was no clashing of interest

---

[1] C.O. 31:2, pp. 32-3, Journals of Assembly, 20 April 1671, letter from Speaker of Assembly to Ferdinando Gorges.

[2] C.O. 31:2, p. 92, Journals of Assembly, 6 Dec. 1671.

there was little unanimity. Barbados alone as yet manifested the zeal for questions concerning the sugar trade and labour supply, later to be the common concern of all the islands. The Leeward Islands retained their paramount desire for safety from the French and reparation for the losses from French attack, while Jamaica, her soil not yet all under cultivation, did not feel any urgent need for reforms in the management of trade. More than half a century was to pass before the common interests of the islands produced common action on the part of their representatives at home. The history of the development of the first half of the eighteenth century is one of gradual growth, the slow gathering in one of the various elements to form the strong combination that fought the battles of the islands in the late eighteenth century.

Planters versus Merchants.—The unification of the interests of the different islands was more natural and easy a work than the co-operation of planters and merchants. From the earliest days of the Restoration there lay between planters and merchants the heavy barrier of unguaranteed credit. To establish a plantation on one of the islands, Richard Ligon stated, the first necessity was to procure supplies: and he described how this might be done by successive mercantile ventures to the island before a settlement was attempted.[1] Such a process was of necessity slow, and in practice a large part of the work of plantation was carried out through the grant of credit by the merchant venturers of London.[2] The burden of debt thus incurred by the colonists was a heavy weight upon

[1] Ligon, *True and Exact History of Barbados*, pp. 109-12.
[2] *Vide supra*, pp. 9-10.

their estates, even at the most prosperous periods of West Indian history: and as time passed, instead of diminishing, the danger increased, as in many cases the sugars consigned for sale to the merchants at home were insufficient to defray the expenses incurred by them on the planters' behalf.[1] The state of affairs, indeed, had not yet reached the position so fatal to the colonies a century later;[2] but it was sufficiently serious, and difficulties between planters and merchants frequently arose. As early as 1671 in the case of Barbados,[3] and 1683 in that of St. Christopher,[4] the unsatisfactory position as regards credits alienated the merchants from the planters' interest: and this situation was continued over the first part of the following century.[5]

The ill-feeling that thus resulted had a definite effect on the methods by which the agents worked in conjunction with planters and merchants at home. In 1713 the conflicting actions of planters and merchants in the affairs of the island was partly responsible

[1] *Vide* Robert Dinwiddie to Newcastle in 1743, C.O. 5:5, f. 205; cited by Pitman, *British West Indies*, p. 137, n. 18. The letter-books of Messrs. Lascelles & Maxwell bear witness to the prevalence of the grant of credit; more by London firms than by those of Bristol and Liverpool. Letter-book, August 1752 – May 1754, p. 341. The statement regarding the merchants of Bristol and Liverpool is borne out by the letters of Isaac Hobhouse, a Bristol merchant trading to Africa and the West Indies. Bristol City Library, Jefferies MSS., vol. xiii, ff. 9–158. *Cf.* also Miss M. S. Morriss, *Colonial Trade of Maryland*, 1689–1715, J.H.U.S. ser. xxxii, Baltimore, 1914, p. 95, for relative positions of London and out-port merchants.

[2] See Sir G. Dasent, *Annals of an Eventful Life*, London, 1870, vol. i, pp. 75–6; and Sir J. R. Dasent, *A West India Planter's Family's Rise and Fall*, Edinburgh (privately printed), 1914, pp. 41–2.

[3] *Vide supra*, p. 49. [4] *Vide supra*, p. 178.

[5] See Pitman, *op. cit.*, pp. 134–6.

for making clear the necessity for appointing an agent. So also James Knight, of Jamaica, writing from London to a correspondent in the island twelve years later, when the agency disputes were not yet settled, described the disadvantages from which the affairs of the island suffered in comparison with those of Virginia. Of all the colonies, Virginia, he stated, had the best means of managing her interests in London. She had two agents, and these regularly twice each month held meetings with the planters and merchants concerned in the island, " and consult with them what is proper to be done for the Service of the Country." To defray the expense of these meetings funds were raised on all goods imported from Virginia, and Knight said they all " go hand in hand without any clashing or Jealousie." This position, Knight commented, " is not very practicable with us " : the Jamaica assembly had alienated the merchants, and when planters and merchants met in England there was constant friction.[1]

Many years were to pass before the difficulties were overcome. There were other questions besides that of outstanding debts. In the second quarter of the eighteenth century the first great gain of the West India interest, the Molasses Act of 1733, had been one in which all sections of the West India interest had combined. The grant of a direct trade to Europe was a different matter. In the face of protests from the merchants, agents and planters secured the passing of the bill through Parliament,[2] and the resulting ill-feeling was long lasting. In 1745 the alliance between planters and merchants of Barbados was still very

[1] B.M. Add. MS. 22677, letter dated 18 March 1725/6. *Vide infra*, Appendix III, pp. 279–80.

[2] In 1739 : see Pitman, *op. cit.*, pp. 172–88.

insecure,[1] and a group of planters of all the islands writing in the same year referred to the " many . . . Instances when the Planting and Mercantile Interest Clash." [2]

Residents versus Absentees.—Yet another difficulty was caused by the disagreements recurrent in the first half of the eighteenth century between resident and absentee planters. The legislatures of Jamaica, Antigua, and St. Christopher during this period passed Deficiency Acts laying additional burdens on absentees : and this caused a measure of ill-feeling which made the co-operation of agents and planters almost impossible.[3]

Yet at the very time of the disputes some measure of co-operation was maintained. The combination of 1733 to secure the passage of the Molasses Act was repeated in 1744 to defeat the proposal to lay an additional tax on imported sugar; again in 1749, this time without avail, to preserve the organisation of the African trade in a joint-stock company, and in 1750–1 to try to force better administration of the Molasses Act.[4] But as soon as the contests were

[1] Letter-book of Messrs. Lascelles & Maxwell, Sept. 1743 – Jan. 1745/6, p. 249, letter dated 2 March 1744/5.

[2] C.O. 177:5, Montserrat Minutes of Council, 16 Oct. 1745.

[3] See Pitman, *op. cit.*, pp. 35–9, especially pp. 38–9, n. 82. In Antigua, the agent being at the time himself an absentee, the acts imposing additional liabilities on non-resident owners specifically mentioned him as exempt. C.O. 8:9, Acts dated 8 June 1742 and 1 June 1744 entitled " An Act for Raising a Tax for paying Public Debts . . ."

[4] Letter-book of Messrs. Lascelles & Maxwell, August 1750 – Aug. 1752, pp. 48–9, letter dated 20 Nov. 1750. Lascelles appears to have been one of the chief promoters of the scheme. It received the assistance of agents John Sharpe (Barbados and Jamaica), James George

over the divergencies reappeared, and were strong enough to prevent any permanent alliances.

In bringing about the measure of unity that was attained, the work of the agent was of the utmost importance. In the middle period of the eighteenth century when the agency disputes in the islands had been settled, when year after year the islands and their representatives at home, at the height of their influence in British politics, sought to secure some new gain for themselves, the islands were fortunate in their possession of zealous and influential agents. The outstanding figures are those of John Yeamans, Samuel Martin, and John Sharpe. From 1733 in the case of Barbados and 1734 in that of Jamaica, John Sharpe was in charge of the agency until his death over twenty years later, while during the last five years of his life he represented also Antigua, Nevis, and St. Christopher. In Antigua, the making of the agency was John Yeamans, official agent from 1727 to 1744 and during the following years acting unofficially on behalf of the island owing to their difficulty in deciding upon a successor. Montserrat, which for a short period made use of the services of Yeamans, found its most satisfactory sponsor in Samuel Martin, who acted also for a few years with less success for Nevis.

The Planters' Club.—Yeamans and Martin were both planters, the friends and associates of James Knight, William Beckford, and others of their fellow-planters in England. And together with them, probably at some date in the decade 1730–40, they formed an association which became known

Douglas (St. Christopher), and Henry Wilmot (Montserrat). C.O. 177:7, Montserrat Journals of Assembly, 21 May 1750, letter of Henry Willmot dated 21 Feb. 1749/50.

as the Planters' Club.[1] The correspondence of Knight and Beckford in the years 1742 to 1745 shows a concern for the prosperity of the Club that suggests some particular interest in it on their part,[2] but it is impossible to assign to them or any other of the members any definite responsibility for its inauguration. The Club included members of all the islands. During the agency of Samuel Martin for Montserrat, the President and council of the island received a letter from the Club, forwarded by John Ashley, a prominent Barbados planter, presumably the Secretary. The Club's letter, the object of which was to appeal for subscriptions, stated that " some Years ago " the sugar planters resident in England had decided " to forme themselves into a Society in London, which takes the Name of the Planters Club," the object being " to promote the Interest of the Sugar Colonys in every Branch of it . . . and to put a stop to many Abuses that had Crept into the Sugar Trade."

The Club appears to have continued its activities for between thirty and forty years ;[3] but the extent of its political importance is not clear. The most vital period of its history was the last decade of the first half of the century closing with the struggle with the Northern Colonies in 1750–1. In 1749 the Leeward Islands proposed to entrust a representation

[1] C.O. 177:5, Montserrat, Minutes of Council, 16 Oct. 1745. B.M. Add. MS. 12431, ff. 116–17, 120–1, letters dated Spanish Town 11 Oct. 1740 and 19 Aug. 1741, William Beckford to James Knight. This is no doubt the association referred to by Pitman, *op. cit.* p. 299.

[2] C.O. 177:5, Montserrat, Minutes of Council, 16 Oct. 1745. *Vide infra*, Appendix III, pp. 280–2.

[3] *Vide infra*, pp. 202–3.

AGENTS, PLANTERS, AND MERCHANTS

to its care,[1] and the Jamaica agent two years earlier was instructed to act in a specific matter in accordance with its advice.[2] It is significant that this is the period when the greatest successes were won for the West India interest, and for them perhaps a large measure of explanation is to be found in the fact that the agents were aided by a powerful body of men, including Beckford, the intimate associate of the Elder Pitt, and a vast number of others whose wealth could command influence in British politics.

The Charge on Trade. — Unlike Yeamans and Martin, John Sharpe was not a planter, and had therefore no place amongst the members of the Planters' Club.[3] He was, however, closely connected with both planters and merchants[4] in his private practice as a solicitor, and perhaps to him is to be attributed the measure of expression granted at about this time to the fundamental identity of interest of all those concerned in the islands. Some years before 1745, probably before the formation of the Planters' Club, there originated a fund to pay the expenses of joint solicitations when these were possible. The date at which this commenced is uncertain. The

---

[1] C.O. 9:20, Antigua Journals of Assembly, 2 Jan. 1748/9. C.O. 177:7, Montserrat Journals of Assembly, 9 Feb. 1748/9. The proposal was disapproved of by Barbados, to whom it was sent by Antigua, and the matter was dropped. C.O. 9:20, Antigua Journals of Assembly, 13 Feb. 1748/9.

[2] *Journals of Assembly of Jamaica*, iii, p. 71, 16 April 1747.

[3] Beckford, however, wrote in 1740 to James Knight: "Remember me to Yeamans, Jack Sharpe, the rest of my friends." B.M. Add. MS. 12431, f. 117, letter dated 11 Oct. 1740.

[4] This appears from numerous references in the letter-books of Messrs. Lascelles & Maxwell.

wording of James Knight's letter of 1726 suggests that it certainly was not in existence at that time, but twenty years later at any rate it was sufficiently long established to be described as " the old fund." The source of these supplies, like those raised by the Virginia interest in 1726,[1] was a charge on all West Indian produce imported by the London merchants. The burden fell on both resident and absentee planters, since the merchants reckoned it as part of the expenses of transporting the sugars, but it was collected by the merchants and required, therefore, co-operation of all sections of the West India interest. In 1745 the Gentlemen of the Planters' Club explained in their letter to Montserrat that the necessity for agreement between planters and merchants much diminished the usefulness of the charge, and suggested its abolition in favour of a system of voluntary contributions. A Barbados merchant in 1746 stated that his firm " constantly paid 1d p Hhd on trade & do believe & others do the same " : and he added it was used to prosecute thieves on the wharves when detected stealing sugars.[2] If the charge ever fell into disuse it must soon have been revived, for in 1769 it was well established as the foundation of another society of the West India interest.

The exacting of the charge on trade, at first sporadic and then a regular incident, is an indication of the approaching development of the form of organisation of the West India interest that was to become permanent. But the progress to greater unity among those concerned in the islands was not a precursor of greater

[1] *Vide supra*, p. 187.
[2] Letter-book of Messrs. Lascelles & Maxwell, Feb. 1745/6 – Aug. 1748, p. 51, letter dated 14 June 1746.

success in their undertakings. After the Peace of Paris the strength of the West India interest slowly declined. The outbreak of the war in America placed the islands in a position of great danger, harassed by the fear of insufficient supplies. The loss of the British possessions in America discredited the cause of colonies : the eighteenth century theories and precepts were passing away and the new spirit of *laisser-faire* in commerce combined with the strivings of humanitarian feelings to diminish the authority hitherto attributed to the voice of the West Indian islands. The zenith of their power was over ; and the new organisations, far more effective and closely knit than those of the previous period, were concerned no longer in gains from their rivals or from the administration, but in defending their interests from attack.

CHAPTER X

THE WEST INDIA COMMITTEE

THE Treaty of Paris, Mr. G L. Beer has stated, " marks a turning-point in British colonial policy in so far that thereafter greater stress was laid on colonies as markets for British produce than on colonies as sources of supply."[1] The change of attitude is important in the history of the relations of the West Indian islands with the mother country. According to the theory which aimed at a self-sufficing Empire, the West Indian islands were, as has often been remarked, ideal colonies. Their plantations produced goods which Great Britain could not supply; and the character of their climate gave little temptation to the establishment of manufactures which would compete with those at home. The passing over of arguments based on this fact, and the preference of Canada as an acquisition of empire to French and Spanish West Indian islands, indicate that new values were being formed, and presage the coming of a new era when the old views, on which the West Indies had based their claims to special favours, would no longer be effective.

The Peace of Paris marks also the climax and the approaching decline of the influence of the West India interest in British politics. At the time of its negotiation the West Indian planters opposed the

[1] Beer, *British Colonial Policy*, 1754-65, p. 139.

THE WEST INDIA COMMITTEE 195

transfer to English rule of new plantations whose products would compete with those of the older islands.[1] In this they were following a long-standing policy, for as far back as 1667 " the Planters and Merchants concern'd in the Island of Nevis & the other Leeward Islands," in petitioning the King for separation of government from Barbados, alleged that the interest of " the Barbathians " was that " these Islands be no more setled."[2] Their suspicions, although probably groundless at the time, typify the trend of feeling in the West Indies.[3] New settlements meant increased competition, and they ranked therefore with the importation of foreign sugars and, in time of war, the classifying of prize sugar as of British origin, as dangers to the prosperity of the islands. The triumph in 1763 was a greater one than those over threatened " breaches of the Acts of Trade,"[4] for there was no recognised principle to which they could appeal. It was probably made possible only by the first movings of the new spirit of colonial policy.

New theories did not operate to check the attempts to enforce the policy of the Acts of Trade. The act of 1764, revising and extending the Molasses Act of 1733, was the epilogue to the colonial policy embodied in the Treaty of Paris. Although the supply of sugar from the British Islands to the whole Empire had been left as difficult as before by the almost negligible accessions of territory in the West Indies, the monopoly

---

[1] See Pitman, *op. cit.*, chapter xiv *passim*.
[2] B.M. Egerton MS. 2395, ff. 455–6.
[3] *Cf.* Letter-books of Messrs. Lascelles & Maxwell, 1750–2, p. 114.
[4] The question of prize sugar arose in 1759. See Letter-book of Messrs. Lascelles & Maxwell, 1757–60, p. 331, letter dated 3 August 1759.

was to remain untouched. West Indian planters and merchants found in these two verdicts the realisation of the ideals of empire for which they had been striving in the preceding years of the century, and which they were to enunciate with diminishing assurance in the fifty years that were to follow.

The Society of West India Merchants.—The zenith of the influence of the West India interest coincided, as far as can be determined, with the growth of more definite organisation. Evidence is lacking as to the exact date at which the development took place, and it appears probable it was gradual in operation, reaching a stage of greater definition in the decade 1760–70. The source of the evolution was the holding of meetings of persons concerned in particular branches of trade, in very general practice throughout the eighteenth century. A writer in *The Universal Spectator and Weekly Journal* of 10th August 1734 made reference to the frequent

> Meetings or Clubs of particular Merchants, either fix'd or occasional, as of the Turkey and Italian Merchants, the Spanish, the Portuguese, the French, the Flanderçan, the German, the Danish, the Swedish, the Muscovite, the Dutch, the Irish, the West India, the Virginia, the Carolina, New York and New England Merchants.[1]

And although probably a margin of exaggeration must be allowed to the writer, it is certain that such meetings were held, as for example of the Portugal merchants in January 1739/40,[2] and, probably in a more permanent organisation, the Society of Merchants Trading to

---

[1] An abbreviated form of the article appeared in the *Gentleman's Magazine*, vol. iv, August 1734, pp. 431–2, under the heading " Proposal for a Merchants' Club."

[2] *London Daily Post and General Advertiser*, Jan. 17, 1739/40.

THE WEST INDIA COMMITTEE 197

Virginia and Maryland.[1] The West India Committee, taking its origin in meetings of merchants analogous to these, gathered political significance from the more public meetings held in times of crisis, and took form in the latter part of the eighteenth century in a general organisation of the West India interest, with whose activities the agents became gradually more closely associated.

The basis of the development was the charge on trade. The reference to its collection in 1746,[2] together with the abandonment a year earlier by the Planters' Club of any attempt to support their action with its proceeds,[3] suggests a possibility for which there is no confirmatory evidence, that at that time some society of merchants came into existence concerning itself with the details of the West Indian trade. Some fifteen years later slight confirmation is obtained by the existence of a letter from the "Chairman of the West India Merchants" to the Duke of Newcastle;[4]

[1] Reference to this Society exists in 1757, P.R.O., Chatham Papers, Bundle 95. Cited by Miss K. Hotblack, *Chatham's Colonial Policy*, London, 1917, p. 49. Evidence is lacking to connect it with the fortnightly meetings of Virginia merchants and planters described by James Knight. *Vide supra*, p. 187. It is uncertain whether there existed a permanent society of North American Merchants in general. At the time of the secession there were meetings of North American merchants analogous to those held by the West India interest, *e.g.* on 4 January 1775, *The Morning Chronicle and London Advertiser*, Friday, 6 Jan. 1775. See also B.M. Add. MS. 8133 C, ff. 91-2. There were also city coffee-houses connected with the North American colonies, as the Maryland Coffee House and the Pennsylvania Coffee House. [2] *Vide supra*, p. 192.

[3] *Vide supra*, p. 192, and *infra*, Appendix IV, pp. 280-2, where citation is made of C.O. 177:5, Montserrat, Minutes of Council, 16 Oct. 1745.

[4] B.M. Add. MS. 32902, f. 458 (Newcastle Papers), letter dated 20 Feb. 1760.

to be followed in 1766 by another letter relating to a dinner to which the West India merchants, following precedents a century old, had invited him.[1] Then again in 1766 reference exists to a "Committee of West India Merchants,"[2] as to which nothing further is known. Finally in 1769 the first definite evidence is to be found, for from that year there are continuous minutes of meetings of West Indian merchants inherited and preserved by the West India Committee.

The character of the Society of West India Merchants was based very largely on the traditional functions of the merchants during the preceding century. Their work was to some degree confined to details of trade. In all branches of commerce questions had to be settled as to freights and taxes of preservation from thieves, and more difficult matters of bonds and warehouses,[3] and the minutes of the society show a large measure of concentration on these points.

If a review is made of the whole history of the Society, undoubtedly this aspect predominates. But in the first twenty years of its existence it had a wider interest of greater importance in connection with the agent's work. If the letter to the Duke of Newcastle in 1760 may be taken as the first evidence of the existence of the Society, it is not without significance that although signed by "Beeston Long, Chairman of the West India Merchants," it conveyed information from "The Agents for the Sugar Colonies & the Merchants," and was accompanied by a memorial

[1] B.M. Add. MS. 32975, ff. 416, 430 (Newcastle Papers).
[2] B.M. Add. MS. 8133 C, ff. 91–2.
[3] *Cf.* Miss M. S. Morriss, *Colonial Trade of Maryland, 1689–1715*, J.H.U.S. xxxii, p. 95.

THE WEST INDIA COMMITTEE 199

from both planters and merchants signed by Lovel Stanhope, as agent for Jamaica, Joseph Pickering, agent for Barbados, and Henry Wilmot, agent for the Leeward Islands.[1] The Society of West India Merchants during this period, although confined in membership to one section alone of the West India interest, showed its capacity to act on behalf of the whole. The fund from which its resources came, the charge on trade, was borne ultimately in large measure by the planters, both resident and absentee. It contained within its ranks, albeit in their capacity as private merchants, Stephen Fuller, agent for Jamaica, and Richard Maitland, agent for Tobago, Grenada, and St. Vincent; and, obtaining reinforcement when it was thought necessary from the planters and the other agents, it took action in matters of general interest to the islands.

General Meetings of Planters and Merchants.—Of wider importance were the measures concerted at general meetings of the West India interest. During the period of the great triumphs of the mid-eighteenth century, the agents, planters, and merchants held occasional meetings to provide for joint representation as to the affairs of the islands. Thus, in January 1743/4 it was said that there had been, in connection with the threatened duty on sugar, " for some Weeks past frequent meetings of the Agents, Planters & Factors, interested in the Sugar Colonies."[2] And similarly in January to March 1750/1 there were several meetings in connection with the complaints the planters and merchants were conducting against

[1] B.M. Add. MS. 32902, ff. 460-1.
[2] Letter-book of Messrs. Lascelles & Maxwell, Sept. 1743 – Jan. 1745/6, p. 83, letter dated 17 Jan. 1743/4.

the illicit trade of the Northern Colonies and the French.[1]

The practice became more general as the century advanced. A reference in the council minutes of Jamaica in 1760 to the accounts of Lovel Stanhope, then agent for the island, gives the impression that meetings of those concerned in Jamaica were frequent, and were, furthermore, considered of such importance to the island as to justify the charging of the expense of attendance amongst the agent's disbursements.[2] So also Stephen Fuller, in his accounts for the years 1760–71, includes numerous entries for expenses at meetings of the West India interest : " Several meetings of the merchants and planters, and at the house of commons " regarding regulations to prevent the smuggling of French brandy ; more meetings, some of them at the Treasury and Custom House, " at the request of the general meeting of the merchants " to secure redress in the affair of the " ship Lawrence " at Montego Bay, unlawfully seized by a customs officer.[3]

[1] On 10 Jan. 1750/1 John Sharpe informed the Board of Trade that " pursuant to their Directions a general Meeting of the Merchants Sugar Planters had been held." C.O. 391:58, 10 Jan. 1750/1. The accounts of Henry Willmot, agent for Montserrat, show that there were several such meetings.

	s.	d.
6th February.—Ditto (coach hire) into the City upon a meeting of the Sugar Colony's about the Memorial	2	0
13th March.—Expenses at another meeting	2	0
19th March.—Ditto	2	0
21st March.—Ditto and dinner	6	0

C.O. 177:7, Journals of Assembly, 21 Nov. 1753.

[2] C.O. 137:32, Bb. 13, 14, 18 Dec. 1760. Cf. meeting of 28 Nov. 1781, Merchants' Minutes, vol. ii.

[3] Reference to this solicitation is made in Merchants' Minutes, vol. i, meeting of 11 April 1769 ; the first entry in the records of the

THE WEST INDIA COMMITTEE 201

"For this," Fuller interposes, "I had the public thanks of the general meeting of the West India merchants." And then there were meetings about the importation of rum into Jersey and Guernsey; still more, to apply without success for the especial exemption of Jamaica from North's Revenue Act. Then there was the drawback on foreign soap;[1] the defence of the island from Spain in case of war; and many other matters all conducted by the agent in conjunction with planters and merchants, and his expenses in connection therewith charged to the island.[2]

Organisation of the Society.—The relation between the Society of West India Merchants and these general meetings of planters and merchants is not clear. The Society held its meetings normally once a month, with some variation in practice. The most usual place of meeting was a room in office of the Marine Society, a charitable organisation established in 1758 to care for the widows and orphans of seamen,[3] but meetings were also held frequently at various city taverns, the London Tavern, more usually used for large meetings, the King's

committee. The earlier meetings mentioned must have taken place before the minutes begin.

[1] See Merchants' Minutes, vol. i, meeting of 3 April 1770. The meeting directed Fuller to attend the Treasury on the point: and he charged it as an item in his accounts. A copy of the accounts is given in *Journals*, vol. vi, pp. 357–8.

[2] Similar meetings took place of the Tobago interest in 1779 and 1783. Merchants' Minutes, vol. ii, meeting of 23 Nov. 1779, and *Gentleman's Magazine*, vol. liii, pp. 173, 535. Also of the planters and merchants of St. Vincents in 1794. Charles Shepherd, *An Historical Account of the Island of St. Vincent*, Appendix xv, p. xxxix.

[3] This Society is still in existence, having its office in Clark's Place, Bishopsgate.

Arms Tavern in Cornhill, and the Jamaica Coffee House. It had a permanent chairman, Beeston Long, an honorary treasurer, Samuel Long, and a paid secretary, James Allen. At the general meetings of planters and merchants Beeston Long at this period always presided, and the summons published in the press was signed by James Allen. Further, many, although not all, of the meetings are recorded side by side with the ordinary meetings of the Society in the Minute Books. Thus the first entry in the minutes is described as a " General Meeting," although there is no indication as to whether planters were present as well as merchants.[1] For the following two years only the ordinary meetings of the Society are recorded; then there is a " General Meeting of West India Merchants "; then, again, a year later a " General Meeting of Planters and Merchants interested in the Sugar Colonies." The explanation appears to be that the Society was the only working organisation available, and therefore formed the kernel of all such meetings, however small the proportion its members bore to the whole.

It is difficult to make any definite statement as to the position at this time of the Planters' Club. Reference to it exists in 1771,[2] and, possibly, in 1775, when a letter was sent to the West India merchants from " Certain Gentlemen of the West India Islands living in London ";[3] but after this it disappears, and either became primarily a social club open to both planters

---

[1] For further details as to the organisation of the Society see article in *English Historical Review*, Oct. 1921, " The London West India Interest in the Eighteenth Century."

[2] Merchants' Minutes, vol. i, meetings of 1 Jan. and 5 Feb. 1771.

[3] *Ibid.*, meeting of 8 Jan. 1775.

THE WEST INDIA COMMITTEE 203

and merchants¹ or vanished altogether. Such references as there are give little impression of any considerable activity. Amongst the names subscribed to the letter of 1775, there appears neither that of George Walker, the Barbados agent, nor of Samuel Estwick, his assistant, although they were both planters, the only agent included being John Ellis, of Dominica. Probably the growth of a highly organised Society of Merchants removed the necessity for political activities on the part of the club, and the interest of the agents therefore declined.

Results of War of American Independence.—The next development in the history of the organisation dates from the period of the War of American Independence. The war brought considerable anxieties to those whose interests lay in the islands. In the earlier stages of the struggle the West India planters and merchants, despite the amicable agreement reached with the North American trade in 1766,² made no attempt to give assistance to those concerned in the continental colonies.³ Their interest was, however,

¹ In 1779 Admiral Keppel was invited to a dinner by the " Society of West India Planters and Merchants." And later in the same year reference is made to a dinner given to Admiral Barrington by " the Club of Planters and Merchants." Merchants' Minutes, vol. i, meetings of 23 Feb. and 21 Dec. 1779. In 1783 a notice was inserted in the public press relative to the founding of a West India Club " to consist of Planters only " (*Morning Herald and Daily Advertiser,* Thursday, 13 March, 1783).

² B.M.Add.MS.8123C,ff. 91–2. *Vide infra,* Appendix III, pp. 284–5.

³ In March 1774 the Society of West India Merchants resolved that certain members of the Commons should be requested to give notice to the Chairman of any proceedings in Parliament likely to affect the interests of the Sugar Colonies. Merchants' Minutes, vol. i, meeting of 9 March 1774. On 18th Jan. 1773 a writer in *The Public Ledger*

roused in September 1774 by the passing of resolutions in the Congress at Philadelphia imposing first a partial and then a total ban on trade with the West India Islands. In January 1775, at the instance of a group of planters living in London,[1] joint meetings of planters and merchants were held and memorials drawn to represent the distress the islands would suffer from the non-importation of provisions from the colonies.[2] Before long there arose, also, the usual concomitant of war, fear of foreign attack. Nor were the apprehensions groundless, for first Dominica fell into French hands and then all the Leeward Islands except Antigua. The old questions therefore appeared of convoys for the trade, and squadrons to defend the islands: of the rating of prize sugar and sugar from the English islands in French possession.[3] All these matters agents, planters, and merchants dealt with in agreement, working together to minimise the danger suffered by the islands through the war.

reproached the planters and West Indian merchants for not having " been alarmed sooner," and taken action that might have prevented the threatened " Destruction to the British Empire."

[1] Merchants' Minutes, vol. i, meeting of 3 Jan. 1775, and *The Gazetteer and New Daily Advertiser*, Thursday, 5 Jan. 1775.

[2] *Ibid.*, meeting of 7 Feb. 1775. Accounts of the meetings of 18, 25, and 31 January and 7 February are given in *The Gazetteer and New Daily Advertiser*, Thursday, 16 Feb. 1775. Other papers give greater details of the meetings, as *The London Chronicle*, Tuesday, 17 Jan., to Thursday, 19 Jan., 1775; *Lloyd's Evening Post*, Wednesday, 18 Jan., to Friday, 20 Jan., 1775; *The Morning Chronicle and London Advertiser*, Wednesday, 8 Feb. 1775.

[3] In 1782, at a general meeting of planters and merchants at which a committee was appointed to meet the Sugar Refiners, it was resolved that attitude to prize sugar could not be altered, but the sugar of their former fellow-subjects in St. Christopher, Montserrat, and Nevis might be admitted. Merchants' Minutes, vol. ii, meeting of 5 June 1762.

THE WEST INDIA COMMITTEE

The Standing Committee.—The prevalence of joint action during this period was productive of a new form of permanent organisation, a definite advance on the Society of West India Merchants. The first indication of it was given in December 1781, when an important innovation took place at a meeting of planters and merchants to discuss questions of defence; instead of the usual Chairman, Beeston Long, the chair was taken by a planter, Nathaniel Bayley.[1] In the following June at a general meeting[2] regarding the importation of foreign sugars, another planter, Richard Pennant, was chairman, and, following the precedent of former occasions,[3] a committee of planters and merchants, including both Fuller and Estwick, was nominated. From this time, or soon after, the committee of planters and mer-

---

[1] *The Public Advertiser*, Monday, 24 December 1781. The meeting took place on the 21st at the London Tavern. See also Merchants' Minutes, vol. ii, meeting of 29 Jan. 1782. On this occasion the petition was signed first by Nathaniel Bayley, "Chairman," then by Stephen Fuller, "Agent for Jamaica" and Samuel Estwick, "Agent for Barbados"; 199 other signatures followed.

[2] At this meeting there attended the one West Indian agent of the eighteenth century who belonged to the provinces: Henry Rawlinson, of Liverpool, agent for the Virgin Islands.

[3] At a general meeting of planters and merchants on 18th January 1775 a Committee was appointed under the chairmanship of Sir Philip Gibbes. At a general meeting of 25th January to which this committee reported it was resolved: "That the Committee be at liberty to adjourn as they see fit, from place to place, and to call a General Meeting when they think proper." The Committee met a general meeting on 7th February, when they were again directed to "continue to sit from day to day, by their own adjournments, untill they shall think proper to report to a General meeting to be called by them." *The Gazetteer and New Daily Advertiser*, Thursday, 16 Feb. 1775.

chants acquired a permanent character, being known as the " Standing Committee." [1]

The new organisation, the centre of which was the Standing Committee, started to keep records separate from those of the Society of West India Merchants in May 1785. The two bodies were distinct by their possession of different chairmen, Lord Penrhyn, formerly Richard Pennant, being the chairman of the new organisation. The same fund supplied the revenues of both, it was administered by the same treasurer, and the same secretary attended to the affairs of both societies. No more definite name was attached in the eighteenth century to the joint organisation than the " West India Planters and Merchants,"[2] the term West India Committee as covering all its sections not being officially adopted until the incorporation by Royal Charter in 1904.[3]

Between the two bodies which functioned side by side in 1785 the division of duties became gradually more definite. The Society of Merchants before the end of the century confined themselves wholly to details of trade. They continued as before to deal with applications made for convoys for merchant vessels in time of war, with the charges made by wharfingers and lightermen, with the policing of wharves. It was they who took part in the negotiations for the establishment of a Marine Police Office,

---

[1] At the meeting of 21 December 1781 the term was first used. It became general about four years later.

[2] Certain nineteenth-century publications of the organisation are to be found under this head in the British Museum Catalogue.

[3] See A. E. Aspinall, *The British West Indies*, London, 1912, chapter xxi *passim*. The title was in general use in the early nineteenth century.

THE WEST INDIA COMMITTEE 207

and who were responsible, together with the authorities of the City, for the construction of the West India Docks. Matters not, like these, directly connected with trade were dealt with by the Standing Committee.

Eighteenth-Century Negotiations.—The two societies continued in existence for over half a century, working together with considerable harmony, but keeping their organisations in large measure distinct. While the Merchants' meetings, however, decreased in functions as the time passed, the Standing Committee gained in importance, fighting for the interests of the islands as their predecessors had done before them. With the Younger Pitt they maintained a constant intercourse, carrying on the tradition established by Alderman Beckford in the days of the Great Commoner. The abolition of the Board of Trade and the American Secretaryship in 1782 did not terminate the practice of consulting with planters and merchants, and numerous questions were submitted to the Committee for advice and information. Thus on 3rd March 1787 the Chairman, Lord Penrhyn, together with Beeston Long, attended Pitt in answer to a summons from him to discuss the lowering of duties on brandy and rum. He informed them of the proportion of the duties which he intended to propose to the House of Commons, and as a result a general meeting was summoned and their resolutions conveyed to Pitt.[1] Likewise in 1791 William Grenville, then Home Secretary, requested the opinion of the planters and merchants as to the amount of additional forces that should be sent to Dominica in view of the negro insurrection there. To this the meeting of 5th April

[1] Standing Committee's Minutes, vol. i, meetings of 5 and 6 March 1787.

refused answer: the troubles, they alleged, were due to "novel and extraordinary ideas respecting the Slave Trade" which had had support from members of the administration, and they alone could decide the measure of defence necessary.[1] Again, in 1792, Pitt asked the sentiments of the West India Planters and Merchants as to certain propositions that had been made to him for the importation of East India sugar at the same duties as British, and to allow the importation under certain conditions of French sugar, and to consider the propriety of a temporary suspension of export of both raw and refined sugar: all, in fact, of the old demands put forward by the refiners from time to time during the preceding century; and met once more by the old arguments as to the system of trade under which the islands had been settled:[2] "An implicit Compact ... for a mutual monopoly."[3]

More frequently the Committee took the initiative in the negotiations with the Government, in accordance with the long-standing functions of the agent, to guard against any menace to the prosperity of the islands and their interests. So upon the submission to Parliament of Pitt's Irish Resolutions in February 1785, the planters and merchants presented a list of queries as to the working of the scheme,[4] clearly manifesting an attitude of disfavour. During the following three months frequent meetings were held

[1] Standing Committee's Minutes, vol. i, meeting of 5 April 1791.

[2] *Ibid.*, meetings of 14, 20, 24, and 28 Feb. 1792.

[3] *Ibid.*, meeting of 28 Feb. 1792.

[4] See Chatham Papers, 352, where extracts are given from the minutes of meetings of the Committee held on 9 and 15 March, 22 April, and 6 May. Also Standing Committee's Minutes, vol. i, meetings of 18 and 31 May, 7 and 14 June.

THE WEST INDIA COMMITTEE 209

and resolutions sent to Pitt, and conferences took place with him, and the revision of the proposals in May shows the strength of the influence exercised by the Committee.[1] Similarly, in 1786 the terms of the Treaty of Commerce with France roused the apprehension of the Committee, and application was made for a reduction of the duty on rum to counterbalance that included in the treaty on French brandy: this time despite prolonged negotiations only a slight concession could be obtained.[2]

Lengthy communications took place also with regard to the establishment of the Sierra Leone Company in 1791. Early in the year a sub-committee was appointed " to consider the Bill respecting Sierra Leone," and on 11th May the first meeting of the committee decided to call a general meeting on the matter.[3] The general meeting resolved that application should be made to Pitt to postpone the bill for a week, a request which was granted; and there followed discussions between Pitt and members of the Committee as to the desirability of prohibiting the cultivation of sugar, or, while allowing cultivation, forbidding export. On 19th May a memorandum was agreed setting forth the attitude of the Committee to the establishment of plantations in the proposed colony: it would show the way to " foreign Nations, who have as yet no Colonies anywhere " : [4] it would supply a

[1] See J. Holland Rose, *William Pitt and National Revival*, London, 1911, pp. 260–1.
[2] Standing Committee's Minutes, vol. i, meeting of 23 Nov. 1786; cf. ibid., meetings of 29 Nov., 6, 12, 13, and 19 Dec. 1786, and of 9, 14, 20, and 28 Feb., 2 and 6 March 1787.
[3] *Ibid.*, meeting of 11 May 1791.
[4] *Ibid.*, meeting of 13 and 14 May 1791.

model of production which the African natives themselves might seek to imitate : if export were forbidden, it would be certain to take place clandestinely in foreign vessels, and many other reasons were alleged why the colony should be wholly prohibited from cultivating sugar, coffee, and pimento, and from manufacturing rum. For such regulations there was ample precedent in the forbidding of tobacco cultivation in Great Britain and slitting mills in North America. And the memorandum concluded :

> In short the continued and prescriptive adoption of the system of local Monopolies throughout the empire, has alone given to the Colonists in the British West Indies the confidence and Spirit they have shown in these several enterprizes.[1]

In the end the Committee failed to obtain their wish,[2] and their last resolution on 23rd May amounted to a withdrawal from their attempts.[3] The conditions of the colony soon removed any fear of dangerous competition.[4]

In all these matters the planters and merchants were working in accordance with principles long accepted in the islands, and expressed in petitions from councils and assemblies during the previous century. Still more close association, however, is to be observed in connection with the movement for the suppression of

---

[1] Standing Committee's Minutes, vol. i, meeting of 19 May 1791.
[2] See 31 George III, cap. 55.
[3] A General Meeting resolved that they could give no estimate of the damage threatened to the West India Island until they had consulted the legislatures of the various islands. Standing Committee's Minutes, vol. i, meeting of 23 May 1791.
[4] T. Clarkson, *Abolition of the African Slave Trade*, London, 1808, vol. ii, pp. 343-4.

THE WEST INDIA COMMITTEE

the slave trade. On the raising of the question as a measure of practical policy early in 1788, a sub-committee was appointed by the Planters and Merchants to conduct the opposition.[1] The agents were all included in the membership, and close co-operation was thus ensured with the islands. The measures taken were, as was always the case when opposition to a bill was desired, petitions to Parliament and the stirring up of friends amongst the members. In April 1789 it was resolved that the City Members should be approached;[2] and applications for assistance were sent to the kindred organisations at the out-ports.[3] The zeal of the Committee continued unabated until the final failure of their aims in 1807. They then devoted their attention to the question of preventing the abolition of slavery, and when this too proved a failure, to the practical purpose of organising the supply of an alternative form of labour, the immigration of East Indians and Chinese.

Nineteenth-Century Developments.—The stress of the contests of the late eighteenth and the nineteenth centuries resulted in a development of the organisation of the Committee. In 1829 a sub-committee of the Standing Committee, the Acting-Committee, was made a permanent feature of the constitution. It was to meet monthly, making reports every six months to the Standing Committee, which was to assemble to receive it. The change was no doubt made necessary by the gradual growth in the numbers of the

---

[1] Standing Committee's Minutes, vol. i, meeting of 7 Feb. 1788. The Committee remained operative for at least four years, receiving constant votes of supplies from the Standing Committee.

[2] Standing Committee's Minutes, vol. i, meeting of 24 April 1789.

[3] *Ibid.*

earlier committee. It had, indeed, lost its character as an executive body responsible to the general meetings of planters and merchants, and had become virtually a full meeting of the West India interest. Henceforth its functions were largely formal, the Acting Committee taking its place in the initiation of business.[1]

Yet a further development took place in 1843. In that year the Society of West India Merchants reviewed its relations with the Standing Committee, and resolved that its continuation as a separate body was no longer necessary. It thereupon, in July, voted its own dissolution, directing such of the society as were not already members of the Standing Committee to join that body.[2] The decision was reached in collaboration with the Standing Committee, who for over four months had been considering a reform of their constitution.[3] The new constitution was passed at a meeting of the 8th May,[4] and anticipated, therefore, the final disappearance of the kindred society. From 1843 there has, therefore, been only one permanent organisation, which after surviving further changes of constitutional form is now known as the West India Committee.

The year 1843 marked also the climax in the relations between the agents and the other elements of the West India interest. The half-century that lay between the establishment of the Standing Committee

---

[1] From this time there are two series of minutes, one for the Standing Committee and the other, far more voluminous, for the Acting Committee. The particulars of the new constitution are given at the end of vol. v of the Standing Committee's Minutes.

[2] Merchants' Minutes, vol. vii, meeting of 7 July 1843.

[3] Standing Committee's Minutes, vol. vii, meeting of 22 March 1843. [4] *Ibid.*, meeting of 8 May 1843.

THE WEST INDIA COMMITTEE 213

and this final development saw increasing importance attached by the Committee to the presence of the agents. Amongst the members of the Committee in the eighteenth century were the agents for Jamaica, Stephen Fuller and Robert Sewell, several agents for the Leeward Islands, John Stanley, Alexander Willock, Charles Spooner, the agents for Barbados, Samuel Estwick and John Brathwaite, Alexander Campbell, of Grenada, and Sir William Young, of St. Vincent. When, in 1788, a sub-committee was appointed to deal with the attack on the slave trade, the colonial agents were included on the ground of their office,[1] and four years later the other agents since appointed were added.[2] And this tendency to include the agents in sub-committees was continued on several occasions in the next century. But it was not until the reorganisation of 1843 that the tendency received definite recognition. It was then resolved as a part of the reformed constitution " That the agents appointed by the West India Colonies . . . . be *ex officio* . . . members of the Acting Committee." [3]

The agents, despite this development, were never wholly absorbed in the committee. In their function of " standing sentrie " lest any harm should be done to the interests of the islands, they acted, indeed, in conjunction with the planters and merchants: in the great struggles over the trade monopoly and the

[1] Standing Committee's Minutes, vol. i, meeting of 7 Feb. 1788. The agents referred to were Stephen Fuller for Jamaica, John Brathwaite for Barbados, John Stanley for Nevis, and Charles Spooner for St. Christopher and Montserrat.

[2] Standing Committee's Minutes, vol. i, meeting of 19 Jan. 1792.

[3] *Ibid.*, vol. vii, meeting of 22 March 1843.

supply of labour all sections acted together. But, in many aspects of their work, the agents proceeded alone, as they had done before this closely organised body had come into being. In particular they retained within their hands the responsibility for soliciting the confirmation of laws; and they fulfilled alone the miscellaneous duties imposed upon them by the islands. The agents never forgot that their "constituents" were the colonists abroad, and if they received valuable aid from the interest at home, to the residents in the islands they recognised their ultimate duty.

CHAPTER XI

SOLICITATIONS IN WHITEHALL AND WESTMINSTER

IN the exercise of nearly all his functions the agent came into contact with the government at home, and the circumstances of this contact made the relationship of a highly complicated character. The old empire grew up in the seventeenth century side by side with the growth of differentiation in the English executive. At the time of the origin of the colonies the centre of the English governmental system, the Privy Council, was still an effective body, having indeed but just passed the zenith of its power: and so colonies were included under its control. They were viewed, indeed, as an expansion of the mother-country, the continuation of the process which had but lately embraced in one jurisdiction the outlying districts of England and Wales. The increasing intricacy of government compelled the functions of government to be more precisely defined in the case of great offices like the Treasury and the Admiralty, and of administrative organs like the Commissioners of the Customs and the Board of Ordnance, the Navy Board, and others, which were only a little less important. It was found necessary also to constitute special authorities to deal with trade and the plantations, now, ever since the Interregnum, bound together. Some of these authorities were standing committees of the

Privy Council, the most famous the Lords of Trade of 1675 to 1696, and the Board of Trade established in 1786, the foundation of the modern office of that name: others were separate councils specially commissioned, as the Board of Trade and Plantations, which remained in operation from 1696 to 1782. None of these authorities, however, took away from the final responsibility of the Privy Council, being dependent upon an Order in Council to give authority to their advice.

During the same period, also, another change took place: the growth in the sphere of Parliament. In colonial as in foreign affairs there had been little Parliamentary interference in the first part of the seventeenth century; but, as the period of discovery and exploration was succeeded by one of settlement, the association of plantations and trade called forth Parliamentary regulation. The reigns of the later Stuarts established precedents for the control by the English Parliament of the trade of the whole Empire, even of that between one colony and another.[1] Further, the period demonstrated the importance, from the point of view of the West Indies, of Parliamentary imposition of import duties on colonial produce and Parliamentary regulation of the African trade. The policy of the Navigation Acts, the duties on sugar, and the methods of carrying on the traffic in slaves were subjects in connection with which the authority of Parliament was constantly being brought before the minds of the West Indian colonists.

The sphere of activity open to the agent was by virtue of these facts almost coextensive with the whole system of the English government. In practice,

[1] 25 Car. II, c. 7.

however, some branches were far more prominent than others, and during the greater part of the eighteenth century, the largest share of the agent's solicitations took place in connection with the Board of Trade and Plantations.

The Board of Trade.—The power of the Board of Trade varied considerably during different periods of its history, depending largely on its indefinite relations with the Secretary of State and the Privy Council. The existence in the office of the Secretary of State for the Southern Department of an embryonic plantation staff in the first half of the eighteenth century indicates the drift of colonial business; the establishment of the American Secretaryship in 1768 marked a further advance; and when in 1782 the new secretaryship and the Board of Trade both disappeared, the Secretary of State for Home Affairs undertook in large measure the control of the plantations, his junctions being absorbed later by the office of the Secretary of State for War and the Colonies. A similar development took place in the authority of the Privy Council. During the period of the Board of Trade's activities there was a growing tendency for the Privy Council or in practice the Committee of the Privy Council to make real its control in the review of colonial legislation, no longer accepting without question all the reports made by the Board. And when the reorganisation of 1782–6 was effected it was in large measure to a committee of the Privy Council, known then, as now, as the Board of Trade, that the function of advising upon colonial laws was assigned.[1]

[1] The history of the growth of machinery is dealt with in *A.P.C.* ii. Preface pp. vi–xi; Andrews, *Guide to . . . the Public Record*

Even the first workings of such developments of necessity affected the authority of the Board.¹ But, nevertheless, there was considerable continuity of functions. The colonial governors corresponded sometimes with the President of the Board of Trade and sometimes with the Secretary of State, sending their dispatches very frequently in duplicate to the two authorities. Matters coming before the Secretary of State were, however, often referred to the Board, and this happened even more frequently when, on more formal occasions, petitions were sent from the islands to the king. The functions of the Board, in making a report to the Secretary of State or the Privy Council on matters referred to it, were in practice identical to those connected with matters originating with the Board, which terminated in a representation to the Council.

The matters dealt with by the Board of Trade, either in the first instance or upon reference from some other authority, embraced almost all the aspects in which the colonies were linked with the administration at home. Among the most frequent items of colonial business were the review of colonial legislation and questions of defence; then there were accusations against Governors, applications for favour from both sides in quarrels in the local legislatures; the drawing up of commissions and instructions to Governors, the appointment of councillors; and a miscellaneous mass of business originating in memorials from persons

Office, vol. i, pp. 20-1, 96-100; cf. E. B. Russell, *The Review of American Colonial Legislation by the King in Council*, New York, 1915, pp. 83-5.

¹ Cf. Dickerson, *American Colonial Government, 1696-1765*, chapter ii, especially pp. 108-9, 112-15.

in England, or paragraphs in the Governor's dispatches, or petitions from the island.

Reference to other Departments.—The Board of Trade, in making the decisions which were embodied in its representations and reports, acted in a large number of cases on expert advice. There were in the first place legal matters, especially in connection with the review of colonial laws, which were referred either to the Law Officers, the Attorney- or Solicitor-General, or, after 1718, to the Standing Counsel of the Board, an officer appointed for this purpose. There were, furthermore, matters coming under the purview of one or another of the great departments of state; business in which duties and customs were involved were referred to the Commissioners of the Customs; the salary of governors and other questions of finance to the Treasury; the provision of troops, convoys, frigates, or stores of war, to the Admiralty or the Board of Ordnance. On many of these matters the agents would be summoned to give explanation as to the policy of the island or to answer any questions arising from them or from the representations made by government departments or other interested persons. In such cases the agent's function would be to attend amongst the several groups of people whom the journal notes as attending at the Board's meetings,[1] and give evidence as required,

[1] *Cf.* Miss M. P. Clarke, "The Board of Trade at Work," in *American Historical Review*, October 1911, pp. 19–20: "... the general arrangement of the Plantation Office must have been similar throughout. With the exception probably of the first temporary location it always consisted of four rooms or groups of rooms. The Council Chamber, where formal meetings of the Board were held, must have been of considerable size, as it was usual to give audience to a number of people at one time. Here the commissioners seem to have sat round

and if necessary employ counsel to plead the cause of his island.

Frequently the part taken by the agent was more independent than this. Perhaps he would find upon summons to the Board that the business submitted to him was of a kind that required constant solicitation; or, in more instances, the order was reversed and the agent took the initiative in bringing before the Board matters in which his island was concerned. Sometimes the memorial was merely a reminder of business lying untouched, and in any case it might be necessary to make several applications before any action was taken. Then there would be references to other departments, and finally the submission of the question to the Privy Council for the issue of the final order. If the memorial was addressed to the Secretary of State or the Treasury, or other department, preliminary conversations would probably take place, and then the matter would be referred to other departments, or the Board of Trade and perhaps, though by no means uniformly, the Privy Council. A petition to the king went first before the Privy Council and then frequently to the committee, which referred it to the Board of Trade or elsewhere for discussion and then drafted an order when the desired reports had been supplied.[1]

a table, each having his own place according to a definite order of precedence. Communicating with this room from one side was that of the secretary, and from another side the waiting-room or rooms—for there were at times several of them—where witnesses, petitioners, visitors of all sorts had to wait till formally admitted to the Board. Besides these there was the clerks' room...."

[1] To some extent this description of the Board's activities is applicable also to the successor appointed in 1786. The later Board, like the earlier, referred matters to legal and other advisers, summoned the attendance of agents, etc. But its powers were on the whole more

SOLICITATIONS

Procedure of the Agents.—The work of the agent in all the cases is well described by the phrase of Governor Handasyd, of Jamaica, when urging the appointment of an agent in 1719. The colonial laws had to be, he said, " dexterously solicited through the several offices " ;[1] the letters and accounts of the agent show that such negotiation was necessary for all the business in which the home government was involved. In 1759 John Yeamans as agent for Montserrat petitioned the King for the supply of stores of war. The first step was a reference to the Committee of the Privy Council, the next from the Committee to the Board of Trade, and returning to the Committee to obtain an order in favour of his request; then a reference to the Board of Ordnance, and an order from that Board for the dispatch of the stores, fees, and gratuities for " expediting " the business being required in each case, and several visits by the agent to the Ordnance Board, at the Tower, and the Plantation Office in King Street.[2]

With the confirmation of laws, even more troublesome negotiations were necessary, made more difficult from time to time by the lack of a full Board, or the dilatoriness of the legal expert whose advice was required. William Nevine in 1721 to 1724, when he was acting as agent for Antigua, St.

overshadowed by those of successive Secretaries of State than had been its predecessors', and its business as far as it related to the colonies tended to become more formal, the real administration falling into the hands of the permanent officials. The arrangement of its establishment was largely similar to that of its predecessors. See P.C. 1:63, B. 22.

[1] *Journals*, vol. ii, p. 297.

[2] C.O. 177:3, Journals of Assembly, 19 Feb. 1739/40. *Vide infra*, Appendix III, pp. 277-9.

Christopher, and Montserrat, drew attention to these obstacles. In February 1721/2 he wrote to the President, Council, and Speaker of Montserrat, describing the progress made in "the Acts now depending wth the Board of Trade." He had not yet been able to get them considered, and though he intended to "continue to Press for a Report" he had no very great hopes of success. A new Parliament was shortly expected "which will Call the Members upon their Elections": all the other colonies were in the same plight.[1] Six months later no advance had been made. The members of the Board were many of them out of town, and the Board was not very frequently summoned. When it did meet the time was so taken up with "Business recommend'd to them by the Ministry to be Imediately Dispatched," that there was little prospect of any attention to the laws. The meeting of Parliament would bring the members to town, but even then there was the expectation of such a busy session that for some time after the meeting there was little likelihood of much advance. Nevine assured the island that he still flattered himself "the Acts of Antigua, Montserrat & St. Christophers will be the first they will go upon," and he contemplated

> a Vigorous Push to that purpose sometime the Latter end of next week or beginning of the following Either by a Fresh Memorial or by Personall Application to such of them as are in Town.

He had obtained a favourable report from the standing counsel, Mr. West, on a number of the acts, and considered therefore that there was "little Danger of

[1] C.O. 155:6, Montserrat, Minutes of Council, 23 June 1722.

their Miscarrying either with the Board of Trade or Privy Councill."[1]

This was in August 1722; in September of the following year no further progress was made,[2] but at last in January an improvement took place. The Board of Trade had been " prevailed " upon to consider the acts and were going to make report in two or three days. They did not think fit to communicate the purport of the report until it was actually signed, but he hoped shortly to send information on this point, and he assured the island that when the acts were sent to the Council Office he would be " as Industrious for Dispatch there " as he had been with the Board of Trade.[3]

The reports were finally made in May, and those acts recommended to be confirmed sent to the Council, where Nevine proceeded further to press for approbation. Many of the acts had been ordered to " Lye by," and in respect of these nothing could be done for some time as the report was based on a desire to test their working. Nevine commented that he found " the Board at Present very much disposed to treat most of the Acts that come from the Colony that way " : and he believed " it will be no Easy matter to Bring them to another way of thinking " ; but when he thought such a decision would be harmful he would " labour by all proper ways to prevent such a Report being made."[4] A few months later the matter was still unfinished, for the Council had

[1] C.O. 155:6, Montserrat, Minutes of Council, 17 Nov. 1722, and St. Christopher, Minutes of Council, 7 Nov. 1722.
[2] *Ibid.*, St. Christopher, Minutes of Council, 13 Sept. 1723.
[3] *Ibid.*, 17 April 1724.
[4] *Ibid.*, 19 Aug. 1724.

referred three of the St. Christopher Acts to the Attorney- and Solicitor-General, and in October Nevine was required to attend " at the Attorney General's chambers "[1] while they were being considered.

The Secretaries of State.—In the transaction of business with the Secretaries of State similar delays were frequent. In 1721 William Nevine as agent for St. Christopher and Montserrat was still treating with the administration regarding the claims of sufferers from French depredations committed during the Spanish Succession War.[2] He had, he told the council and assembly of Montserrat, held interviews with Lord Carteret, the Secretary of State for the Southern Department and " another Great Lord wth out whose protection & Countenance " no success could be expected.[3] A little later, in 1724, Nevine was commissioned by Governor Hart to secure the grant for him of 500 acres of the French land in St. Christopher. The Governor had opened the negotiations by an address, which Nevine took in the first place to the Chancellor of the Exchequer, an action explained by the fact that the office was then held by Walpole. He was told to deliver it to the Duke of Newcastle, the successor of Carteret, and he accordingly took it to Charles Delafaye, the Duke's secretary, who promised " to gett it referred . . . to the Treasury . . . as soone as he could gett a Leisure

[1] C.O. 155:6, St. Christopher, Minutes of Council, 19 Dec. 1724.

[2] The negotiations included a proposal for Nevine to attend the Congress of Cambrai. In 1743, during the agency of Samuel Martin, directions were sent him from the island to attempt to reopen the negotiations. C.O. 177:5, Minutes of Council in Assembly, 28 May 1743.

[3] C.O. 155:6, Montserrat, Minutes of Council, 23 June 1722.

SOLICITATIONS

Minute of his Grace." This was in May.[1] By the time of his next letter, written in October, no action had been obtained. Nevine said that he had been lately to Windsor to see the Duke. But he was informed that since his appointment as Secretary the Duke " had not had it in his power to fix a day for the Consideracon of the West India affairs." In any case there was little hope of a favourable decision and Nevine appears to have abandoned the negotiations.[2]

Nor was it only with the Board of Trade and the Secretaries of State that the agents had relations. In time of war agents, planters, and merchants all made representations to the Admiralty,[3] the Secretary at War,[4] and Commander-in-Chief;[5] and other offices, the Victualling Office,[6] the Treasury,[6] the Postmaster-General,[7] were approached from time to time.

Fees and Gratuities.—In securing the attention of officials to West Indian business there does not seem to have been more than the normal use of the payment of fees and gratuities. For the issue of

[1] C.O. 155:6, St. Christopher, Minutes of Council, 19 Aug. 1724. The letter is dated 16 May.

[2] C.O. 155:6, St. Christopher, Minutes of Council, 19 Dec. 1724. No doubt it was Nevine's failure in this affair that caused the hostility of the Governor. *Vide supra*, p. 150, n. 4. For other examples of negotiations with Secretaries of State see B.M. Add. MSS. 32921, 32923, 33065-7, 32905. Also Merchants' Minutes, vol. i, meeting of 5 May 1772.

[3] Merchants' Minutes, vol. i, meetings of 2 Jan., 6 and 16 Feb., 3 March, 6 Aug., 6 Sept. 1776.

[4] *Ibid.*, vol. i, meeting of 30 Oct. 1776.

[5] *e.g. ibid.*, vol. ii, meeting of 29 Jan. 1782.

[6] *e.g. ibid.*, vol. i, meeting of 7 March 1775.

[7] *e.g. ibid.*, vol. ii, meeting of 24 Jan. 1782.

226 COLONIAL AGENTS OF WEST INDIES

all official documents regular fees were charged,[1] and these appear repeatedly amongst the agents' disbursements. In addition there were certain distributions of gratuities. Jeaffreson in 1682 urged the island of St. Christopher to make Blathwayt, then Secretary to the Lords of Trade, their "friend" by a present of £20.[2] William Nevine, in describing his solicitations of 1721 to 1724 regarding the Leeward Islands' laws, represented to St. Christopher the desirability of making a present to the standing counsel, Richard West, suggesting that it would be "Convenient if not necessary" to give him a "hansome fee" on all acts which the island judges to be "of Importance enough to be anxious about their fate."[3] Later Nevine paid the Attorney- and Solicitor-General ten guineas each in connection with three St. Christopher acts.[4]

It was seldom that the agents were unnecessarily generous.[5] John Yeamans, as agent for Antigua, in 1735 presented in all, five guineas to Samuel Gellibrand,

[1] *Report of the Commissioners appointed by an Act of Parliament to inquire into the Fees . . . in the several Public Offices . . .* London, 1793.

[2] Jeaffreson, *op. cit.*, vol. ii, p. 14. He had no doubt learnt the necessity for such payments by experience. Earlier in the year he had encountered great difficulties in negotiating the transportation of malefactors because of his unwillingness to pay the fees.

[3] C.O. 155:6, St. Christopher, Minutes of Council, 7 Nov. 1722.

[4] *Ibid.*, 19 Dec. 1724.

[5] The only exception seems to have been the Leeward Islands' Commissioners of 1690–7. They appear to have spent vast sums on gratuities, charging to the Island of Nevis within three years two presents of £374 10*s*. and £300 respectively to "the Lord P.," and three presents of 100 guineas each to the "Secretary of the Plantations," besides £141 16*s*. to Povey. C.O. 155:2, Nevis, Journals of Assembly, 21 Oct. 1697.

then in the first year of his office as deputy-secretary to the Board of Trade. The only other gratuities paid by him in the year 1735-6, besides small sums to porters and messengers, were to William Sharpe for " extraordinary trouble and dispatch " in transacting business in the Council Office.[1] So also in his accounts with Montserrat in 1740 the total paid in gratuities to officials was only eleven guineas, which was shared by various clerks in the Ordnance Board.[2]

Relations with Parliament.—The more expensive and troublesome part of the agent's functions lay in his solicitations to Parliament. Frequently both the islands and their representatives proceeded, not by petition to the king or memorial to a subordinate branch of the executive, but by petitions to one or other of the Houses of Parliament. This was the method of procedure in all the more important gains of the West India interest in the eighteenth century,[3] and in the defensive actions after the period of aggression was over. In Parliament, also, the strength of the islands was not derived from extensive bribery. The West Indian planters were personally wealthy, and able, therefore, to incur the expenses attendant upon an election, but there is little evidence of concerted corruption by them in the concerns of the islands. Even for the defence against the attacks on slavery and the slave trade the West India Committee of London raised only between four and

[1] C.O. 9:9, Minutes of Council, 5 July 1736.
[2] C.O. 177:3, Journals of Assembly, 28 Aug. 1742.
[3] The agitation over the illicit trade between the Northern Colonies and the French West Indies in 1730-3 commenced by petitions to the King, but the sphere of action was transferred to Parliament early in 1731. Pitman, *op. cit.*, pp. 250-4.

five thousand pounds in the last twelve years of the century.

The applications to Parliament made by the agents and other members of the West India interest were facilitated by the frequent presence of agents, planters, and merchants in the House of Commons. If the agent himself were not a member of the House, a relative frequently undertook the task for him, as Rose Fuller[1] did for his brother Stephen. If this was not possible and none of the other planters or merchants were considered suitable, application was made to the City members. As a rule, during the eighteenth century the strength of the West India interest in the House of Commons was great enough to permit not only presentation of petitions, but a considerable measure of support for any motion proposed in the House.

In the House of Commons in the middle of the eighteenth century the West Indian group was a formidable section, comparable to that of the returned " nabobs " from the East.[2] One of the agents for Massachusetts Bay asserted in 1764 that the state of parties in the Commons was unfavourable to them, " 50 or 60 West India voters can turn the balance on which side they please ";[3] and twenty years earlier it was com-

---

[1] M.P. for New Romney, Maidstone, and Rye successively.

[2] *Vide* Chesterfield, *Letters to his Son*, 19 Dec. 1767; cited by Lecky, *History of England in the Eighteenth Century*, London, 1892, vol. iii, p. 369.

[3] *Jasper Mauduit, Agent in London for the Province of the Massachusetts-Bay*, Massachusetts Historical Society, 1918, p. 149, n. 1. The quotation is from a letter from Israel Mauduit, associate agent, dated 3rd March 1764, in Mass. Arch., lvi, 412. *Cf. Remarks on the Letter Address'd to Two Great Men*, London, 1760, pp. 46–7. Cited Beer, *British Colonial Policy*, 1754–1765, pp. 135–6, n. 1. Also *An*

mented that many Members of the Commons " were either by themselves or their friends, deeply concerned in one part or other of the Sugar trade, and . . . the cause . . . was always popular in the House of Commons.[1] In gaining their ends at home such a source of strength was of the greatest possible value to the agents.

Moreover, the same painstaking solicitations are observable as in the negotiations with the departments of the executive. The description given by Henry Lascelles of the agitation to defeat the sugar imposition in 1744 shows the trouble taken by an organised system of interviews to secure the adherence of ministers and opposition. Agents, planters, and merchants held meetings together: they drew up a statement of their case against the tax, procured the adherence of William Pitt and other members of importance, and painstakingly visited in little "committees" of two or three persons all the members of Parliament then in town,[2] besides making a bargain for mutual assistance with the Scottish and Irish linen interests.[3]

The history of the abolition of the slave trade shows

Examination of the Commercial Principles of the Late Negotiations, London, 1762, p. 28, and *Writings of Benjamin Franklin*, edited by Albert Henry Smyth, iv, p. 243, and Jasper Mauduit's letter of 1764, *Mass. Hist. Soc. Coll.*, ser. 1, vol. vi, p. 193, cited Beer, *op. cit.*, p. 158, n. 2.

[1] *Parliamentary History*, xiii, p. 639.

[2] *Parliamentary History*, vol. xiii, pp. 640-1; *cf.* Letter-book of Messrs. Lascelles and Maxwell, Sept. 1743 – Jan. 1745/6, p. 95. The account is confirmed in its main features in C.O. 177:5, Minutes of Council in Assembly, 26 May 1744.

[3] *Parliamentary History*, vol. xiii, pp. 652-3; *cf.* Letter-book of Messrs. Lascelles and Maxwell, Sept. 1743 – Jan. 1745/6, p. 113.

the same methods in practice. Co-operation was sought from every possible source, especially from the merchants at the out-ports: through the medium of the agents the activities of the West India interest in London were co-ordinated with the measures taken by the islands. In this case, in addition to the steps formerly so frequently taken, interviews with ministers and members of Parliament, an attempt was made to tie the hands of the House by a moderate measure of reform. The idea was conceived by a society formed under the direction of Sir William Young, a prominent planter of Antigua, member of Parliament since 1784 for a Cornish borough:[1] the society comprised all those members of both Houses that had estates in the West Indies, including Charles Ellis, member for Seaford.[2] Ellis in 1797 proposed in the House of Commons a motion for the issue of instructions to governors of the West Indian islands to recommend to the assemblies to adopt measures to ameliorate the condition of the slaves. The motion was carried, although the former action of its supporters roused some suspicions. It was well received in the islands, to whom it was communicated in advance by the agents, and steps were taken to pass laws to meet its advice.[3] This victory achieved its purpose in affording a pretext

[1] Young had been deputed by the planters and merchants interested in the Island of Tobago to attend the French Court upon the negotiations over the Treaty of Versailles. He became later (in 1807) Governor of Tobago. *Vide sub nom. D.N.B.*

[2] *Vide sub nom. D.N.B.* and *Gentleman's Magazine*, Oct. 1745, p. 419. His family was related to that of the Beckfords and Longs.

[3] Account of these proceedings is given in a communication from Sir William Young to the Island of Antigua inserted in the *Minutes of the General Legislature of all the Islands* held at Basseterre in March–April 1798. C.O. 152:76.

for the allegation that the House had thereby expressed its preference for gradual as opposed to immediate abolition.

Mr. E. P. Tanner, in writing of the colonial agencies of the North American colonies, speaks of the agent as "a general lobbyist." This same description applies to the West Indian agents as well. The functions ascribed by Povey to the personal agent of the Governor, of watching his interests, and warning his friends when danger threatened, may well be taken to describe the agents of the whole island in the eighteenth century. The circle of the islands' friends was large and powerful, the agent himself was one amongst them, often one of the most prominent. The long period of the agitation against the slave trade shows the strength of the system which agents, planters, and merchants had built up; for the history of the abolition movement, marked by the growth and final victory of an organisation comparable to the West India Committee for its longevity, was one of continuous fighting against the almost overwhelming power of interest. The failure of this struggle was for the West Indian colonies an important stage in their decline. And, with the decline, the agent, despite the continuance of his office for nearly half a century, lacked the influence to maintain the eighteenth-century tradition of close intercourse with ministers, government officials, and the members in the House of Commons.

CHAPTER XII

THE DISAPPEARANCE OF THE AGENCIES

IF the Peace of Paris marks one turning-point in British colonial policy, another has yet to be found somewhere in the period between the recognition of American independence and the settlement of 1815. The Revolutionary and Napoleonic Wars, like those of half a century earlier, brought new colonies to the Empire. Not only was the fate of Tobago at last settled in favour of British rule, while St. Lucia also became once more British; but two further colonies were added to the West Indian group, Trinidad, formerly in the possession of Spain, and, on the mainland, the Dutch settlements of Essequibo, Demerara, and Berbice, soon to be known as British Guiana. These colonies, like the acquisitions of 1763, raised constitutional problems for British statesmen to solve. But the decision in the case of the " new colonies " differed considerably from the treatment given to Canada and the " ceded islands." In 1763 the colonies, immediately upon the conclusion of peace, were made the subject of a proclamation [1] establishing the normal type of colonial government, an executive appointed by the Crown, and an elected assembly. Before 1815 the universal application of this common type had been abandoned.

[1] See A. B. Keith, *British Colonial Policy*, 2 vols., London, 1918, vol. i, pp. 1-4.

DISAPPEARANCE OF THE AGENCIES

There were, indeed, special reasons why a representative assembly was considered unsuitable in the particular colonies concerned; but there were also general principles involved. Many factors combined to raise doubts as to the value of the old system: the revolt of the American colonies, the early difficulties of Canada, the perpetual quarrels in the West Indies, and, perhaps most potent of all, the problem of the suppression of the slave trade.[1] And so in the early years of the nineteenth century each colony received separate treatment, disregarding the traditional forms. In Tobago alone, where representative institutions had been granted in 1763, the old system was revived. On the mainland the existing constitution was in large measure retained. St. Lucia and Trinidad shared the fate of other " new colonies," such as Ceylon and the Cape, and were ruled by a Governor and nominated council, with no representative element.

The Crown Colony System.—In Trinidad, St. Lucia, and the mainland settlements, it was therefore impossible that an agency law should be passed on the model of those of the old colonies. Yet in the minds of the administration an agent had long been considered necessary, and colonial governors tended to assume that some form of agency was essential. Trinidad led the way, appointing an agent by resolution of Governor and council in 1801;[2] Demerara followed in 1804;[3] and thus there came into existence a new type of agents owing their position to the executive of the colony,

---

[1] *Cf.* Dispatch from the Earl of Liverpool to Governor Hislop of Trinidad, 27 Nov. 1810. *Parl. Papers*, 1810–11, xi. 333.

[2] C.O. 295:20, " Statement respecting the Agency of Trinidad."

[3] C.O. 323:217, Treasury, Adam Gordon to Viscount Howick, 24 Jan. 1832.

and in no way to the free choice of the inhabitants.[1] The executive was appointed by the Crown, and an obvious possibility existed for patronage from home. After some difficulty this right of recommendation was established, and secured as the monopoly of the Colonial Office.[2] Fifteen years after the conclusion of the Napoleonic Wars nine such agencies existed for various parts of the Empire and six were held by Colonial Office clerks. In 1833 a reorganisation took place of the work of these agents; the greater number of the agents were pensioned, and two of them henceforth transacted the business of the whole. They were known as the "Agents General of the Crown Colonies," and the office they controlled has continued to the present day under the title "Crown Agency Office."[3]

The years following the settlement of 1815 provided thus an answer to the problem that puzzled English statesmen in the time of the Napoleonic Wars. There was now an alternative to the representative system of colonial government: there was the crown colony system, and side by side with it there had grown up a new form of agency, the crown agents. In both, one feature characterised them as distinct from their older counterparts: the Colonial Office held far closer control. The crown colonies were more readily held in leash when there was no assembly to contest for

[1] *Cf.* the appointment in 1764 of Purbec Langham as agent for Grenada, and Richard Cumberland as agent for Quebec. These, however, were appointed by royal warrants. (P.R.O.) T. 28: 1, p. 14.

[2] C.O. 295:20, "Statement respecting the Agency of Trinidad"; and B.M. Add. MS. 37847, pp. 81–8.

[3] *Parl. Papers*, 1881, lxiv. 589 (C. 3075). The title does not imply any connection with the earlier office of Crown Agents, *vide supra*, p. 169, n. 2.

power: the crown agents, although not wholly under official directions, were less subject to outside influence. And it may well have seemed that the new system was better than the old: for in the nineteenth century, clashing of interests in the West Indies was common; the abolition of the slave trade and slavery, the adoption of free trade, brought the colonies and mother-country into conflict.

The economic and financial distress of the mid-nineteenth century caused the defeat of the colonists in this contest, and in many of the islands abandonment of their representative institutions marked their final surrender. The dependence of the islands on royal protection for internal defence, always an important factor in their history, became of predominant significance as the century progressed and was responsible in Jamaica for the reorganisation of the government. In other islands decline of population or the burden of finance were determining factors in the same development.[1] Before the end of the century all the islands except the Bahamas and Barbados had undergone constitutional reform. It was in the course of this struggle and before its end that the colonial agencies disappeared.

There were many factors leading to the abolition. The West Indian colonial agency in its character belonged essentially to the eighteenth century. It came into existence to meet the difficulties latent in all systems of colonisation where the central government is far removed from the outlying parts; and, especially, to provide a solution for the many problems

[1] *e.g.* in the case of the Virgin Islands, C.O. 239:78, letter dated 22 July 1845. The Council had passed resolutions in 1841 and 1845 as to the difficulty in finding nine persons to constitute the assembly.

arising from the form of government characteristic of the old Empire. Every aspect of its constitution stands in immediate relation with some feature of eighteenth-century history. While for their appointment and control the agents looked to the legislatures of the colonies, their work in England was determined to a very great degree by the eighteenth-century parliamentary and administrative systems and the attitude of government, equally typical of the times, towards the representations of persons whose private interests claimed consideration.

Nineteenth-Century Changes.—With the progress of the nineteenth century there were many changes affecting the position of the Empire. The introduction of steamships and telegraphs made communications with distant colonies less dilatory, and the assertion of British sea-supremacy in the Napoleonic Wars, unchallenged for a century to come, relegated to the past that constant danger of interruption that made difficult the intercourse of mother-country and colonies in the preceding era. Further, the period of the Industrial Revolution closed in a time of constitutional as well as social reforms. The House of Commons underwent reconstruction, losing much of its character as a sphere for influence. The Reform Bill of 1832, imperfect though it was, abolished or reduced the representation of small boroughs where wealthy West Indians could obtain seats, and no longer were there at a political crisis a group of "West India voters" to determine the cause in favour of the islands. Change also occurred in the agents' relation with the administrative offices. The report made in 1793 by Parliamentary commissioners appointed to inquire into fees charged in government

DISAPPEARANCE OF THE AGENCIES

offices[1] was indicative of a policy leading to the substitution of salaries for the fee system, and with the growth of the modern civil service, to a great degree, the function of the agent in " dexterously soliciting " business through the hands of officials was no longer required.

The change in administrative procedure started with the passing of Burke's Sinecure Act in 1782.[2] The abolition of both the American Secretaryship and the Board of Trade and Plantations left the control of the colonies divided between the Secretary of State for Home Affairs and successive committees of the Privy Council appointed in 1784 and 1786, known once more as the Board of Trade and Plantations.[3] But the change was greater than this suggests. From the beginning, the work of the new Board of Trade was more formal than that of its long-lived predecessor, for the greater part of its functions was carried out in practice by its permanent officials, first Grey Elliot and then George Chalmers. Their offices were placed in close juxtaposition to those of the Privy Council and the Home Secretary, and the normal conduct of colonial business was much simplified by the easy intercourse of officials.[4] In 1801, when Lord Hobart became Secretary of State for War and the Colonies, a further unification of control

[1] *Vide supra*, p. 226, n. 1.   [2] 22 George III, c. 82.

[3] A paper describing the division of functions as arranged in 1786 is in C.O. 5:2 : it is printed in Andrew's *Guide to Materials . . . in the Public Record Office : The State Papers*, pp. 100–1.

[4] Details of the establishment are in (P.R.O.) B.T. 3:1, p. 1 (26 Aug. 1786); B.T. 5:4, pp. 11–14 (25 Aug. 1786), pp. 210–11 (10 March 1787); B.T. 5:8, pp. 39–42 (14 May 1792). The Committee of 1784–6 had no establishment ; its functions were similar to those of the Board of Trade in the nineteenth century ; *cf.* B.T. 5:1, pp. 51–6 and *passim*.

took place. This department took over from the Home Office all colonial affairs, and from this time the function of the Board of Trade became in colonial matters more purely advisory. The Colonial Office, henceforth, was the sole medium of executive action in connection with the colonies.

Within the Colonial Office elaboration of duties proceeded in the first half of the nineteenth century, thereby much simplifying the passage of colonial business. In the middle of the century it was looked upon as the best organised of Government offices: a condition largely due to the long service of James Stephen.[1] By 1845 an officer had been appointed whose special function it was "to retain in his custody the original transcripts of all Colonial Enactments and to watch over the various formal proceedings to be taken on each until it is ultimately disposed of by the Queen in Council."[2] And, although the reference of colonial acts to the Board of Trade for report continued to the second half of the century,[3] the responsibility recognised by the Colonial Office obviated the necessity for the work of the agent in following through the various stages of confirmation the acts of the colonial legislature.

The changes in organisation were not alone responsible for the decline in the functions of the agent in connection with the confirmation of laws. The appointment of a Secretary of State, part, and at a later time the whole, of whose functions was to consider the business of the colonies, had the

---

[1] *Vide sub nom. D.N.B.*

[2] C.O. 23:120, Draft 89 to Gov. Mathew, 4 Oct. 1845.

[3] *Cf.* Alpheus Todd, *Parliamentary Government of England*, vol. ii, 2nd ed., pp. 639, 790-1; and *Parl. Papers*, 1847-8, xlii. 371.

DISAPPEARANCE OF THE AGENCIES 239

effect of bringing about the development of rules of policy in colonial affairs and the drawing of the control of the colonies into the maelstrom of party politics.[1] In all aspects of his work the strength of the influence of the agent declined as this development progressed. The break-up of the system of English society which was one aspect of the Industrial Revolution was accompanied by a great decline in the respect paid to private interests. It is true, indeed, that the influence of rivalries of interest has survived these changes, but at no time in the nineteenth century was the power of interest so great as when eighteenth-century administrations strove to balance against one another the northern colonies and the West Indies, sugar planters and sugar refiners. The service of the agent was no longer so much required in seeing that the West Indies did not suffer in the competition for official favour.

The Agents in the Nineteenth Century.—For the West Indies the downfall of interest was achieved in the great struggle that ended in the abolition of the slave trade and slavery. The first manifestation of its decline was in connection with the question of trade. In the eighteenth century some of the most striking of the agents' achievements had been in the control of the sugar market, the maintenance of the mercantilist economic system so far as it affected the islands. With the close of the century the admission

---

[1] Lines of policy can be traced in the eighteenth century; *cf.* E. B. Russell, *Review of American Colonial Legislation by the King in Council*, pp. 109–201. But the impression gained from colonial correspondence in the nineteenth century is that policy and precedent to a great extent were substituted for the earlier " continual lobbying " as determining the course of action.

of prize sugar, East Indian sugar, and foreign sugar gradually destroyed the old profitable monopoly of the West Indian planters. With the old system there disappeared much of the concern with which those interested in the West Indies had watched the imposition of sugar duties. Competition rather than the weight of duties determined the price of sugars as soon as competition was admitted, and so another source of the call on the agents' activities was gone.

There remained, then, a number of miscellaneous duties the care for which would naturally fall on the agent. And in the nineteenth century these were by no means unimportant in character. Between the abolition of the slave trade and that of slavery not only were there many occasions when action in England with reference to the treatment of slaves roused the apprehension of all the islands, but in 1818 the constitution of the Leeward Islands came under review with the reorganisation of the government.[1] The year before the abolition of slavery, in January 1832, there started a long agitation on the part of Barbados and the Leeward Islands for the repeal of the four and a half per cent. duty, an end finally to be reached in 1838;[2] and during this same period, ever since the early years of the century, the interest of the colonies had been turned to the problem of the supply of labour from the East. But even matters as fundamental as these did

[1] From 1818 to 1871 Antigua and Montserrat formed one government, St. Christopher, Nevis, and the Virgin Islands another.

[2] The agents were responsible for initiating this struggle, C.O. 318:114. It is interesting to compare the method taken to abolish the tax with that used in originating it. The action of the legislatures of the islands in repealing the acts making the grant was reinforced by an Act of Parliament.

not seem to the islands to justify the retention of the agents. In 1848 a member of the Barbados House of Assembly asserted that there had been for some years little for the agent to do: that his office had not been abolished earlier was due to the respect of the assembly for his long services.[1] So also in St. Christopher all parties agreed in 1850 that the agency was " useless."[2]

The Economy Movement.—The readiness of the islands to abandon the maintenance of agents, over which for so many years they had struggled in the previous century, was due mainly to considerations of finance. The revolution of West Indian society accomplished by the abolition of slavery had an immediate effect in paralysing the economic condition of the islands. The Bahama Islands had never resigned the financial grants made to them at the time of the settlement of the Loyalists after the American War, but now other colonies also required subsidies from the home government.[3] And as they ceased to be self-supporting, or as it became apparent that this end could not long be delayed, pressure from England and their own desire for economy combined to produce a rigid censoring of all branches of expenditure. In many of the islands the termination of the agency synchronises with the abolition of other offices.

[1] C.O. 31:56, p. 40, 21 March 1848.
[2] C.O. 239:89, Lt.-Gov. Mackintosh to Earl Grey, No. 53, 8 Aug. 1850, and copies of correspondence enclosed.
[3] It was proposed in 1833 that Parliamentary grants should be made to cover the cost of salaries formerly paid out of the 4½ per cent. C.O. 318:114, Agent, letter dated 17 Feb. 1833. This was actually put into force after the abolition of that duty.

The responsibility for this movement of economy is difficult to divide. In 1850 an official of the Colonial Office noted on the back of a letter relative to the agencies that "endeavours have been frequently made on the part of this office to induce the legislatures of West Indian Colonies to forego the appointment of agents on the ground of their uselessness."[1] Five years earlier an act of the Virgin Islands appointing a new agent was disallowed: the appointment was "totally useless," and "not to be justified . . . in a colony labouring . . . under great pecuniary difficulties":[2] and in the same year a similar act passed in the Bahama Islands was annulled; there was no necessity for an agent and the colony could not afford one.[3] But in other cases, Jamaica, Barbados, and the Leeward and Windward Islands, there is no evidence of suggestion from home: the impulse to abolition appears at any rate to have come from the colonies themselves.

For desiring the abandonment of the agencies, there were other motives besides those of finance. Both in the colonies and at home there were doubts as to the value of the agents' services. At the time of the final struggle over the abolition of slavery several of the colonies considered the possibility of appointing persons to be sent to England as "delegates" to advocate the views of the planters. The Colonial Office refused without question to receive

---

[1] C.O. 239:89, Despatch No. 53, 8 Aug. 1850. Minute signed H. T., 3 Sept. 1850.

[2] C.O. 239:77, Draft No. 216, 15 Aug. 1845.

[3] C.O. 23:120, Despatch No. 68, 10 Feb. 1845. Minute on back, and Drafts following. The Board of Trade reported on this Act; but a minute from the Colonial Office outlined the report beforehand.

DISAPPEARANCE OF THE AGENCIES 243

any such emissaries : "His Majesty's Government cannot recognise any other than the regular Colonial Agents":[1] but the suggestion indicates the dissatisfaction of the colonies with the work of the agents,[2] a dissatisfaction expressed a few years later by the legislature of the Bahamas in an attempt to reorganise the agent's office.[3] Governors also repeated at this time their old assertion of misrepresentation through the agent. Thus Sir Lionel Smith, of Barbados, in 1833 complained that the agents had lately departed from their " original object. . . . A Superintendence or Watch over the mercantile Interests of the Colonies" and had " done infinite mischief as Political Representatives."[4] In this case the Governor was assured that the Colonial Office was fully aware of the difficulty that might arise from intercourse with agents, and that for the future copies of all important communications from them should be sent to him.[5] But the distrust remained, and while there is no evidence that the abolition of the agencies was caused by its operation, it may well have made easy the steps by which the abolition took place.

In each island the abolition seems to have proceeded separately : and there were few obstacles. After the agencies for the Virgin Islands and the Bahamas had disappeared, Jamaica was not long to follow, for the last agent, Edward Burge, was not reappointed when his

[1] C.O. 323:214, circular letter dated 10 Oct. 1832.

[2] *Cf.* proposal inserted in the *Barbadian*, 2 Feb. 1833, for dispatch of special representatives to assist J. P. Mayers : lack of local knowledge hampered the agent.

[3] C.O. 23:109, Despatch No. 101 ; describes character of act appointing an agent passed on February 1841. The act was disallowed.

[4] C.O. 28:111, letter dated 18 Nov. 1833.

[5] *Ibid.*, draft letter following above.

period of office terminated in 1847. In Barbados there was some discussion in the assembly, but finally the office was abolished in 1848,[1] despite a protest that the principle *quamdiu se bene gesserit* was the one on which he had undertaken the appointment.[2] In Dominica the abolition dragged on for ten years, the first motion taking place in 1842 and the final decision in 1852.[3] In Tobago it was achieved without difficulty; in St. Christopher it was necessary to disprove an idea that the agent had a claim to compensation,[4] but the feeling in favour of abolition was unanimous. By 1852 all the agencies were abolished. The islands were left to the unaided care of the West India Committee, until one by one they started the practice of making use of the crown agency office.[5]

The history of the West Indian agents, while apparently it terminates in the office of Crown Agents for the colonies, has left another legacy to the present time. Before the West Indian agencies had ceased, their example had spread not only to the new colonies, which had no representative institutions, but to the rapidly developing communities of North America whose history had started while the ideas of the old colonial system were still prevalent. In Canada and Nova Scotia in the first half of the nineteenth century there were appointed agents whose position was identical with that of the eighteenth-century agents of the West Indies and the thirteen continental colonies. Their growth was not unattended

[1] C.O. 31:56, pp. 37, 40, 42, 64.
[2] *Ibid.* pp. 100–4. The appointing act was annual.
[3] C.O. 74:26, p. 6, and C.O. 74:28, Journals of Assembly, 10 Feb. 1852.
[4] C.O. 241:37, pp. 39–43.   [5] C.O. 323 : 256, Agent.

with difficulties, and their history did not continue without interruption. But they survived after the old system of colonial government had lost its supremacy, and they passed on their tradition to the newer communities on the other side of the Pacific. The middle years of the nineteenth century saw the first appearance of separate agencies for New South Wales and South Australia, to be the forerunners of other such agencies in all parts of the Empire. And as these colonies developed, as the system of responsible government took the place of administration by the aid of a representative assembly, the position of these agents tended to assume a greater political significance. In 1880, when negotiations were in progress for the appointment of the first High Commissioner of Canada, a request was put forward that the Dominion representative should be accorded a quasi-diplomatic standing at the English court.[1] To this English ministers could not agree;[2] but the proposal indicates the increased importance which was beginning to be assigned to colonial sponsorship in England. It is reminiscent of the time when a hundred years earlier a member of the Barbados assembly claimed for the agent of his colony the position of a foreign minister residing at "some distant state."[3]

For the West Indian agency such a status was not possible. The agent's relations with the home government were not at any time a matter of negotiation. In the seventeenth century, indeed, Christopher Jeaffreson had spoken of the difficulty of soliciting

[1] *Parl. Papers*, 1880, xlix (C. 2594, p. 5).
[2] *Cf.* Keith, *op. cit.*, vol. i, pp. 342–3.
[3] C.O. 31:36, Journals of Assembly, p. 122, 3 June 1772.

the business of St. Christopher unless he were given an official recommendation to the government; but normally the agent was accepted with little investigation and no formality by the authorities at home with whom he had to deal. The West Indian agency was essentially for the accomplishment of definite aims : to secure the application of sufficient care and interest in the affairs of the colony in England ; to provide information on points of which the home government was ignorant. There were few theories as to its character, and it was only by long practice that it came to be regarded in the eighteenth century as the natural accompaniment to a British colony. When in the nineteenth century its constitutional position was defined the time was not long in coming when the whole system was superseded. It vanished because the conditions under which it had served were no longer prevalent. So long as they remained it possessed a definite place in colonial administration, and if its history is considered as a whole from the time of early experiments to that of its downfall it must be concluded that in the accomplishment of its purpose it was successful.

APPENDIX I
THE AGENCY OF BERMUDA

THE history of the Bermuda Islands proceeded on lines different from those noticed in the West Indies. The only group with which they are at all comparable is the Bahamas, which were, like them, a port of call and a centre of trade in salt with the American mainland. The Bermudas were amongst the earliest of the island colonies to receive settlers, and their assembly came in order of date second only to Virginia. Down to the period of the Restoration, however, the islands were under the control of a chartered company, and until its dissolution in 1684 constitutional progress was slow. Then there followed a century of prosperity terminating with the American War. It was during this period that the agency was established.

From the earliest times of royal government personal agents were maintained by successive governors,[1] but it is with the year 1705 that the colonial agency properly begins. In September of that year a resolution was passed by the assembly " that an agent be appointed in England to soliciate and manage all publick matters and affairs relating to these Islands," and it was further agreed that Charles Noden, a London merchant, should be the agent. He was granted a yearly salary of £35 currency, and he was to hold office until Governor, council, and assembly should otherwise determine.[2] Noden continued as agent until he was discharged in 1714, although upon some occasions his action was supplemented

[1] *Cf.* C.O. 391:5, pp. 184, 219; C.O. 391:8, pp. 129-31, 143; C.O. 391:11, pp. 387-8.
[2] C.O. 40:2, Journals of Assembly, p. 94, 25 Sept. 1705.

APPENDIX I

by the sending of embassies from the islands.[1] At the end of this term he was succeeded by Sir John Bennett and his brother Thomas, but these were not regularly constituted agents, as is shown by the dispute over their salary.[2] Finally, in 1724 a formal appointment was again made. A London merchant, of the same family as the first agent, Ralph Noden, was voted as agent, to act under the direction of Governor, council, and assembly. He was given a salary of £40 currency.[3] This Noden remained as agent until 1750, when he lost office through the controversies of the islands. Governor William Popple was in 1747 involved in difficulties and accusations, and Noden came into disrepute in consequence.[4]

Again the islands had recourse to agents sent over for the purpose. Henry Tucker and Vincent Mathias acted as agents from 1757 to 1762. Then a regular appointment followed, another merchant, John Pigott, being constituted agent.[5] The outbreak of the American War brought again dissensions and distrust; and Henry Tucker once more was put in charge of an embassy, one of the chief objects of which was to conduct charges against the Governor.[6] Then in 1784, when these difficulties were ended, a merchant was again appointed, John Brickwood,[7] who remained as agent until his death in 1829. He was succeeded by Edward Winslow,[8] a barrister, who, being appointed for four years, and until "the end of the next session of the Legislature thereafter," retired in 1834.[9]

[1] E.g. in 1707–8; *ibid.*, 5 Dec. 1707, 1 March 1707/8.
[2] *Ibid.*, 6 May 1713; C.O. 40:3, 16 Nov. 1720; *ibid.*, 1 Aug. 1721; 6 March 1722/3.
[3] C.O. 40:3, 22 July 1724.
[4] C.O. 40:6, Council in Assembly, 3 Feb. 1747/8. An attempt to supersede him was made in 1729. C.O. 40:3, 7 Feb. 1728/9.
[5] C.O. 40:9, 9 April 1762.
[6] C.O. 40:20, Journals of Assembly, 8 July 1779.
[7] C.O. 40:23, Journals of Assembly, 1 May 1784.
[8] C.O. 40:30, Journals of Assembly, 26 Jan. 1829. Winslow received 100 guineas a year.
[9] C.O. 40:32, Journals of Assembly, 21 July 1835.

THE AGENCY OF BERMUDA

No successor was named, and the office lapsed. By this time the financial position made avoidable expenditure impossible.

The agency of Bermuda presents points both of similarity and contrast to those of other islands. In the constitution of the office, the similarity is great. The agents were, indeed, appointed by resolution and not by act, but this had been done in Nevis down to the middle of the eighteenth century. Control was effected by committees of council and assembly; the systems of correspondence and accounts were alike. In functions, too, no difference seems perceptible. But in the organisation of work in England there is considerable contrast. The West India interest had no concern in them; they acted alone: hence perhaps the frequent use of embassies from the islands. The agency, although on the same lines, was really a separate institution developing itself to meet the needs of the islands which it served, and disappearing when such service seemed no longer justified.

APPENDIX II
LIST OF WEST INDIAN COLONIAL AGENTS, 1660–1860.

I. Barbados

1671–1672. Edward Thornburgh.
1676–1677. Edward Thornburgh.
1685. Peter Colleton, Henry Drax.
1691–1694. Edward Littleton, William Bridges.
1695. Edward Littleton, William Bridges, Francis Eyles.
1705. Sir John Stanley, William Bridges, Melatiah Holder, William Cleland.
1706–1707. Sir John Stanley, William Bridges, Rowland Tryon.
1709. William Heysham, John Royley.
1711–1714. William Heysham.
1714–1715. James Campbell.
1715–1716. William Heysham, Joseph Micklethwaite, John Lloyd.
1716–1719. Joseph Micklethwaite, John Lloyd, George Bampfield.
1719–1720. John Lloyd, George Bampfield, Alexander Stevenson.
1723–1726. Charles Worsley, John Huggins, John Sharpe.
1727. Charles Worsley, John Sharpe.
1735–1736. John Sharpe, Peter Leheup, George Lewis Tissier.
1738–1756. John Sharpe (1756, Joseph Pickering, assistant agent).
1757–1763. Joseph Pickering (Thurston Blackman, assistant agent).

LIST OF WEST INDIAN AGENTS

1763–1778. George Walker (Samuel Estwick, assistant agent).
1778–1792. Samuel Estwick.
1792–1805. John Braithwaite.
1805–1823. Gibbes Walker Jordan.
1823–1831. George Carrington.
1831–1848. John Pollard Mayers.

II. JAMAICA

1682–1687. Charles Littleton, William Beeston.
1688. Ralph Knight.
1693–1704. Bartholomew Gracedieu, Gilbert Heathcote.
1722–1725. Alexander Stephenson, Edward Charlton.
1728–1731. Charles Delafaye.
1731–1733. John Gregory, Charles Delafaye.
1733–1756. John Sharpe.
1757–1763. Lovel Stanhope.
1764–1794. Stephen Fuller.
1795–1806. Robert Sewell.
1806–1812. Edmund Pusey Lyon.
1812–1831. George Hibbert.
1832–1846. William Burge.

III. LEEWARD ISLANDS

1. GENERAL

1674. Ferdinando Gorges.
1690–1697. Bastian Bayer, Christopher Jeaffreson, Jeffry Jeffryes, Joseph Martin, Richard Cary.
1698. Joseph Crispe, Joseph Jory.
1704. Richard Cary.
1705. Joseph Jory.

2. ANTIGUA

1698–1708. Richard Cary.
1712–1713. Sir John St. Leger.
1716–1723. William Nevine.
1728–1744. John Yeamans.

1751–1756. John Sharpe.
1757–1781. Henry Wilmot.
1781–1789. Alexander Willock.
1790–1798. William Hutchinson, John Burton.
1798–1840. Anthony Brown.
1841–1843. Nicholas Nugent.
1845–1851. Edmund Nugent.

3. Nevis

1699–1726. Joseph Jory.
1726–1744. Thomas Butler.
1744–1750. Samuel Martin.
1751–1756. John Sharpe.
1757–1775. Henry Wilmot.
1778–1785. John Stanley.
1785–1806. Charles Spooner.
1806–1821. Patrick and James Colquhoun.
1821–1848. James Colquhoun.

4. St. Christopher

1682–1690. Christopher Jeaffreson.
1706–1716. Stephen Duport.
1716–1724. William Nevine.
1724–1733. Thomas Beake.
1733–1740. Richard Coope.
1740–1751. James George Douglas.
1751–1757. John Sharpe.
1757–1773. Henry Wilmot.
1773–1784. William Payne Georges.
1784–1790. Charles Spooner.
1790–1808. Anthony Hart, Charles Thompson.
1808–1811. Anthony Brown.
1811–1818. James Akers.
1818–1823. Alexander Cray Grant.
1825–1851. James Colquhoun.

LIST OF WEST INDIAN AGENTS

5. MONTSERRAT

1718–1729.	William Nevine.
1737–1742.	John Yeamans.
1742–1749.	Samuel Martin.
1749–1773.	Henry Wilmot.
1773–1785.	William Payne Georges.
1785–1790.	Charles Spooner.
1790–1840.	Anthony Brown.
1841–1845.	Nicholas Nugent.
1845–1848.	Edmund Nugent.

IV. BAHAMA ISLANDS

1760–1785.	Richard Cumberland.
1785.	Grey Elliott.
1785–1792.	Anthony Stokes.
1792–1826.	George Chalmers.
1826–1833.	Edward John Lack.

V. VIRGIN ISLANDS

1774.	William Payne Georges.
1776–1777.	John Pownall.
1783–1796.	Henry Rawlinson.
1796–1801.	Robert Dougan.
1802–1845.	Patrick and James Colquhoun.
1845.	Patrick Colquhoun.

VI. TOBAGO

1770–1775.	Richard Maitland.
1775–1783.	John Spottiswood.
1794–1802.	John Petrie.
1823–1827.	Robert Douglas.
1827–1842.	Patrick Maxwell Stewart.
1842–1850.	James Colquhoun.

APPENDIX II

VII. St. Vincent

1767–1775. Richard Maitland.
1792–1805. Sir William Young and William Manning.
1806–1844. Patrick and James Colquhoun.
1845–1850. James Colquhoun.

VIII. Grenada

1767–1775. Richard Maitland.
1775–1776. Edward Montague.
1776–1785. Alexander Campbell.
1785–1812. Charles Spooner.
1812–1815. William Lushington, Benjamin Broughton.
1815–1825. Joseph Marryat.
1825–1831. William Manning.
1831–1849. Joseph Marryat.
1849–1850. Thomas Hankey.

IX. Dominica

1771–1784. John Ellis.
1784–1805. George Rose.
1816–1826. Patrick and James Colquhoun.
1826–1852. James Colquhoun.

X. Bermuda

1705–1713. Charles Noden.
1713–1724. Sir John and Thomas Bennett.
1724–1750. Ralph Noden.
1762–1786. John Pigott.
1786–1828. John Brickwood.
1831–1834. Edward Winslow.

APPENDIX III

DOCUMENTS ILLUSTRATIVE OF THE HISTORY OF THE WEST INDIAN AGENCIES

1. Letter from Thomas Povey to William, Lord Willoughby of Parham, London, 15 March 1672/3. [B.M. Egerton MS. 2395, ff. 487–9.]
2. Letter from Gentlemen Planters of Barbados in England to Deputy Governor, Council, and Assembly of Barbados, London, 14 December 1670. [C.O. 31:2, Journals of Assembly, pp. 15–17.]
3. Minutes of Meetings of the Committee for the Concern of Barbados. [C.O. 31:2, Journals of Assembly, pp. 37–9, 104–5.]
4. Letter from Gentlemen Planters of Barbados in London to Assembly of Barbados, 1 May 1671. [C.O. 31:2, Journals of Assembly, pp. 45–9.]
5. Instruction to Governor of Jamaica, 24 August 1702. [Plantation Register, iii, p. 50.]
6. Instruction to Governor of Jamaica, 16 March 1721/2. [Plantation Register, v, p. 247.]
7. Speech of Governor William Shirley to Council and Assembly of the Bahama Islands, 6 May 1760. [*Journals of the Lower House of Assembly of the Bahama Islands*, ii, pp. 38–40.]
8. Acts of Appointment:
    i. Antigua, 22 December 1698. [C.O. 8:1, No. 109, pp. 89–91.]
    ii. Jamaica, 11 February 1731. [C.O. 139:13, No. 49.]
    iii. Jamaica, 10 December 1767. [C.O. 139:23, No. 105.]
    iv. St. Christopher, 3 July 1773. [C.O. 240:12, No. 36.]
    v. Canada, 7 May 1880. [*Parl. Papers*, 1880, xlix, p. 7 (C. 2594).]
9. Letter to Colonel Jory from the General Legislature of the Leeward Islands, 25 June 1705. [C.O. 155:3, Minutes of General Council in Nevis.]

256 APPENDIX III

10. Letter from Richard Maitland to President and Speaker of Grenada. [C.O. 104:4, Journals of Assembly, 12 March 1760.]
11. Letter to George Chalmers from the Honble. Robert Stirling, member of the Committee of Correspondence of the Bahama Islands. February 1794. [B.M. Add. MS. 22900, f. 216.]
12. Accounts of John Yeamans with the Island of Montserrat, 1738–1739. [C.O. 177:3, Journal of Assembly, 5 June 1740.]
13. Letter from James Knight, London, 18 March 1725. [B.M. Add. MS. 22677, ff. 1–2.]
14. Letter from Planters' Club to President and Council of Montserrat. [C.O. 177:5, Minutes of Council, 16 Oct. 1745.]
15. Letters from Henry Lascelles to Correspondents in Barbados. [Letter-book of Messrs. Lascelles and Maxwell, Sept. 1743–Jan. 1745/6.]
16. Minutes of Meeting of West India and North American Merchants, 10 March 1766. [B.M. Add. MS. 8133 C, ff. 91–2].
17. Minutes of Meetings of Society of West India Merchants and of West India Planters and Merchants. [Merchants' Minutes, i, pp. 117–18 ; ii, Meeting of 29 May 1781 ; Standing Committees' Minutes, i, pp. 21, 25, 51–2.]
18. Minutes of Bristol West India Club. [Minute Books of Bristol West India Club, Merchants' Hall, Bristol.]

The following extracts from the manuscript materials used in the preparation of this monograph have been placed together in an appendix, because, while they appeared necessary to an understanding of the subject, they are too long to be inserted conveniently in the text. The first six extracts illustrate the origin of the agencies, traceable in part to the interested designs of Thomas Povey, in part to the party politics of the Barbados planters, in part to the deliberate encouragement of the home Government. The speech of Governor Shirley (No. 7) gives evidence of the degree to which the agencies developed late in the history of the office were founded upon the model of the older agencies. The series of Acts of Appointment (No. 8, i–iv) shows the variation in the form adopted by the various islands,

ILLUSTRATIVE DOCUMENTS 257

and indicates in the case of Jamaica the growth in the organisation of the office in the eighteenth century. The Canadian Act of 1880 (No. 8, v) is inserted to make possible a comparison of the constitution and functions of the West Indian and Dominion agencies. The work of the agents in England is shown in the letters and accounts sent by them to the colonial legislatures (Nos. 9–12), in the unofficial correspondence of members of the West India interest in London (Nos. 13–15), and in the records of the organised bodies of the West India interest in London and other ports (Nos. 16–18).

1. LETTER FROM THOMAS POVEY TO WILLIAM, LORD WILLOUGHBY OF PARHAM, LONDON, 15 MARCH 1672/3. [B.M. Egerton MS. 2395, ff. 487–9.]

. . . I doe in the first place, laie it down for a ground that whosoever shall bee engaged in such a distant Government as yr Lopp now is ought before hee adventures upon it, to secure to Himself as many as Hee can of the Principall Ministers neare the King and as many of the principall Persons whose Trade or busyness relate to that Place; who may represent things heere to the best Advantage, and bee readie to encounter that Envie, and Malice and Misreport, and Mistakes, which doe most certainly persecut forreigne Employments especially when a Populaice is concerned in them. Nor will it bee enough to bespeak the Favour, and Good will of men in Power, unless some fitt Person bee selected, to make due, and seasonable applications, and to awaken, and stirr upp and bring to Action that kindness, and adhearencie, which will bee, in a manner fruitless, if not minded and sollicited, and applyed to the Occasion to which their interposition is necessary. It being sufficient in them to Continue well inclin'd but it is to bee the work of some other diligent Person who is as it were to stand sentrie and bee watchfull, and give the Alarm when their Assistance is oportune, and requisite. . . . And surely the Discretion and Reputation of that Man are verie lowe, who will adventure himself upon a Trust, and appear to man (in an) Employment of that Nature, unless such previous things be considered and putt into his hands, as may prepare and qualify Him. Such as are Copies of Comissions, Instructions, Orders, Letters of other materiall Papers, from England relating to the Government. Which are to bee registred by him, that Hee may have a recourse to them, as occasion calls for them.

For his better Direction and Vindication it is necessarie that 2 or 3 particular Friends about Court and as many in the Cittie, bee desired to receive Him, and advise with Him, when any matter offers, which may require consideration and Councell. By whose consent and approbation, Hee may adventure upon some things in which singly Hee may too much distrust or perhaps Presume upon his own judgment by either of which Affairs may suffer.

It may bee fit to recomend Him to the Good Confidence (of) the Ministers heere, and such others as are concerned and may probably bee addressed to by Him.

For his Continuall Information everie shipp that comes homeward ought to bring Letters from the Governor or his Secretarie to him: In which all the Transactions of the Island are to bee conveyed, that Hee bee not a stranger even to the least Things, as well as to the Greatest, which are oftentimes better understood; and represented by knowing former circumstances.

He ought first to receive his Letters to which everie Master of the Shipp should bee obliged as far as conveniently may bee; it tending not a little to the Disadvantage of the Governour, that the King, or his Ministers or the Exchange, bee possessed or prejudiced by letters or Suggestions of others, before his own Letters, and such as are intrusted by Him, bee first heard.

And because the Temper of the Place, may bee the better understood. It may bee fitt Hee should knowe at least the names of such as are of the Councell, which of them are Complying; which opposing; and what Correspondencies they have on the Exchange. And who is speaker of the Assemblie, and who the most Popular and Troublesome upon the Island. Which Motions will bee Necessarie, if any Complaints shall bee made heere, against, or relating to the Government.

And nothing being more likely to occasion Complaints or Discourse than the Matter of Money, Hee should knowe how the farme of the 4 and $\frac{1}{2}$ p cent is managed; and by whom. How that Revenue is answered or Employed. And what Directions the Governour hath received thereupon. And by what means and allowances the Government is supported. . . .

ILLUSTRATIVE DOCUMENTS 259

2. Letter from Gentlemen Planters of Barbados in England to Deputy Governor, Council and Assembly of Barbados, London, 14 December 1670. [C.O. 31:2, Journals of Assembly, pp. 15–16.]

. . . The Parliament are laying a very heavy Imposition on Suga^{rs} and are lyke to put the Rates in favour of the Portugall Sugars, and Refine^{rs} of England, which wee are Labouring to withstand, and besides o^r Constant personall Attendance upon the Buisness, wch is very Burthensome unto us, wee are some of us alsoe at Great expense, and how Longe wee shall thinke it our Interest at ou^r pticular Charge and Labour to withstand a Generall Inconveniency wee Leave you to Judge, wherefore wee humbly advise you to Lodge some stock in England in the hands of such men as you dare trust, for defraying the charges of this nature, or that shall arise upon any other publique Concern of Barbados which money shall not be Issued out But by the Order under the hands of such men and such a number of those men as you shall Appoint whereof A, B, C, D or any two of them, shall be two, and in the Order to mention to what use the money Issued is to be put, wee doe also desire that you would allow a Sallary to a person of some quallity who shall constantly attend the sevarals Councells and from time to time give notice to us what is in Agetation Relateing to Barbados and with our Advice draw up and prepare such things as are necessary, keepe a Register of the Orders drawne upon your treasury for money, and from time to time Remitt Coppyes of them to you By which you will perceive how you^r monyes are Disposed of and whether to the Advantage of the publique or noe. this Agent wee will bee ready to Countenance and Assist with ou^r presence upon any occasion. And doe further Advise that he may be some one concerned in Barbados otherwise he may have distinct Interest from you And be mischievous unto you, and for his sallary to settle from yeare to yeare that he may have his whole Dependance upon the assembly and know itt is the People of Barbados that Imploy him, which will prevent the haveing such an officer Imposed upon you from hence Or by you^r Governo^r which shall come there who haveing generally distinct Interest from the People and putting him in, may make him promote his Interest and not the Islands. . . .

APPENDIX III

3. MINUTES OF MEETINGS OF THE COMMITTEE FOR THE CONCERN OF BARBADOS. [C.O. 31:2, Journals of Assembly, pp. 37–9, 104–5.]

January the 28th 1670.

The names of the Committee then appointed for the Buisness of Barbados.

His Excellency the Lord Willoughby
Sir Peter Colleton
Sir Paul Paynter
Coll. Henry Drax
Coll. Phillipp Bell
Coll. Thomas Middleton
Edward Pye Esq.
Thomas Wardall Esqr.
Mr Jacob Lucie
Mr Constant Sylvester
Mr John Bowden
Major John Gregory
Capt. Ferdinando Gorges

Any three to be of the Quorum

The abovesaid Committee haveing appointed to meet at the Cardinall Capp in Cornhill on Friday next being the third day of Feb^{r}y at three of the Clock in the afternoone, and after, Friday weekly at the same hower, to Consider, Act and doe all things they shall see Requisite and needfull for the Good of the Island of Barbados and to issue out any money that is in the hands of Mr. Jacob Lucie for the ends aforesaid and to employ such pson or psons as they shall see convenient for the service aforesaid.

A true Coppy p Edw. Thornburgh.

At a Meeting of the Committee for the Concern of Barbados, February ye 3^d 1670.

Present

Sir Peter Colleton
Coll. Henry Drax
Capt. Ferdinando Gorges

Coll. Thomas Middleton
Thomas Wardall, Esq.

It is ordered by the Committee that a Letter be Drawne to the Assembly of Barbados in answer to theirs Received the seaventeenth november last, and to Insist upon the heads now Resolved upon, and

ILLUSTRATIVE DOCUMENTS 261

anythinge else that shall be thought Convenient in prosecution thereof and to be presented at ye next meeting of this Committee on Thursday next.

Ordered that this Committee doe to morrow Consult wth his excellency the Lord Willoughby and Desire his assistance to take a Convenient time to wayte on the Lord Lauderdale in order to the procuring a free trade from Scotland to Barbados especially for men servants. That Sir Peter Colleton and Coll. Henry Drax are Desired by this Committee to entertaine a Parliament Solicitor to follow and negotiate the present Buisness about the Imposition voted by the Parliament to be Layd upon Sugars.

That wee have appointed Edward Thornburgh to be ou^r Agent to attend this Committee, and he is ordered to Buy a Booke, and make a Register of all things transacted by this Committee and follow our Directions.

That Mr. Jacob Lucie bee ordered to pay Edward Thornburgh Ten pounds for the Defraying the Charge of this Committee for which he is to bee accountable to this Committee.

> The Committee Adjourn till Thursday next being the nineth present at eight of the clock at the Cardinall Cap Taverne in Cornhill.

A true Coppy per Edw. Thornburgh.

. . . . .

At a Meeting of the Committee for the publique Concerne of Barbados. Feb^{r}y 28th 1670.

Present

His Excellency Will: Lord Willoughby
Sir Peter Colleton Barronett.   Tho. Wardall, Esqr.
Coll. Henry Drax   Edw. Pye Esq.
Capt. Ferdinando Gorges   Coll. John Searle.

Sir Peter Colleton, Coll. Henry Drax and Capt. Ferdinando Gorges are Desired to take care to be at Westminster Hall Daily till the new Imposition on Sugar be Determined and upon notice from them, all the Gentlemen Planters concerned in Barbados are Desired to give their Attendance there, And Edward Thornburgh upon Appointment from them is ordered to give them all notice and likewise to attend at Westminster himselfe.

Ordered that Mr. Jacob Lucie pay unto Edw: Thornburgh Ten pounds for Defraying the charge of this Committee for which he is to be accountable to this Board.

A true Coppy per Edw. Thornburgh.

. . . .

Att a Meeting Novemb^r the 22nd 1671.

Present

His Excellency Wm. Ld. Willoughby
Sir Peter Colleton, Barronet   John Bowden Esqr.
Sir Tobias Bridge, Knt   Col. John Searle
Col. Henry Drax   Fer Gorges esqr.
Col. Tho. Middleton   Mr. Jacob Lucie
Col. Phillip Bell   Major John Gregory
Edw. Pye Esqr.   Major Robt Legard.

Twas this day putt to the vote, first whether or noe itt would be any prejudice to Barbados that any Planter or member of this Committee should subscribe to the stock of the new Royall Company. Carryed on the negative (nemine Contra dicente).

The members of this Royall Company consisting of the Principall men, in the Government of this nation, It was secondly putt to the vote.

Whether, or noe it be for the Interest of the Island of Barbados, that as many of the Gentl. Concerned there as have money to spare and are willing to putt itt in should become members of that Company, whereby they may be in some measure, able to Influence, the Councells of that company for the Good of Barbados.

Carryed in the affirmative.

A true coppy p. Edw. Thornburgh.

4. LETTER FROM GENTLEMEN PLANTERS OF BARBADOS IN LONDON TO ASSEMBLY OF BARBADOS, 1 MAY 1671. [C.O. 31:2, Journals of Assembly, pp. 45–9.]

LONDON, *May day* 1671.

. . . As soon as the Parliament was mett they fell to consider how to Raise money for the Kinge, and at Length agreed, (among other things) to lay an Additional Duty upon fforraigne Commodities Amongst which sugar was mentioned as one, which wee noe sooner knew of But wee Applyed our selves to the Councell of Plantations shewing how Ruinous it would be to lay a ffarther Imposition upon that trade that was sinking of itts selfe and needed rather ease than new Loads And Desired theire mediation with the kinge and Parliament to keep off the tax, from the Sugars of the English Plantations And after that wee Applyed our selves to severall of the Leading members of the house of Commons, And then it was that wee began to perceive that the Refiners had been the Cheife Instruments of bringing sugars upon the stage, who haveing fformerly Laboured to gett the Planters Prohibitted from makeing any Improvement of theire sugars, by sun-Drying Claying etc : And ffinding they were not able to carry itt that way, Concluded that if they could gett the Parliament in ye minde to gett a tax on sugars they should by theire Interest in the House get the Rates soe proportioned as should in effect amount unto as much, In which they Laboured at ffirst Clandestinely and ere wee were aware, got one ffarthing p pound to bee Rated on Browne Sugars one penny upon the white sugar of the English Plantations, and two pence upon the white sugars of portugall with which Rates (though much in ffavour of the Refiners) wee were not much Dissattisfyed considering the vast Advantage wee had over Portugall. And that you could by Laws of yor owne Restraine the Dammage mighte bee Done by the Refine^{rs} But the Portugall merchants haveing Dispersed Papers amongst the members, setting forth how Advantagious a trade, theirs was to the nation, and what Damage it would Receive if theire sugar should be taxed higher than ours And haveing Alsoe a great party in the House, they gott theire sugar Reduced to the same Rate wth ours, And the Refiners ffinding theire party strong in the House, and secretly encouraged (as wee Conceive) by the merchants trading to Barbados, who held theire Clubbs wth them, began openly to pretend to have a third sorte of suga^{rs} taxed at halfe penny (vizt) All sundryed and browne Clayed sugars, which now pass at the Custome house, as Browne Sugars and were to doe the same in the Intended Imposition, In which both Promised themselves these Advantages, the Refiners that they should by underselling you, beat you out of any Improvement of yor muscovado sugars and become sole Buyers of the other, The merchants thought they should by that meanes finde the quicker vent, for theire sugar Received for Debts In order to wch ye Refiners Disperst the enclosed Papers amongst the members of the House of Commons and wee were then Advised by our ffriends to print the papers inclosed and Disperse it allsoe to all the members which wee did And the Refiners answered what Related to them as you may see by the Coppyes sent, to which wee Replyed And both wee, the Refiners and the merchants put in Petitions, to be heard at the Commons Barr which was Graunted, wee shewed how Ruinous this tax would bee to the Plantations, . . . the House of Commons finding us thus positively contradicted by men who had lived in Barbados and therefore not Believing what we had said Continued fixed in theire former, votes of one penny and one farthing and Letting Portugall sugars stand in equally with us, and soe past itt, We therefore Resolved not to sitt downe thus: and knowing the Lords to bee men unconcerned and of more discerning Judgmen then the generallity of the Commons made our Addresses to them . . . soe that All partyes were againe heard by a Committee of Lords Wee Prest as before the Lisbone merchants Joyned with us Against the proportion between white and Browne sugar But Divers Barbados merchants and the Refiners prest feircely for the middle sort which now they Desire mighte bee sett at three ffarthings But both Joyned with us In our Desires of haveing the Portugall sugars set higher though wee knew that was Impossible, ffor the Lords will not soe much as pretend to a power of encreasing any tax, wherefore all the Releefe wee could hope for, was the Lowering of Browne white sugars and the keeping out of the three farthings sort and letting the Portugalls stand . . . And the merchants possitive Contradiction of what wee said kept many of the Lords a great while in Doubt whether it were the Interest of the sugar Planters in Generall not to have a middle sorte and to ease white sugars or noe, And wee undoubtedly had had the same success here, that wee had wth the Commons had not the Lord Willoughby who was one of the Comittee, and Infinitely concerned for you, with great efficacy convinced the Lords of the mistake the merchants were Runing them upon, of a poor browne sugar Planter, with wch theire Lordshipps being sattisffyed Reduced white sugars to two ffarthings and a half and kept off the middle sorte, pretended to by the merchants, and soe Returned the Bill with the Amendment on white sugar to the Commons who presently flew into a heate and voted the Lords had noe righte to abate of any ayd Graunted to the Kinge and sent them that message about which haveing Divers Conferences and both Adhearing stiffley to their priviledges the Kinge thought fitt to Prorogue the Parliament till the sixteenth of Aprill, next by which meanes the Bill fell, and wee are eased of this tax for the present.

Thus wee have showne you with how great Difficulty wee kept off your Ruine and hope wee have Convinced you how necessary it is to have the merchants tradeing to Barbados concerned in your Improved sugars, by your passing some Lawe for their Receiveing of theire Debts now standing out In these sorts, and by a Lawe of your owne Compelling all Contracts for the ffuture, to be made in money which though at first it may prove a Little troublesome, yet, itt will avoyd the great objection, the Refiners and merchants soe feircely urged, that browne sugar was the mony of the Plantation, and what the merchant Received in exchange of the Provision and manufactures of England carry^{ed} to the Plantation by which meanes you will alsoe seperate the merchants Interest and the Refiners, which should they continue united may prove too powerfull for us should the Parliament at theire next sitting thinke a laying an Imposition, upon sugar.

. . . . . .

wee thinke it not amiss for you to send two or three hhds of very good double or trebble Refined sugars which wee may finde opportunity to bestow for yor Advantage.

Yo^r most humble & ffaithfull servants

	Fer Gorges	P. Colleton
	John Bawden	Henry Drax
	Paul Paynter	Thomas Wardall
	John Searle	Edw. Pye
		James Lucie

5. Instruction to Governor of Jamaica, 24 August 1702.
[Plantation Register, iii, p. 50.]

We do hereby Inform you after the Expiration of the Act now in force for raising money in Order to the better carrying on the Solicitation of the Publick Affairs in England, to consent to a new Law for the purpose, provided that such Levy do not Exceed three hundred pounds sterling yearly; but in case you shall not then think fit to agree to such a Law, Our Will and Pleasure is, that the Persons desiring the same be permitted to make voluntary Contribution for discharging the Expence of their Sollicitations; Provided such contributions do not Exceed three hundred pounds Sterling p annum. And we do likewise think fit that when any complaynt shall be intended against you Notice shall be immediately given you thereof, by the Complainant with the charge against you in writing, to the end you may make timely preparation for your defence.

6. INSTRUCTION TO GOVERNOR OF JAMAICA, 16 MARCH 1721/2. [Plantation Register, v, p. 247.]

And whereas upon the Expiration of an Act passed in Our Island of Jamaica in the year 1693 Entitled An Act for raising Money to solicit to England the Affairs of this their Majestys Island, the Assembly did pass a Bill for the same purpose wherein Our Council were entirely excluded, from any share in the Management thereof, We do hereby empower you to give your Consent to a New Law for raising Money to Solicit the Affairs of our said Island to England, Provided that such Levy do not Exceed three hundred pounds sterling yearly and that two of Our Council in Conjunction with five of ye Assembly or be named by their respective Bodys be thereby Authorized to exercise the Several Powers given them by the former Act passed in 1693.

7. SPEECH OF GOVERNOR WILLIAM SHIRLEY TO COUNCIL AND ASSEMBLY OF THE BAHAMA ISLANDS, 6 MAY 1760. [*Journals of the Lower House of Assembly of the Bahama Islands*, ii, pp. 38–40.]

A Message from His Excellency the Governor was delivered by yᵉ Secretary as follows.

GENTLEMEN OF THE COUNCIL AND LOWER HOUSE OF ASSEMBLY,

As I find you have no standing Agent in London to sollicit the affairs of these Islands upon any Emergencys at the Several Boards of State within the Departments of which the regulation of them lies, I think it incumbent upon me to recommend the appointment of one to you as a matter, which very nearly concerns the welfare of the Government.

All the English Governments in North America, whether Charter, Proprietory, or those Governed by the kings Commission, in the same manner with this have either Standing Agents at Home, as have likewise all his Majestys Colonys in the West Indies, the Bahama Islands alone are without any. The Universality of this Practice among all the other Colonies, which is founded upon their long Experience of the advantages resulting to them from it shews in the strongest manner the expediency of this Policy; the necessity indeed of which is evident from its own Nature without citing precedents.

It is well known what a multiplicity of national Business the several before mentioned Boards have constantly under their Consideration and of course must require a close attendance of some Person residing upon the spot, who are duly authorized by the Colonies to appear before them in their behalf to press on an hearing of those Points which they may have depending there Otherwise the effectual consideration of any Representations which may be made from the Colonies either by address of their respective Assemblys or their Governors letters upon their most material Interests must at least be greatly Postponed, besides this it frequently happens that two particular Colonies have disputes which must be decided at Home, or points are moved in Parliament upon the application of some Bodies of men for laying general Restrictions upon the Colonies or of particular Persons for obtaining Monopolies (as was lately done for leave to Monopolize the Manufacturing of Salt in America) all which require the constant attention of standing Agents to oppose them even before their constituents can have regular Notice of those measures.

The Bahama Islands Gentlemen have already some Interests, and will soon have others more valuable depending upon his Majesty's favour, the solliciting of which in the most effectual manner at the several Boards, thro' which the consideration of them must pass absolutely require your immediate appointment of an Agent, and I would observe to you, that it has been found by Experience that the Utility of an Agent very much depends among his other Qualifications to promote the interest of his Constituents, upon his having a favourable Access to the Boards before which he is to Sollicit them.

W. SHIRLEY.

8. ACTS OF APPOINTMENT. i. ANTIGUA. 22 DECEMBER 1698. [C.O. 8:1, No. 109, pp. 89–91.]

AN ACT for electing an Agent from time to time for this Island, appointing a Recompence for his trouble, and settling Methods for the better Management of that trust.

WHEREAS our Remoteness from the Court of England renders us under the Necessity of appointing some person, or other to negotiate the severall Laws made in this Island for Confirmation by Royal Assent, or otherwayes appearing on our behalf on many occasions,

APPENDIX III

Wee therefore the Governor, the Council, and Assembly of this Island, most humbly pray your Sacred Majesty, that it may be enacted.

And be it, and it is hereby enacted by the authority of the same, that the Commander in Chief, Governor, or President for the time being shall once every year (or oftner, if Mortality shall so occasion) choose or Nominate some fitt person by, and with the consent of the Council and Assembly of this Island, to be their Agent, not only to represent their affairs by solliciting at His Majesties Court the Confirmation of such Lawes as shall from time to time be remitted for that end, but all other Matters, and things as shall at all times be recommended by the severall persons authorised by this Act to that purpose.

And for the better direction, and Management of such who shall happen to be from time to time so chosen, or Nominated, It is hereby enacted and ordained by the authority aforesaid, That noe Agent for this Island whatsoever shall observe or take notice of any other Orders, or directions relating to His Majesties passing the severall Laws of this Island transmitted to him by any person, or persons whatsoever, but such onely as he shall receive from the Commander in Chief of this Island, Governor, or president for the time being, and the speaker of the Assembly thereof joyntly signed by them; Nor observe any other orders relating to any Remonstrance, or Complaint of any Grievance, except what shall come to him from under the hand of the Speaker for the time being, by the advice, and consent of the Assembly Nor observe, or take notice of any Minutes of the Council, and Assembly as copied out of the Assembly bookes, but such allone as shall be signed by the said Speaker of the Assembly, and attested by the Clerk (pro tempore) of the same. All which Orders, and directions being duely observed, and kept by such chosen agent, he shall have, and receive for his trouble and care (to be remitted him by the Treasurer for the time being, out of the publick of this Island) one hundred pounds sterling Money of England, besides his needfull charges, and expences reimbursed by said Treasurer, who is hereby declared to have full power, and authority to remitt the same.

And it is further enacted by the authority aforesaid that what person soever shall happen to be first chosen as Agent for this Island, the time of his Agency shall commence from the first day of January next ensuing to date of this Act, and continue for one whole year, and noe longer (except again chosen from the succeeding year, or years in manner aforesaid), And when at any time after a New Agent shall be chosen by virtue of this Act, it is declared to be the true intent, and meaning hereof That on such choice, or alteration notwithstanding the former Agents acting should end by the expiration of the limited time of one year as aforesaid, yet the said former agent is hereby fully authorised, and empowered to negotiate all affairs pursuant to the foregoing directions as fully, and amply as if the said time was not expired, untill orders to the contrary be given by the Commander in Chief, Governor, or President for the time being, with the advice and consent of the Council, and Assembly of this Island. On the Receipt of which Order all the power invested in such former Agent shall wholly cease; and entirely devolve upon the succeeding agent, who shall be chosen as aforesaid in his stead, and place.

Allwaies provided, and, it is the true intent, and Meaning hereof, that the said Agent, or Agents who shall at any time hereafter be so succeeded in their Stations, shall have, and receive out of the Treasury of this Island as aforesaid, a proportionable allowance for such surplusage of time above one year as abovesaid according to such yearly appointment as is before sett down in this Act, or otherwise agreed on with them by the authority of the same.

And be it further enacted by the authority aforesaid That if any person or persons whatsoever shall think themselves agrieved by any Remonstrances or Complaint made pursuant to this Act, and shall endeavour a Remedy at Law against the Speaker, or any Member of the Assembly for anything contained in such complaint, or Remonstrance, the said Speaker, or any Member of the Assembly so molested, shall plead the General Issue, and give in this Act in evidence, Which shall be received by the Justices, and Jury and be allowed by the Court, and Judgment shall be entered for the Defendant, which shall be a perpetuall Barr to any such plaintiff or plaintiffs; any Law, Custom or Usage to the Contrary notwithstanding.

Dated at St. Johns the twenty second day of December, sixteen hundred ninety eight, and in the tenth year of the Reigne of King William over England, Scotland, France, and Ireland, Defender of the Faith, etc.

ii. JAMAICA. 11 FEBRUARY 1731. [C.O. 139:13, No. 49.]

AN ACT for appointing an Agent or Agents in Great Britain to sollicite the Passing of Laws and other the publick Affairs of this

APPENDIX III

Island, And Impowering certain Members of the Council and Assembly, during the Intervals of Assembly from time to time, as Occasion shall be, to give Instructions for such his Management.

WHEREAS it is absolutely necessary that the Inhabitants of this Island should have One or more Persons fitly Qualifyed in Great Britain fully Impowered to Sollicite the Passing such Laws and to Transact such other Publick matters as shall be from time to time Committed to his or their care for the good of the said Island. Be it therefore enacted by His Majesty's Governor Council and Assembly And it is hereby enacted by the Authority of the same That Charles Delaffaye Esqr and the Honourable John Gregory Esquire be and are hereby nominated and Appointed Agents in Great Britain for this Island for the purpose aforesaid And that the Honble Richard Mill and Edward Charlton Esquires two of the Members of His Majesty's Council of this Island and John Stewart Esqr. Speaker of the present Assembly or the Speaker of the Assembly for the time being Dennis Kelly, Alger Pestell, Andrew Arcedeckne and George Ellis Esquires five of the Members of the present Assembly shall be and are hereby Impowered and Appointed to be Commissioners for Instructing and directing the said Agent in his Sollicitations pursuant to such Powers and Authoritys as the said Commissioners shall from time to time receive from the Council and Assembly when sitting Provided Nevertheless that the Commissioners before mentioned or the Major part of them, whereof One of the Council shall be one, may from time to time in the Interval of Assemblys or upon any emergent Occasions give to the said Agents in Great Britain such further Instructions as they shall think fitt for the Publick Service of this Island And in case of the death Absence or refusal of any of the Commissioners before mentioned That then if a Councillor, the Council or the Major part of them shall chuse out of their body or if an Assembly man such person or persons of the Assembly as the remaining or surviving Commissioners of the Assembly or the Major part of them shall think fitt to chuse in the room of him or them which shall remove dye or refuse And that the Person and Persons so chosen shall be Impowered to Act to all Intents and purposes as if he or they had been mentioned or appointed by name in this Act And in case it shall be thought fitt to alter the aid Agent or Agents or to continue them or either of them for longer time the said Commissioners or the Major part of them (whereof One of the Council shall be one) are hereby Impowered to remove them or either of them And in such case or in case of their or either of their deaths to Nominate and Appoint another Agent in Great Britain who shall and is hereby Authorized to Act as if herein named And be it further enacted by the Authority aforesaid That the Commissioners hereby Appointed shall Enter Copies of all and every their proceedings in pursuance of this Act in a fair Book to be bought and kept for that purpose Which proceedings or any of them shall and are hereby directed to be laid before the Governor Council and Assembly for the time being when sitting, as often as the same shall be required And the said Commissioners shall have no manner of ffee or Reward or any Allowance for their Trouble and Care in their Transactions pursuant to this Act (the Charges of a Clerk and Books Excepted) And be it further Enacted by the Authority aforesaid That the said Agents shall be paid at the rate of Three hundred pounds sterling money of Great Britain per Annum for such time as they shall continue Agents for their Care and trouble in and about the Affairs of this Island in Great Britain And that the same shall be remitted to them by William Crosse Esquire His Majesty's Receiver General from time to time when and as often as he shall be required so to do by the Commissioners herein before named or the Major part of them (Whereof One to be of the Council) together with such Charges as they shall find he or they may have expended in or about the Publick business of this Island And this Act to continue and be in force for Twelve Months from the Passing thereof and no longer.

11th *February* 1731.

iii. JAMAICA. 10 DECEMBER 1767 (Additional clauses only). [C.O. 139:23, No. 105.]

. . . And provided, further, that in Case a difference of opinion should at any time happen between the Two Bodies of Commissioners hereby appointed wherein each of them adhere unanimously to their different Opinions, then and in such case the Commissioners of each Body shall be and they are hereby Empowered to act seperately anything in this Act contained to the Contrary hereof in any wise notwithstanding.

. . . .

And be it further enacted by the Authority aforesaid That any two of the Commissioners hereby appointed shall and may during the Intervals of Assembly, Open all and every the packets and Letters, which from time to time shall or may come from the Agent for this Island directed to the Commissioners of Correspondency hereby appointed. And that as often as it shall, or may be Necessary during the Intervals of Assembly for the said Commissioners to meet for the drawing up and transmitting of Letters, in Answer to such Packetts or Letters so received from the Agent, or for any other of the purposes and Businesses herein before mentioned, any Two of the said Commissioners shall and may from time to time appoint a Certain Day for the meeting of all the Commissioners. . . .

. . . And be it further enacted by the Authority aforesaid that the Room, in which the present Assembly is now Convened in the Town of Sant Jago de la Vega, and no other shall be the place of meeting of the Commissioners or any Five of them for the Transacting of all the several Matters and Businesses which they, or any Five of them are hereby Required empowered, or Authorized to Transact, And be it further Enacted by the Authority aforesaid that the Commissioners hereby Appointed shall cause fair Copies of all their proceedings in pursuance of this Act together with the names of the Commissioners present at each meeting to be duly entered in a Book to be kept for that purpose which proceedings or any of them shall be, and they are hereby directed to be laid before His Honor the Lieutenant Governor or the Commander in chief of the Island, And the Council and Assembly of this Island for the time being when sitting as often as the same shall be Required.

iv. St. Christopher. 3 July 1773. [C.O. 240:12, No. 36.]

An Act for repealing a former Act Intituled " An Act for appointing Henry Wilmot Esquire . . . " and for appointing William Payne Georges Esquire Agent for the said Island, in the Room of the said Henry Wilmot, and for settling a proper Salary upon him during the time of his Agency.

Whereas by an Act of this Island of Saint Christopher " An Act for appointing Henry Wilmot Esquire Agent for the Island of Saint Christopher, in Great Britain, in the Room of John Sharpe Esquire, lately deceased, and for settling a Salary upon him during the Time of his Agency " It is Enacted that Henry Wilmot Esquire be, and he is thereby appointed to be Agent for the said Island in the Kingdom of Great Britain.

And whereas the said Henry Wilmot by his Neglect, and Inattention to the Affairs of the said Island, and omitting to keep up any kind of Correspondence, or Intelligence with the Public thereof, for a long time past, hath rendered it highly expedient to appoint some other Person in his Room, who will attend to the Duties of his Appointment, We therefore your Majestys most Dutiful, and Loyal Subjects the Governor in Chief of all your Majestys Leeward Charibbee Islands in America, the Council and Assembly of your Island of Saint Christopher taking the same into Consideration, have chosen William Payne Georges Esquire to be Agent for the said Island, And We do most humbly pray your most Excellent Majesty that the said Act appointing the said Henry Wilmot Esquire Agent for the Island may be repealed.

(Two paragraphs rescinding Act of 1757 and enacting the appointment of Georges at a Salary of £100.)

And whereas it hath been usual, and customary for the Agents hitherto appointed, to make extra Charges for their Personal Trouble, and attendance, in transacting the Publick Affairs of the said Island, in consequence whereof, many and divers extravagant Bills of Accounts have been transmitted against the Publick of the said Island, for remedy whereof, for the future, Be it, and it is hereby further enacted by the Authority aforesaid that for and in consideration of the above Premisses the further sum of One Hundred Pounds Sterling Money of Great Britain, over and above the said Sum of One hundred Pounds herein before granted, be paid to the said William Payne Georges or his Executors or Administrators, as the case shall happen for and during the time he shall so continue Agent as aforesaid, at the Times and in the Manner prescribed for Payment of the said other Sum of One Hundred Pounds, herein before granted, which sum of One Hundred Pounds shall be deemed, and taken by the said William Payne Georges, in lieu of all and every claim, or Demand whatsoever, which he may have, or make against the Publick of the said Island for his Personal Service, Trouble, and Attendance, in the Transaction of their Publick Affairs; except all such Demands as he may . . . Occasionally, or from Time to Time, advance, expend, or be out of Pocket, on account of the Publick of the said Island, and by their Direction. . . . Provided Always and it is hereby Enacted by the authority aforesaid that this Act shall not be in force untill His Majestys royal approbation and Confirmation thereof. . . .

v. CANADA. 7 MAY 1880. [*Parl. Papers*, 1880, xlix, p. 7 (C. 2594).]

AN ACT for the appointment of a Resident Representative Agent for Canada in the United Kingdom.

WHEREAS the growing and varied interests of the Dominion render it expedient that Canada should appoint a Representative Agent in the United Kingdom, to watch over those interests, who shall be duly accredited in Her Majesty's Imperial Government: therefore Her Majesty by and with the advice and consent of the Senate and House of Commons of Canada, enacts as follows :—

1. The Governor may, under the Great Seal of Canada from time to time appoint an officer to be called "The High Commissioner for Canada" who shall hold office during pleasure.

2. It shall be the duty of the High Commissioner:

   (1) To act as Representative and Resident Agent of the Dominion in the United Kingdom, and in that capacity to execute such powers and to perform such duties as may from time to time be conferred upon and assigned to him by the Governor in Council:

   (2) To take the charge, supervision and control of the immigration offices and agencies in the United Kingdom, under the Minister of Agriculture:

   (3) To carry out such instructions as he may from time to time receive from the Governor in Council respecting the commercial, financial and general interests of the Dominion in the United Kingdom and elsewhere.

3. The High Commissioner shall receive a salary of not more than $10,000 per annum, and the same shall be payable out of any unappropriated moneys forming part of the Consolidated Revenue Fund of Canada.

9. LETTER TO COLONEL JORY FROM THE GENERAL LEGISLATURE OF THE LEEWARD ISLANDS, 25 JUNE 1705. [C.O. 155:3, Minutes of General Assembly held in Nevis.]

S^r

The General Council and General Assembly of ye Leeward Charibbee Islands, now met together at Nevis, haveing Intire Confidence in ye great Diligence you will use in getting ye several Acts now past by ym to be Confirm'd by her Majesty: The Commander in Chief hath Thought fit to remit ym in yor Care, desireing They may wth all convenient speed, be laid before ye Lords Comissioners of Trade and ye plantations, after wch all possible Application be made for her Majesties Royal Assent. And if any of them should be Repealed, or Laid by for further Consideration, We intreat yt yo{u} would Inquire as far as yo{u} can into ye Reasons wch were ye Cause thereof, and comunicate ym to us. We likewise desire yo{u} would frequently correspond wth ye Treasurer of each Island, That no one Island may be in ye Dark or Ignorant of what becomes of these General Laws, wch we think so very beneficial to ye whole. We have order'd yo{u} Fifty Pound, sterling, for yor care and pains in this matter over and above any charge it shall put yo{u} to, wch we shall take Care to remit to yo{u} from ye Treasurer of each particular Island according to their several proportions. We are wth due respects

Sr

Yor most humble Servt

JOHN JOHNSON
THOMAS BELMAN

NEVIS, *June 25th* 1705.

10. LETTER FROM RICHARD MAITLAND TO PRESIDENT AND SPEAKER OF GRENADA. [C.O. 104:3, Journals of Assembly, 12 March 1768.]

LONDON 23 *Octob{r}* 1768.

GENTLEMEN,

In consequence of an Order from the Lords of Trade I attended their Board on the 16th Instant When several Petitions signed by some of the Inhabitants of Dominica, some Merchants here in London and Liverpool were read Complaining of their Want of a Legislature and the hardships their Trade Laboured under by being Obliged to apply to Grenada on many Occasions and praying a Seperate Government. I had received no Instructions from you on this Head Yet as your Agent, I thought it my Duty to appear against any plan to Dismember the Government, I carried with me Sir George Colebrooke and some other of the principal proprietors here, I made it Appear plain that all the Complaints could be remedied without Makeing it a separate Government upon which Sir George Colebrooke as well as the Other Proprietors present Declared their Oppinion unanimously against the separation Notwithstanding they had signed the petition for it. It seems this projectors of this scheme proposed to be at the additional expence themselves (I mean by raising the Money by a Tax) This made Sir George Declare so strongly against it. The Board was strongly pr(e)poss(ess)ed in favour of the Plan, but were Much staggerd at what was said against it, and I am now in Doubt whether they will report in favour of the separation as was given out to be certain.

You no Doubt know there is a board of Customs appointed for North America. The Commissioners are to reside at Boston; when the Instructions for the Board were Making out the Lords of the Treasury sent for Mr. Long and myself (who generally attend the Ministry on West India Business) to attend their Board and give Our Oppinion whether it would be Convenient or Not to have Our West India Collectors under the Direction of the North America Board. The intention of the Act was so and the Inclination of the Commissioners of the Customs here, wanting so, and the Inclination of the Commissioners of the Customs here, wanting to ease themselves of much trouble was so likewise. Mr. Long and myself painted the inconveniency in so Strong a light; that I find an Order from the Treasury to the Commissioners were, to Manage all Matters relating to us as Usual. The Planters and Merchants here Approved of Our Conduct in this Matter, and I hope my behaviour in this as well as the Dominica Affair may Meet with your Approbation.

I have the Honor to be with Great regard
                Gentlemen, Your most Obedient
                and faithfull humble Servant,
                        RICHARD MAITLAND.

11. LETTER TO GEORGE CHALMERS FROM THE HONBLE ROBERT STIRLING MEMBER OF THE COMMITTEE OF CORRESPONDENCE OF THE BAHAMAS ISLANDS. FEBRUARY 1794. [B.M. Add. MS. 22900, f. 216.]

NEW PROVIDENCE. *Feb'y* 18th 1794.

SIR,

As there are not a sufficient Number of the Gentlemen who form the Committee of Correspondence, now on the Island, there cannot be an official Answer to the last letter you favored us with, transmitted by this Opportunity: I therefore as an Individual of that body, think it my duty to acquaint you, that your Letter, inclosing a Copy of your Memmorial relative to the Turks-Island business, came safe to our hands: and was received with unanimous approbation of the Board, and the warmest expressions of thanks for the indefatigable attention you have exercised on behalf of the Colony. Indeed, Sir, the Measures you have adopted, and vigilence with which you have seized every opportunity where the interest of this Colony has been concerned, leaves us nothing but gratitude to offer: As any instructions we should presume to give must fall short of the mode, and end which your prudence would adopt, and your attentive perseverance would procure. As soon as a sufficient number of the Committee to transact business can be convened, We shall fully answer yours: and if in the mean time any thing material shall occur, we shall acquaint you with it, but leave the manner of transacting it to your sole Management, as we are perfectly convinced of your Abilities and good wishes for the wellfare of your Constituents.

Permit me, Sir, to make you a tender of my best services in this part of the World, and to assure you I shall be happy in receiving your Commands.

I have the honour to be, with great respect, Sir
Your most Obedient and very humble Servant,
Rob$^{t.}$ Sterling.

George Chalmers Esqre.
Colonial Agent for the Bahama Islds.

12. Accounts of John Yeamans with the Island of Montserrat 1738–1739. [C.O. 177:3, Journals of Assembly, 5 June 1740.]

John Yeamans Esq, Acctt against the Publick of Montserrat.
D^r

1738.	Paid the Council Office Bill on the Petition for Stores as follows. Viz^t			
	Order of Reference to the Committee 3.2.6.			
	Committees Reference to the Board of Trade, 2.2.6.	7	7	6
	Order of the Committee. 2.2.6.			
Feb^{ry} 8.	Coach hire to Board of Trade . .	0	1	0
9.	Chair hire to the Widows Coffee house and home 3/ on Spanish Depredations I charge ¾ to Antigua and to Montserrat ¼	0	0	9

			£	s	d
	10.	Coach hire twice into the City to meet the Comittee on Spanish Depredations 8/ ¼ is	0	2	0
	11.	Ditto into the City 2/ ¼ is	0	0	6
Febry	22.	Coach hire to the D: of Bedford 1/ ¼ is	0	0	3
	23.	Coach hire on Ditto 2/6 ¼ is	0	0	7½
	28.	Ditto on Ditto 3/ ¼ is	0	0	9
1739.					
April	20.	Votes sent	0	1	0
May	20.	Coach hire to D: of Newcastle 2/6 ¼ is	0	0	7½
		To the share of the last Application to Parliament Alloted to Montserrat the whole expence being £636.19.4	20	3	0½
		(Charge of Coppying Vizt	1	0	5¾)
Octob	30.	Letters	0	2	2
	2.	Chair hire from Cockpitt ¼ is	0	0	3
	6.	Chair hire to the Cockpitt 1/6 ¼ is	0	0	4½
	7.	Coach hire into the City 3/ ¼ is	0	0	9
	17.	Coach hire 1/ ¼ is	0	0	3
	21.	Ditto to King Street about Stores	0	1	6
Novembr	27.	Coach hire about Ditto	0	0	3
	30.	Paid Report of the Board of Trade about Stores	1	1	0
		Coach hire to the Tower to the Office of Ordnance	0	4	0
	31.	Ditto	0	4	0
Novemr	31.	Paid for pamfletts	0	4	0
		Paid for Council Office Fees for Comittees Reference to the Board of Ordnance with Copy of the Report of the Board of Trade Petition and list of Stores	3	2	6
		For an Omission in the Fee charged on two former References in this Affair	1	0	0
		Coach hire to the Tower	0	4	0
Decemr	1.	To Two Years Salary due this day	160	0	0
		December 1st 1739	£195	3	5¾

ILLUSTRATIVE DOCUMENTS

Charges Issued since I sent a Coppy of the Account above. The Expence of the last years generall Sollicitation amounted in the whole to £644.17.—being somewhat more than what I have charged the following Division of the same being Agreed to be as the most reasonable by all the Agents Viz^t

To Jamaica ⅓	£214 19 0
To Barbados ⅓	£214 19 0
To the Leeward Islands ⅓ . .	£214 19 0

The Division of the Leeward Islands was as follows vizt

To Antigua ¾ of ⅛ being £107 9 6 . . .	80	12	0½
To St. Kitts ¾ of ⅛ ,, ,, ,, . . .	80	12	0½
To Montserrat ¼ of ⅛ ,, ,, ,, ,, . . .	26	17	5½
To Nevis ¼ of ⅛ ,, ,, ,, ,, . . .	26	17	5½
	£214	19	0

13. LETTER FROM JAMES KNIGHT, LONDON, 18 MARCH 1725. [B.M. Add. MS. 22677, ff. 1–2.]

LONDON, *March the* 18*th* 1725.

SIR,

According to my promise in the last letter, I had the honour to write you, I shall now acquaint you with the method, that the Virginians take, in managing their affairs which are under the best regulations of any of the Colonies: tho' indeed I am of Opinion, such a plan is not very practicable with us: as I despair of ever seing that harmony, and good Agreement among the Gentlemen of our Island, as there is between them.

They have two Agents on Sallary, who constantly meet the planters and merchants twice a month, and consult with them what is proper to be done for the service of the country: they very justly consider their Interests the same and dependant on each other, therefore go hand in hand, without any clashing or Jealousie. A Treasurer is appointed to pay the Charges, and receive the Contribution of 6^d per hogshead on every hogshead imported. tho' such a plan may not be alltogether feasible amongst us, yet something of the kind, may be thought of, by a person of your Judgement and Penetration : which may probably remove all Suspicions and Animosities, when the Gentlemen of our Island in England and the Merchants meet together : especially if the Assembly have a greater regard to the trading Interest, which is most capable of serving the Island here. I need not point out the methods of doing this, you are Sensible of their Complaints particularly in imposing a duty, on negroes imported as well as exported : were it laid on Exportation only, it would not be murmured at : but both is thought unreasonable and inconsistent with the practice of other countrys.

It is worth considering that both Interests are in danger of being destroyed, by the South Sea Company : who are not content with what they have allready monopolised, but are now Aiming at the African Charter, and an exclusive Trade, should they bring this scheme to bear, I need not tell you how much, the value of your Estates will be lessened And therefore it becomes more and more necessary to bethink. I am informed that Mr. Richard Harris has been named and voted for in the Assembly as to be their Agent : I do assure you without any regard to my personal Attachments, to that Gentleman, I am of opinion he will be a proper person And that as he has the Interest of Trade and the Island, very much at heart, and in all respects a publick spirited man, he may be prevailed on, to be one on such conditions as I have mentioned.

.   .   .   .   .   .

So that you may perceive in what light we are set nor can I refrain telling you, that the Addresses and minutes of the Assembly, are not yet come home the reason a Certain person gives for not sending them, his Secretary was dead, and he could not get them Copyed in time.

14. LETTER FROM PLANTERS' CLUB TO PRESIDENT AND COUNCIL OF MONTSERRAT. [C.O. 177:5, Minutes of Council, 16 Oct. 1745.]

MR PRESIDENT AND GENT. OF THE COUNCIL.

The Sugar Planters that Reside in England being Desirous to promote the Interest of the Sugar Colony's in every Branch of it, as far as Lay in their Power : and to put a stop to many abuses that had Crept into the Sugar Trade, thought that the first step to be taken for promoting these Ends, wou'd be, for the Gentlemen belonging to the several Islands, to unite into one Body : and Accordingly they did some years ago, form themselves into a Society in London, which takes the Name of the Planters Club.

It must be obvious to every body, that a Society of this kind, can't go any great Lengths, in effecting the purposes for which it was Erected, without some Fund to support it : as Law suits upon some Occasions may be Necessary, and a Great many other expences will Unavoidably Attend such an Undertaking. The Club indeed thought for a long time, that they shou'd be Aided in the Carrying on of their Intentions, by the Contribution of One penny p hogshead whenever it was called for, in a Case wherein the whole Planting Interest was Concerned, but there are many other Instances besides that, mentioned in the printed Reasons, where the Planting and Mercantile Interest Clash ; and therefore We are Convinced, that it is Absolutely necessary, for the good of the Sugar Colonies, that the Old Fund of One Penny p hogshead shou'd be Abolish'd and a new one (by way of Voluntary Subscription to be under the Management of the Planters) substituted in its Room, such a Subscription therefore We have begun here. . . .

We thought it wou'd be much better to put this Subscription into the Shape of a meer Voluntary Contribution, than to Desire Gentlemen to pay any Certain sum, for every hhd. of Sugar they shou'd send to London, as many perhaps wou'd have a Dislike to let all the world know what Crops they make. And tho' the Planters in England have made it a rule to themselves, not to subscribe less, than Two pence p Hogshead, Yet as every Gentleman, subscribes a sum in Gross, without mentioning any Number of hogsheads, and that sum is left entirely to himself ; this we think will remove that Objection.

. . . .

We must Desire that every Gentleman, that does subscribe will sign an Order to his Correspondent here in London to pay that sum, and that he will Please to Forward that Order to William Perrin and John Spooner Esq^{rs}. at the Jamaica Coffee house in London, or to deliver it to yourself, to be forwarded by you, if you wou'd Please to take that trouble upon you : We have got a Number of those Orders printed (to save Trouble) and have likewise sent them to you in the same Box with the other papers.

We are, Gentlemen,
Your hble Serv^{ts}

James Gordon	Gage
James Egan	Rumney
Francis March	Montfort
Will Beckford	N. Codrington
Francis Beckford	Ch^s Long
John Yeamans	Jere French
A. Walter	Henry Barham
Sam^L Martin	John Pennant
Ed^D Charlton	Henry Evans
Ja^s Knight	John Sutton
Edw^D Garthwaite	Colin Campbell
Theol Taffe	Rich^D Salter
Sam^L Greathead	W^M Perrin
D. Mathew	W^M Holder

To The Honble. the President and Members of
His Majesty's Island of Montserrat.

15. LETTERS FROM HENRY LASCELLES TO CORRESPONDENTS IN BARBADOS. [Letter-book of Messrs. Lascelles and Maxwell, Sept. 1743 – Jan. 1745/6.]

Letter dated 17th January 1743/4 to James Bruce,
(Relating to Sugar imposition of 1744.)

The Agents and some others were deputed and did wait on Mr. Pelham with an abstract of the Case . . . Besides sending the case to every Member of both Houses, we go about to visit the Members at their several places of abode, and divide ourselves (Agents, Planters and Merchants) into little Committees to attend them in the diff^t Quarters of this great Town. Our G.M. with 3 more, had the City Members in their beat this morning, and really some of them are odd people, but they were all of our side, but not to be much regarded, as they are of the Minority that opose the Court. We found a d——lish staunch Man for us, whom Mr Knight used to call by the name of forty-one

Heathcott, but that Man would have been of our side, without any regard to the merit of our Cause, merely to gratify his own natural propensity to opposition. So far we had wrote last night, to-day our G.M. with the same 3 Deputies, had the Quarters of 30 and odd Members to beat up . . . The Courtiers were extremely civil, and said they had read our Pamphlett, which they thought well wrote, but as they were not versed in the knowledge of Trade, they must suspend their opinion till our arguments come to be debated in Parliament, and they Assured us they had great tenderness for Trade and especially for that of the Sugar Colonies. But Doddington (tho' it's believed he wants as much to be a Courtier again as any one, and was they say refused, absolutely by the King to be taken in upon the last change, because he had treated Lord of Orford with the utmost ingratitude, in spurring at him, when he discovered he would fall, and therefore offered him the first kick o' the Orse to throw him down) expressed great zeal for us, but said that all other trade was already ruined by exorbitant Taxes, and ours was the last whereon any money could be raised and the ministry must raise money though it ruined us. He promised to speak for us in the House, and words he said cost nothing and they really were not worth more than they cost, on this occasion. Some of the courtiers told some of our Deputies, of another Committee, that our Pamphlet, was only declamatory and by no means argumentative . . .

Letter dated January 17th 1743/4 to Genl. Applewhaite, pp. 82-3.

The agents waited again upon Mr. Pelham with an abstract of the Case. He said, he would carry it with him into the Country, where he was going during the Holy Days, and read it: but whatever his own sentiments might be, the rest of the ministry were of opinion that an additional Duty upon Sugar would be born by the Consumers, and it was resolved therefore to bring a Bill for that purpose into the house, the Case was then published, and we got a Dozen from the Printers for our friends in B'dos. . . . The printed Case has been sent to the respective house of every Member of Parliament in Town. The Agents, Planters and Merchants, have also agreed and divided themselves into several small parties to attend upon the several Members, and many of them have already been addressed upon the subject and everyone of them will be sollicited personally before the Bill comes into the House. All people that have any Interest with such as have Influence with

Members are also Courted, and People in general seem to think as we do, in opposition to the Bill. Copies of the case have also been dispersed to the several Sea Ports of the Kingdom, besides publishing it in the Evening Post and nothing shall be wanted to make the Clauses popular, and if possible to get this d——d Bill as much abhored as the Excise Scheme. We have the greatest fears, nevertheless, that the Ministerial party will carry their Bill, yet some people have hopes of the contrary, because many of that side will divide and be for us, and they say we are sure of every Man in the opposition to the Ministry, we shall soon know the event as the Bill will be speedily brought in. There are great Divisions among the present ministry. Lord Carterett is said to be in high favour and wants to carry all before him, and that he has treated the Duke of Newcastle as insolently as if he had been a footman. Mr Pelham is a Man of Spirit, and they say will not submit to the favourite, and that there is now a tryal of skill which of them shall be the primier. Would to God they would divide also upon the Bill, but that is too good a thing to expect.

16. MINUTES OF MEETING OF WEST INDIA AND NORTH AMERICAN MERCHANTS, 10 MARCH 1766. [B.M. Add. MS. 8133 C, ff. 91–2.]

At a Meeting of the Committee of the West Indian and North American Merchants at the Kings Arms Tavern 10 March 1766.

AGREED unanimously that such Points as are adjusted at this meeting shall have the general concurrence and Assistance of the whole Trade on both sides to carry them into Execution.

AGREED that the Duty on the foreign Molasses Imported into North America be reduced to one penny sterling per gallon and that every possible method be adopted to enforce the full and just collection of that Duty.

AGREED that the Importation of foreign Rum to North America continue to be prohibited.

AGREED that foreign Sugars, Coffee and Cocoa be allowed to be imported as Articles of Commerce into those places only of North America w(h)ere regular Custom houses are Established, these to be lodged in Warehouses under the care of the Kings Officers with liberty to export them to any part of Europe under such regulations as Administration may judge proper, if landed in Great Britain to be deposited free of Duty in the King's Warehouses till exported.

ILLUSTRATIVE DOCUMENTS 285

AGREED that all foreign Cotton and Indigo be allowed to be imported into North America and the British Islands merely as Article of Commerce free of Duty and to be exported from thence to Great Britain only under the Regulation of Enumerated Articles.

AGREED that the consumption of foreign Sugars be permitted in North America on payment of a Duty of 5 shillings per hundredweight.

AGREED that all sugars imported into Great Britain from North America be deemed foreign and Warehoused.

The Duty of 7 shillings per hundred on English Coffee and ½ per pound on Pimento to be taken off.

Duty on Wines to be altered.

17. MINUTES OF MEETINGS OF SOCIETY OF WEST INDIA MERCHANTS AND OF WEST INDIA PLANTERS AND MERCHANTS. [Merchants' Minutes, i, pp. 117–18 ; ii, Meeting of 29 May 1781 ; Standing Committee's Minutes, i, pp. 21, 25, 51–2.]

May 6th, 1777.

. . . . .

It having been observed that several Gentlemen concerned in the West India Business have neglected to pay the Charges on Trade which is the sole Fund for supporting the expences of the Society, the Secretary is ordered to apply to all Gentlemen and in the name of the Society to request the regular Payment of Trade as essentially necessary to the Interest of the Islands at large, the present Income being insufficient to support the present unavoidable extraordinary expences.

May 29, 1781.

. . . . .

Resolved,

That Mr. Fuller be desired to print his Petition to Parliament presented the 28th May 1781.

The two following Petitions were presented on Monday the 28th of May.

To the Hon. the Commons of Great Britain in Parliament assembled.

The Petition of the Planters and Merchants interested in, and trading to the British Sugar Colonies, whose names are hereunto subscribed for themselves and others,

APPENDIX III

Humbly sheweth,

That your Petitioners are greatly alarmed, by observing in the Votes of this Hon. House, that the Sugar Refiners of London have applied to Parliament for leave to bring in a bill to reduce the duties on foreign prize sugars, for the consumption of Great Britain, to an equality with the duties on British plantation sugar.

That the West India Islands have been settled and cultivated upon the faith of the whole system of the commercial laws of Great Britain whereby the exclusive privilege of supplying the British consumption has hitherto been secured to them without interruption, and if that faith were forfeited by the introduction of foreign sugar, so as to deprive the planters of that increase of price which forms their natural relief under the pressure of those enormous duties, expences and losses, wh. have of late years fallen upon them, the most fatal consequences must ensue to the sugar colonies, and to the navigation commerce, revenue, and manufactures of Great Britain thereon dependent.

That unless your Petitioners could have relied on such exclusive right, they would not have risqued such immense sums as are invested for the increase of the Colonies : and that if the enjoyment thereof shd be rendered precarious, by encouraging even an idea that so great a system of comercial law may be broke in upon, for slight and temporary causes, even if such cd. be proved to exist, the consequences must be highly injurious to the credit of the sugar colonies, must tend directly to prevent their further extention, and thereby weaken the source from which alone the very manufactory in question can be permanently fed, and wh. can never flourish but in proportion to the encouragement given to the cultivation of our own Colonies.

(The Petition is followed by one to similar effect from Stephen Fuller, as Agent for Jamaica.)

LONDON TAVERN, *24th February* 1786.

Standing Committee of West India Planters and Merchants.

. . . . .

Mr. Saml Long reported to the Meeting that he had received a letter from Mr Steele of the Treasury, which was read, as follows,

TREASURY CHAMBERS, *Feby* 23 (1786).
DEAR SIR,
I am directed by Mr Pitt to acquaint you in answer to your letter to me of yesterday's date, that in consequence of the Resolution which the West India Merchants and Planters came to in June last Orders were sent to the several Governors of the West India Islands early in the Month of August, that they should take the most effectual means in their power, by a co-operation with the Planters etc. to prevent and destroy, if possible, the illicit Trade which has been carried on to so considerable an extent in their several Governments. If you wish for any farther Confirmation upon the subject from Mr. Pitt himself for the purpose of laying his Answer formally before the Committee be so good as to let me know it in the course of the evening.

I am, etc.
(Signed) THOS STEELE.

At a Gen'l Mtg of the W.I Planters and Merchants held at the Marine Society's Office 14th of Feb. 1787.

. . . .

Mr Pitt's Answer of the 13th Inst. . . . was . . . read as follows :
DOWNING STREET, *February* 13*th* 1787.
SIR,
Having been out of Town I did not receive till Yesterday the favor of your Letter, enclosing the Resolutions, of the Gen'l Mtg of West India Planters and Merchants. Tho' I should be very desirous of shewing all the Attention in my Power to the Sentiments and Wishes of the Meeting I cannot see sufficient Ground for thinking that a Reduction of more than 3^d. in the Duty on Rum wd be necessary, in case the Duty on Brandy should be fixed at 7/–. It will be my duty to propose a Resolution in the Cttee on the Fr. Treaty, that the Duty on Brandy *should not be higher* than that sum : At the same time, it is my Intention to propose a separate consideration of the Duties on Imported Spirits in an early Period of the Session, and some farther Reduction of the Duties, both on Brandy and Rum, with a view to the prevention of smuggling : but I do not conceive the Reduction ought to take place in such a Proportion as the Mtg appear to have had in view to their second Resolution. I have entered into these Particulars from wishing to apprize you as fully as I can of the present state of this Business, and of my Sentiments upon it.

Previously to making any more specific Proposal in Parliament on the subject, I shall be happy in an Opportunity of receiving any farther communication which the Meeting may think proper.

I have the Honor to be
Sir
Your most obedient
and most humble Servant,
(Signed)   W. Pitt.

18. Minutes of Bristol West India Club. [Minute-books of Bristol West India Club, Merchants' Hall, Bristol.]

Bush Tavern (Bristol) 28th Jany 1782

At a meeting of several gentlemen interested in the West India Trade, it being unanimously the opinion that a New West India Society should be formed, upon the General Principles and for similar purposes, for which the former Society was established :—with this or some such similar restriction, viz—that no stranger whatever shall at any time be invited as a Guest, unless it be by a Card from the Secretary, and with the particular aprobation of the President.

Resolved—That Dinner be ordered at this House for Twelve Persons on Tuesday next 5 February, and that cards be sent to all the Gentlemen who have been at any time members of the late Club,—requesting either their attendance or a note signifying their intention of becoming, and declining to be Members of this New Society, and that at that Meeting such further regulations be considered of, as may then be thought requisite.

That a copy of this resolution be sent with each card.

That Mr. Richd Bright be appointed Secretary for the Year ensueing.

We whose Names are hereunto subscribed agree to become Members of the New West India Society.

Wm. Miles.   (15 other names.)

Merchants Hall, 3rd June, 1789.

The West India Merchants came to an Agreem^t for raising a fund as copied after the Entries of the Day.

A Copy of this Agreem^t is to be sent to Mr. Allan accompanied with a Letter now settled—see same in the Hall Letter Book.

BRISTOL, *June 3rd* 1789.

We the Subscribers being Merch[ts] trading to the West Indies do agree that in order to provide a Fund for the expences which will attend the opposition to the Abolition of the Slave Trade. We will be answerable for sixpence p Hogshead and Puncheon and so in proportion for all other Articles on our Imports with this port from the Sugar Colonies from the 24 April 1789 to the 24 April 1790 to be paid to the Treasurer of the West India Society here for the time being immediately on Importation and to be applied for the beforementioned purpose under the direction of the Majority of the Subscribers or of a Committee by them to be apptd.

APPENDIX IV
NOTE ON AUTHORITIES
I. CONTEMPORARY MATERIALS
(A) DOCUMENTS

Throughout the period of their history the West Indian colonial agents had no official locality for their work. They carried on their duties at their own private residences, passing to and fro to City coffee-houses and taverns, where they met planters and merchants concerned in the West Indies, or to Government Departments scattered over London from the Tower to Whitehall. There were therefore no repositories of records formed in the course of the agents' work. The agents were, it is true, required to supply to the island for which they acted details of their expenditure in the transaction of the islands' affairs and reports of their activities, but if any copy of these was retained by them it was preserved among their private papers. As one agent gave way to another, the papers were lost to the agency. Thus in 1743, when the agent for Montserrat was requested to revive an application made twenty years before, he was given directions by council and assembly as to the means by which he might be able to trace the agent formerly employed in order to gather information from him, and secure also access to the private papers of a West Indian merchant who had assisted the agent in the work. There are, therefore, no series of documents which may be regarded as the formal records of the agency. Their place may, however, be held to be taken by four main classes of papers closely resembling records in their character: they may be included under the following heads:

1. The Private Papers of Agents.
2. The Archives of the Islands.
3. The Archives of the Home Government.

NOTE ON AUTHORITIES

4. The Records of West India Planters and Merchants in England.

1. Private Papers of Agents

Of private papers of agents few have been found: moreover, they refer to various islands and various periods, and form therefore a quite insufficient source for the history of the office. They are valuable, however, in giving details, unavailable elsewhere, especially of the manner in which the agent pursued his aims. The following list indicates their extent:

B.M. Add. MS. 11411 B.M. Egerton MS. 2395	Letter Book 1655–1660, and collection of papers belonging to Thomas Povey. These volumes cover the period of Povey's connection with the early history of the agency.
Jeaffreson MSS. (in private possession).	Letter Book of Christopher Jeaffreson, agent for St. Christopher, 1682–1686.
B.M. Add. MS. 22676	Letters of James Knight, unofficial agent for Jamaica in 1728.
B.M. Add. MSS. 22900, 22901, 22902.	Letter Books of George Chalmers, agent for Bahama Islands, 1794–1826.
P.R.O., C.O. 261:9	Letter Book of Sir William Young, agent for St. Vincent, 1794–1802.
Stapleton MSS. (deposited in the John Rylands Library, Manchester).	Accounts of Sir William Stapleton with his personal agents, William Freeman and Patrick Trant, 1672–1684.

2. The Archives of the Islands

The second class of evidence presents no lack of material. The agent was appointed by the island legislature, to it he was responsible for the carrying out of the functions with which he was entrusted. His correspondence was conducted partly with the governor, but mainly with the council and assembly; his salary and charges were paid by the island treasurer. One of the chief sources of the agents' history, it would naturally follow, would be the archives of the island which he represented. It is unfortunate that West Indian archives have been at present very little used by historical students. For the earlier periods they are not complete, but a study of them would no doubt reveal many details of West Indian administration at present unknown. It has not, however, been found possible to make use of them for the present work.[1]

The incompleteness of the islands' records and their inaccessibility to the English student are in part compensated for by the existence in England of duplicates of all colonial sessional papers and acts of colonial legislatures. The duty of transmitting acts for confirmation by King in Council was made clear in instructions to governors from the year 1672,[2] and within a few years of that date directions, repeated from time to time, were sent to councils and assemblies to send home duplicates of their proceedings. There are therefore in English official custody series of both acts and sessional papers which, if their occasional omissions bear witness to the defalcation of governors or to losses in transit, provide on the whole a fairly complete record of the activities of the island legislatures. And the lack even of the volumes of correspondence receives partial compensation from the fact that interspersed in journals of assembly and minutes of council there are, intermittently it is true, but with considerable frequency, copies of letters sent to the agent, and of letters and enclosures received from him.

The colonial acts and sessional papers are preserved mainly in the Public Record Office; they are classified there under the colony to which they belong.[3] Each series comprises large number of

---

[1] A brief description of them is given in *Second Report of the Royal Commission on Public Records*, vol. ii, pt. ii, 1910, Cd. 7545, pp. 115–120. A report upon them has been prepared for the Carnegie Institute, Washington, but it has not yet been published.

[2] The endorsements of the acts show that this instruction was obeyed sometimes by the enclosure of the acts in the Governor's despatches and sometimes by their transmission through the agent.

[3] Their locality can be traced by means of Lists and Indexes No. 36, *List of Colonial Office Records preserved in the Public Record Office*, London, 1911, and, as far as the sessional papers are concerned, they are calendared up to the year 1708 in *Calendar of State Papers, Colonial, America and West Indies*. These classes of documents for the West Indies and other colonies are at present deposited in the Cambridge Prison. A note as to them is to be found in the *Cambridge Historical Journal*, vol. i, October 1923.

volumes, the papers in which are arranged in chronological order. In addition to these series there are dispersed amongst other classes of Colonial Office records various acts or groups of acts. The only one amongst these of value in the history of the agency is an Entrybook of the Appointment of Agents for the Colonies dated 1750–1774.[1] This is a late eighteenth or early nineteenth century compilation, containing verbatim copies of acts and of other instruments of appointment.

Copies of early acts, entered upon their confirmation by King and Council, also exist in the first two volumes of the Plantation Register in the Privy Council Office, relating to the years 1677–1702. Upon occasion these volumes supply omissions from the Colonial Office series of acts, the most notable instance in connection with the agent being the Jamaica Act of Appointment of 1693.[2]

No complete lists of the titles of colonial acts exist, but considerable value attaches to the several editions of the acts of the various islands published at varying dates in the seventeenth, eighteenth, and nineteenth centuries. In all cases these collections contain the full entry only of those acts that were in force at the date of compilation; others being cited by their title alone. In some cases the date of expiry or repeal is inserted. One such collection, the *Laws of Barbados, collected by W. Rawlin* . . . (London, 1699), is the only source available for the Barbados Agency Act of 1695.

The series of sessional papers are in two main divisions, Journals of Assembly and Minutes of Council, but in most of the islands the work of the Council in its legislative capacity during sessions of the assembly are recorded separately as Minutes of Council-in-Assembly. The series of sessional papers is not complete for any island, and is very defective in the seventeenth century. As in the case of colonial acts, gaps in the series can be in part supplied from legislative records bound together with governors' dispatches and other documents in the various series of original correspondence.

For the Leeward Islands, the sessional papers afford considerable difficulties. The early minutes and journals of the Leeward Islands have been interspersed in order of date amongst the papers of the miscellaneous series C.O. 1 created by Mr. W. N. Saintsbury from a variety of sources, upon his compilation of the *Calendar of State*

---

[1] C.O. 324:60.   [2] Plantation Register, ii, pp. 249–53.

APPENDIX IV

Papers, Colonial, Vol. I. Further, the series entitled "Leeward Islands" has little or no relation to the existence of a General Legislature of all the Islands: its name signifies merely that it contains miscellaneous collections of the proceedings of the various islands bound together in common volumes. The records of the general legislature are not distinguished in any formal way from those of the separate islands, for they appear amongst the papers of the island at which the meeting was held,[1] and in some cases even the endorsement provides no guide.[2]

For two of the colonies [3] series of journals of assembly have been printed, the Bahama group and Jamaica. The Jamaica Journals, comprising fourteen large folio volumes and one additional volume of index, were compiled in the years 1811-29, by order of the House of Assembly. They were formed, as is stated in the Preface to vol. i, by the collation with manuscripts extant in the colony of those in English official custody, and where neither of these sources provided adequate material, extract was made from a variety of contemporary narratives. It is unfortunate that the source of such subsidiary matter is not always given. The Journals of the Bahama Islands are a century later in date. Their production is due to the researches of Mr. Harcourt Malcolm, Speaker of the Bahamas House of Assembly. Mr. Malcolm has used copies of the journals, both in the islands and at home, and like the compilers of the Jamaica Journals, he has found deficiencies; these, however, have not been bridged by narratives, but notes of available sources are inserted.

---

[1] Thus the minutes of the General Legislature of 1698 are amongst the proceedings of Montserrat (C.O. 155:2, p. 533); of 1705 amongst those of Nevis (C.O. 155:3, Journals of General Assembly of all the Islands, 23 May 1705); of 1710/11 in those of Antigua (C.O. 9:2, Minutes of General Council and Assembly, 22 February 1910/11).

[2] The confusion arises from the title "At a meeting of the Governor General Council and Assembly." This has been misread in the calendar on one or two occasions, e.g. *C.S.P.*, vol. ix, p. 488. The only safe guide is the list of persons present.

[3] There are also for most of the colonies printed series of journals starting in the middle of the nineteenth century. But although some start before the abolition of the agencies, the earlier sections are incomplete and of little value.

NOTE ON AUTHORITIES

The following list indicates the series of colonial legislative records available in England, at the Public Record Office:

	Acts.	Sessional Papers.
Antigua	C.O. 8	C.O. 9
Bahamas	C.O. 25	C.O. 26 [1]
Barbados	C.O. 30	C.O. 31
Bermuda	C.O. 39	C.O. 40
Dominica	C.O. 73	C.O. 74
Grenada	C.O. 103	C.O. 104
Jamaica	C.O. 139	C.O. 140 [2]
Leeward Islands	C.O. 154	C.O. 155 [3]
Montserrat	C.O. 176	C.O. 177
Nevis	C.O. 185	C.O. 186 [3]
St. Christopher	C.O. 240	C.O. 241 [3]
St. Vincent	C.O. 262	C.O. 263
Tobago	C.O. 281	C.O. 282
Virgin Islands	C.O. 315	C.O. 316

3. THE ARCHIVES OF THE HOME GOVERNMENT

The third class of material, the Archives of the Home Government, again provide a mass of relevant matter, relating especially to the work of the agents in England. With almost every branch of the home Government the agent came into contact, Parliament, the Privy Council, the Secretary of State, the successive Committees and Councils for Trade and Plantations, the Treasury, Admiralty, the

Printed series, *Journal of the Lower House of Assembly of the Bahama Islands*, 1728-1786, 5 vols., Nassau, 1910. Verbatim print, with index for each session.

[2] Printed series, *Journals of the Assembly of Jamaica*, 14 vols., Jamaica, 1811-1829. Verbatim print, containing also in vol. i historical extracts covering years for which records could not be found. Additional volume containing indices for each volume of the Journals bound together.

[3] Early records, Antigua: Minutes of Council commencing 1670. C.O. 1:25, No. 55, 49; No. 81; No. 49. Nevis: Minutes of Council commencing 1672, Journals of Assembly commencing 1680. C.O. 1:28, No. 60, 44; No. 65, 45; No. 78, 48; Nos. 23 and 79, 49; No. 83, 53; No. 4, 57; No. 40, 58; No. 43. St. Christopher: Minutes of Council commencing 1672. C.O. 1:28, No. 69, 51; No. 98, 57; No. 48.

APPENDIX IV

Board of Ordnance, the Commissioners of the Customs, with all of these authorities the agent was frequently concerned. And therefore, dispersed amongst the records of these bodies, may be found numerous references to the activities of the agent, giving together an almost exhaustive mass of evidence as to the agent's work. That it is not quite exhaustive is due to the prevalence of unofficial unrecorded intercourse between agents and members of administration or of Parliament of which the accounts written by one or the other of the parties concerned are the only guide: for this reason great value is to be attached to the private collections of the manuscripts of Newcastle, Pitt, and other ministers.

Amongst this corpus of material some discrimination is possible as to relative importance. The most valuable of the sources included under this head are the papers of the successive Committees, Councils, and Commissions into whose hands from time to time the business of the plantations was entrusted; and of these the Committee of the Privy Council of 1675 to 1696, commonly known as the Lords of Trade, and its successors the Board of Trade and Plantations of 1696 to 1782, and the Privy Council Committee of the same name established in 1786, cover nearly the whole of the period of the agency. Parliamentary and Privy Council records are of considerable importance, but in the former case the importance is variable, being paramount only on occasions of serious crises in West Indian affairs, and in the latter constant reference is not essential because the frequency with which the matters in which the Council was concerned were referred at one stage or another of the proceedings to the advisory body, the Committee or the Board.

The following list indicates the locality of these series:

i. The Privy Council.

The Privy Council Register in the Public Record Office (P.C. 1) contains minutes of meetings of Council, and of committees not sufficiently permanent to acquire series of records of their own (e.g. Committee for Trade and Plantations, created July 1660, and committees of the period 1696–1782). The papers relating to the activities of the Privy Council are to be found partly in the Public Record Office series of "Unbound Papers," and partly in the Plantation Register at the Privy Council Office.

The Privy Council Register and the Unbound Papers have been calendared for the period 1613–1783, so far as they relate

NOTE ON AUTHORITIES

to colonial affairs. The series comprises six volumes under the title *Acts of the Privy Council, Colonial*; vols. i–v refer to the Privy Council Register, and the sixth to the Unbound Papers.

ii. Committees of the Privy Council.

(*a*) "The Lords of Trade," 1675–96. Minutes are in C.O. 391:1–8 (Public Record Office). Correspondence and other papers are included in the miscellaneous series C.O. 1, down to the year 1689, and from that date in two series for each colony, classed as "Original Correspondence" and "Entry Books."

(*b*) The Boards of Trade, 1784 *et seq*. Minutes for the period to 1837 are in the Public Record Office under the classification B.T. 5:1–44; correspondence and other papers under B.T. 1–4 and B.T. 6. B.T. 6:153–169 contain Orders in Council referring to Colony Laws (with correspondence) for the period 1802–36.

iii. Boards commissioned to deal with colonial affairs.

(*a*) Council for Foreign Plantations, 1660–4. Minutes are in the Public Record Office, in the miscellaneous series C.O. 1 (C.O. 1:14, No. 59); correspondence and other papers are in the same series distributed under a date classification.

(*b*) Councils for Foreign Plantations, 1670–2 and 1672–4. Minutes are in the Library of Congress, Washington, U.S.A.;[1] heads of proceedings are in C.O. 5:1 (Public Record Office), and have been printed with additions from other sources in C. M. Andrews, *British Committees, Councils, and Commissions for Trade and Plantations, 1622–1675*, Appendix, pp. 133–151. Correspondence and other papers are distributed under a date classification in series C.O. 1.

(*c*) The Board of Trade and Plantations, 1696–1782. Minutes are in the Public Record Office, series C.O. 391:9–89. The early volumes relating to the years 1696–1704 are calendared in the *Calendar of State Papers, Colonial, America and West Indies*; from 1704 they are being printed verbatim under the title *Journals of the Commissioners for Trade and Plantations*. Correspondence

---

[1] They were formerly amongst the manuscripts of Sir Thomas Phillips, being purchased by him in 1836 through William Thorpe. While in the possession of Phillips they were used by Sir R. H. Schomburgk in his *History of Barbados*.

and other papers are classified in two series for each colony as follows :

	Original Correspondence.	Entry Books.
Antigua	C.O. 7	C.O. 393
(See also Leeward Islands)		
Bahamas	C.O. 23	C.O. 24
Barbados	C.O. 28	C.O. 29
Bermuda	C.O. 37	C.O. 38
Dominica	C.O. 71	C.O. 72
Grenada	C.O. 101	C.O. 102
Jamaica	C.O. 137	C.O. 138
Leeward Islands	C.O. 152	C.O. 153
Montserrat (see Leeward Islands and Antigua)		
Nevis (see Leeward Islands and St. Christopher)		
St. Christopher	C.O. 239	C.O. 407
(See also Leeward Islands)		
St. Vincent	C.O. 260	C.O. 261
Tobago	C.O. 285	C.O. 286
Virgin Islands (see Leeward Islands and St. Christopher)		

These papers are calendared in the *Calendar of State Papers, Colonial Series, America and West Indies*, which has now reached the year 1708. The value of the volumes of the *Calendar* varies considerably, the later volumes being the most reliable. The detailed character of the information required for the history of the agencies has made reference to the original documents generally necessary.

Next in importance to the records of the councils and committees to which colonial affairs were entrusted are the papers of successive Secretaries of State: and at some periods these are the most important of all. The official sources for the correspondence of Secretaries of State in colonial matters are the several series of "Original Correspondence" and "Entry Books" listed above, the correspondence of the Secretaries of State following on in the same series that of the Board of Trade of the period 1696–1782. There is also a Letter Book of Agents' Correspondence with Secretaries of State, 1801–10, C.O. 324:115. Unofficial sources of value are as follows :

    B.M. Add. MSS. 32686–32992, 33028–33030. Correspondence of Duke of Newcastle, Secretary of State for Southern Department.

NOTE ON AUTHORITIES

P.R.O. Chatham Papers, 19, 90 ; 352.   Correspondence of the Elder and the Younger Pitt.

Hist. MSS. Commission : *Report on the Manuscripts of the Earl of Dartmouth,* vol. ii, 1895.   Papers of the Earl of Dartmouth, Secretary of State in the American Department.

Hist. MSS. Commission : *Report on the Manuscripts of Mrs. Stopford Sackville, of Drayton House, Northamptonshire,* vol. ii, 1910.   Papers of Lord George Germain, Secretary of State in the American Department.

In addition to the regular series of official records for each island, there are miscellaneous series classified as C.O. 5, C.O. 318, C.O. 323, in which much matter of value can be found.

4. THE RECORDS OF WEST INDIA PLANTERS AND MERCHANTS IN ENGLAND

The last main class of sources provides much valuable material for the agents' activities. They are all unofficial and in private hands.

By far the most important are the records of the West India Committee of London (14 Trinity Square, E.C.3).

The relevant volumes of minutes are as follows :

i. Minutes of Society of West India Merchants.

    Vol. I. April 1769—April 1779
    Vol. II. June 1779—August 1783.
    (Vol. III. is missing.)
    Vol. IV. August 1794—December 1802.
    Vol. V. April 1803—July 1804.
    Vol. VI. September 1804—July 1827.
    Vol. VII. January 1828—July 1843.

ii. Minutes of Sub-Committee of Society of West India Merchants, 1799.

iii. Minutes of Standing Committee of West India Planters and Merchants.

    Vol. I. May 1785—December 1792.
    Vol. II. February 1793—April 1801.
    Vol. III. December 1801—June 1804.
    Vol. IV. February 1805—March 1822.
    Vol. V. March 1822—April 1829.

APPENDIX IV

Vol. VI.   April 1829—February 1834.
Vol. VII. April 1834—May 1850.

iv. Minutes of Acting Committee of West India Planters and Merchants.

Vol. I.   May 1829—July 1833.
Vol. II.   July 1833—June 1843.
Vol. III. June 1843—December 1844.
Vol. IV.   January 1845—July 1851.
Vol. V.   January 1852—February 1857.

The Records of the Societies at the Out-Ports are of minor importance :

i. Minutes of Bristol West India Club, 1782–98.
    (Preserved at Merchants' Hall, Bristol.)
ii. Minutes of Glasgow West India Association, 1802–9.
(Preserved by West India Committee, 14 Trinity Square, E.C.3.)

(B) SUPPLEMENTARY SOURCES.

In addition to these four classes of authorities, there are various others of less importance. Contemporary publications making reference to the agency are few, although useful details as to personnel can be obtained from various periodicals. The agents themselves, or their friends the planters and merchants, frequently published tracts and pamphlets setting forth the claims of the West Indies to the favour of administration, but of the agency itself these make as a rule no mention. The most valuable collection of contemporary material is contained in the private letters of merchants, planters, and others who came into contact with the agent in the course of his work. The references to the agent are comparatively few, but for the general conditions under which he worked these afford very great assistance.

The most important volumes are as follows :

1. LETTERS OF PLANTERS, MERCHANTS, ETC.

Letter Books of Messrs. Lascelles & Maxwell, merchants trading to Barbados. (In possession of Messrs. Wilkinson & Gaviller, 34 Great Tower Street, E.C.3.) This is a valuable and extensive series containing much material relative to trade : the first seven volumes only have been used.

NOTE ON AUTHORITIES

Vol. I. March 1739/40—February 1741/2.
Vol. II. September 1743—January 1745/6.
Vol. III. February 1745/6—August 1748.
Vol. IV. August 1750—August 1752.
Vol. V. August 1752—May 1754.
Vol. VI. May 1754—July 1756.
Vol. VII. September 1768—July 1772.

Jefferies MSS., vol. xiii : African Slave Trade, ff. 9–158 (Bristol City Library). — Letters of Isaac Hobhouse & Sons, merchants trading to Africa, North America, and the West Indies, 1723–50.

Bodleian MS. Rawlinson, Letters 66. — Letter Book of J. C., a merchant trading to the plantations in the years 1706–16.

Jasper Mauduit, Agent in London for the Province of Massachusetts Bay, 1762–1765. Mass. Hist. Soc., 1918.

B.M. Add. MSS. 12402–12440, 18270–18275, 18959–18963, 21931–22639, 22676–22680. — Papers collected by Edward Long.

2. TRACTS AND PAMPHLETS.

Campbell, John . . *Candid and impartial considerations on the nature of the sugar trade.* . . . London, 1763.

Franklin, Benjamin . . *The Interest of Great Britain Considered, with regard to her Colonies, and the Acquisition of Canada and Guadaloupe* . . . London, 1766.

Glover, Richard . . *The substance of the evidence on the petition presented by the West India planters and merchants to the House of Commons* . . . London, 1775.

Littleton, Edward . . *The Groans of the Plantations.* London, 1689.

APPENDIX IV

Perrin, William	*The Present State of the British and French Sugar Colonies considered.* London, 1740.
Postlethwayt, Malachy	*The African trade the great pillar and support of the British plantation trade in America* ... London, 1745.
(Anonymous)	*The Alarm Bell: or Considerations on the present dangerous state of the sugar colonies* ... London, 1749.
	Appeal to the candour of the People of England, in behalf of the West India Merchants and Planters. London, 1792.
	The Case of the British Sugar Colonies. London, 1732.
	The Present State of the British Sugar Colonies consider'd ... London, 1731.
	Thoughts on Trade in General and West India in particular ... London, 1763.

There are a number of tracts of interest also amongst the series of Thomason Tracts in the British Museum (catalogued 1908). Others, mainly manuscript, are to be found amongst the Colonial Office Papers in the Public Record Office, classified as C.O. 325:1-4 and 6.

3. Periodical Publications

The most valuable of these are London newspapers, *e.g. London Chronicle, Morning Chronicle, London Advertiser, Gazetteer and New Daily Advertiser, Public Ledger*, etc., a collection of which, made by Charles Burney, is in the British Museum: and annual periodicals, Chamberlayne's *Angliæ Notitia* (1669-1755), *Royal Kalendar* (1767-1850), *Annual Register* (1758 *et seq.*), and *Gentleman's Magazine* (1731 *et seq.*).

4. Historical Works

Lastly, there are historical works relating to the affairs of the West Indies, the greater number of them written in the eighteenth century. In some respects these are contemporary in character.

NOTE ON AUTHORITIES

The writers were frequently themselves concerned in the islands or had recently been visiting them, or were personally conversant with the work of the agents in conducting their business in England; and therefore their references to the agents' history, although for the most part scanty and devoid of any indication as to the authorities on which the statements rest, have an interest as showing the conception of the agency prevalent at the time at which they wrote. Of these, two are of outstanding importance: John Oldmixon's *The British Empire in America*, first published in 1708, which contains some useful details as to the early years of the Barbados agency; and Edward Long's *History of Jamaica*, dated 1774, which devotes a chapter of great interest to the position and functions of the agent.

The following list indicates the most useful of such works:

* Atwood, Thomas . . *History of the Island of Dominica.* London, 1791.

Beckford, William . . *Descriptive account of the Island of Jamaica.* London, 1790.

Blome, Richard . . *Description of the Island of Jamaica* . . . London, 1672.

Browne, Patrick . . *Civil and natural history of Jamaica.* London, 1789.

* Bruce, Peter H. . . *Memoirs of P. H. Bruce* . . . London, 1782.

Davies, John, of Kidwelly . *History of the Caribby Islands.* London, 1666. (Translation from Charles Rochefort: *Histoire Naturelle et Morale des Iles Antilles de l'Amérique.* Rotterdam, 1658.)

Du Tertre, Jean B. . . *Histoire general des Antilles habitées par les Français.* Paris, 1667–71.

Gage, Thomas . . *New Survey of the West India's* . . . London, 1655.

Edwards, Bryan . . *History, civil and commercial, of the British colonies in the West Indies* . . . London, 1793–4.

Graves, John . . . *A Memorial: or a Short Account of the Bahama Islands* . . . London, 1708.

An asterisk indicates those titles which have been reprinted or published by Frank Cass, London.

Labat, Jean B. . .	*Nouveau Voyage aux isles de l'Amérique.* Paris, 1724.
* Ligon, Richard	*A true and exact History of the Island of Barbados* . . . London, 1657.
* Long, Edward	*The History of Jamaica* . . . 3 vols. London, 1774.
Oldmixon, John	*The British Empire in America* . . . 2 vols. London, 1708.
Pownall, Thomas	*Administration of the Colonies.* London, 1774, 5th edition.
Suckling, George	*An historical account of the Virgin Islands, in the West Indies.* London, 1780.
Stokes, Anthony	*View of the Constitution of the British Colonies, in North America and the West Indies . . . down to the present period* . . . London, 1783.
Thomas, Sir Dalby	*An historical account of the rise and growth of the West India Collonies.* London, 1690.
(Anonymous)	*Memoirs of the first settlement of the island of Barbados . . . to the year 1742* . . . London, 1742. *Relation de l'isle de Barbados* . . . Paris, 1774.

II. MODERN WORKS

The extent to which these documentary and other sources for the history of the agency have been utilised by modern historians is not very great. The first pioneer in the still insufficient modern historical literature of the West Indies was Sir R. H. Schomburgk, whose *History of Barbados*,* published in 1848, is still the authoritative work on the island with which he deals: and is distinct from the works of earlier writers by the inclusion of valuable references to authorities. Schomburgk, however, makes only accidental references to the agent. A little later Mr. W. H. Gardner, in his *History of Jamaica*,* a work containing much of interest

NOTE ON AUTHORITIES 305

but not comparable to Schomburgk's for scholarly presentation, makes no reference to the agents. The only modern surveys on the subject of the agent is a brief sketch by Sir Charles Lucas in the article entitled " British Colonial Administration and its Agencies " in the *Oxford Survey of the British Empire : General Survey*, and an article in *The Political Science Quarterly* of March 1901 by Mr. E. P. Tanner, on " The Colonial Agencies of the Eighteenth Century " : the latter, however, deals entirely with the North American colonies, and is apparently based entirely on sources available in the United States.

The following lists indicate the main modern works of importance for the study of the subject :

(a) *Guides to Material and Bibliographies.*

Andrews, C. M. . . *Guide to the Materials for American History to 1783 in the Public Record Office of Great Britain*, vol. i. The State Papers, Washington, 1911, vol. ii. Departmental and Miscellaneous Papers, Washington, 1914.

Andrews, C. M., and Davenport, F. C. *Guide to the Manuscript Materials for the History of the United States to 1783, in the British Museum, in Minor London Archives, and in the Libraries of Oxford and Cambridge.* Washington, 1907.

Cundall, F. . . . *Bibliographica Jamaicensis.* Kingston, Jamaica, 1902.
Bibliography of the West Indies (excluding Jamaica). Kingston, Jamaica, 1909.

Higham, C. S. S. . . *The Colonial Entry-Books. A brief guide to the colonial records in the Public Record Office before 1696.* Helps for Students of History, No. 45, London, 1921.

20

APPENDIX IV

Malcolm, Harcourt . . *List of Documents relating to the Bahama Islands in the British Museum and the Record Office, London.* Nassau, 1910.

Newton, A. P. . . *An Introduction to the Study of Colonial History.* Helps for Students of History, No. 16. London, 1918.

(Anonymous) . . . *Bristol Bibliography.* Bristol, 1912.

Journal of the Institute of Jamaica. Kingston, Jamaica, 1899.

List of Works relating to the West Indies in the New York Library. New York, 1912.

Second Report of the Royal Commission on the Public Records. London, 1910–14.

(*b*) *Historical Works bearing immediately upon the History of the Agents.*

Cundall, Frank . . *Historic Jamaica.* London, 1908. Contains a list, not complete, of the Jamaica agents.

Doyle, William . . *The Colonies under the House of Hanover.* 5 vols. London, 1901–10.

Higham, C. S. S. . . *The Development of the Leeward Islands under the Restoration,* 1660–1683. Cambridge, 1920. Contains references to the early agents of the Leeward Islands: based throughout on original materials.

"The Accounts of a Colonial Governor's Agent in the Seventeenth Century." *American Historical Review,* January, 1923. Based largely on the private papers of Sir Miles Stapleton, i.e. the accounts, etc., of the agents of Sir William Stapleton, Governor-General of the Leeward Islands, 1672–86.

NOTE ON AUTHORITIES

Keith, A. B. . . *Responsible Government in the Dominions.* 3 vols. London, 1912.

Lucas, Sir C. P. . . "Colonial Administration and its Agencies," comprising part of *General Survey*, vol. i, of the Oxford Survey of the British Empire. Oxford, 1914.

Osgood, H. L. . . *The American Colonies in the 17th Century.* 3 vols. New York, 1907-10.

* Pitman, F. W. . . *Development of the British West Indies,* 1700-1763. New Haven, Connecticut, 1917. Not only valuable as detailing economic conditions at the time of the growth of the agency, but of direct use in tracing the work of the agents through its extensive documentation.

Russell, E.B. . . . *Review of American Colonial Legislation by the King in Council.* Columbia Studies in Hist., etc., Baltimore, 1915. Contains a discussion of functions of agent in connection with the confirmation of colonial Acts.

Tanner, E. P. . . "Colonial Agencies in England during the Eighteenth Century." *Political Science Quarterly*, March 1901.

(c) *Other Works*

Andrews, C. M. . . *British Committees, Commissioners, and Councils of Trade and Plantations,* 1622-75. J.H.U. Studies in Hist. & Pol. Sci., Baltimore, 1908. *The Colonial Period.* New York and London, 1912.

Aspinall, A. E. . . *The British West Indies: their history, resources and progress.* London, 1912.

APPENDIX IV

Atchley, C. . . . *Historical Geography of the British Colonies.* Vol. ii, *The West Indies.* Oxford, 1905.

Bell, H. C. . . . "British Commercial Policy in the West Indies, 1785–1793." Article in *English Historical Review*, July 1916.

Beer, G. L. . . *The Origins of the British Colonial System,* 1578–1660. New York, 1908.
The Old Colonial System, 1660–1754, 8 vols. (to 1688). New York, 1912.
British Colonial Policy, 1754–65. New York, 1907.

* Breen, R. H. . . . *St. Lucia: Historical, Statistical, and Descriptive.* London, 1844.

* Bridges, E. W. . . . *Annals of Jamaica.* 3 vols. London, 1828.

Clarke, M. . . . "Board of Trade at Work." Article in *American Historical Review*, October, 1911.

* Coke, Thomas . . . *History of the West Indies.* . . . 3 vols. Liverpool, 1808–11.

* Cunningham, W. . . *The Growth of English Industry and Commerce.* . . . Fifth edition, 1912, Modern Times, Parts I and II.

Davis, N. Darnell . . *Cavaliers and Roundheads of Barbados,* 1650–2. George Town, 1887.
An early impression of Barbados. s. sh. fol. London, 1913.
Pages from the Early History of Barbados, 1627–59. S. sh. fol. 1909.

* Davy, John . . . *The West Indies, before and since Slave Emancipation.* . . . London, 1854.

Dickerson, O. M. . . *American Colonial Government,* 1696–1765. Cleveland, Ohio, 1912.

Egerton, H. E. . . *Short History of British Colonial Policy.* Fourth edition. London, 1913.

NOTE ON AUTHORITIES

* Gardner, W. J.	*History of Jamaica.* New edition. London, 1909.
Malcolm, Harcourt	*The Bahamas House of Assembly.* Article in the *Empire Review*, March 1905.
Martin, R. M.	*History of the Colonies of the British Empire in the West Indies.* . . . London, 1843.
Morriss, M. S.	*Colonial Trade of Maryland*, 1689–1715. J.H.U. Studies in Hist. and Pol. Sci. Baltimore, 1914.
Oliver, V. L.	*History of the Island of Antigua.* . . . 3 vols. London, 1894–9.
* Poyer, John	*History of Barbados.* . . . London, 1808.
* Schomburgk, Sir R. H.	*History of Barbados.* . . . London, 1848.
* Shephard, Charles	*Historical Account of the Island of Saint Vincent.* London, 1831.
* Southey, Thomas	*Chronological History of the West Indies.* London, 1827.
* Woodcock, Henry Iles	*History of Tobago.* Ayr, 1867. *Caribbiana.* . . . London, 1907, etc.
Wrong, Hume	*Government of the West Indies.* Oxford, 1923.
Young, Sir William	*The West India Common Place Book.* London, 1807.

There are further a large number of references of interest to be found in the Reports and Papers of the American Historical Association; for which see *Report* . . . *for the Year* 1914, Part II, General Index to Papers and Reports . . . 1884–1914, 1918.

INDEX

Absenteeism, prevalence of, 14–16, 175–6
Absentees, difficulties with residents, 188–9
Admiralty, reference of colonial business to, 219, 225
Agents, assistant for Barbados, 160–1
——, colonial, early analogies and growth, 10–20, 27–9, 31–3, 40–1, 46–78 *passim*; Povey's schemes, 34–7; first appointment, 52–3, 69–70, 74–6; attitude of home government to, 34–5, 37, 55, 73–4, 77, 87; acts of appointment, 79, 95–7, 267–75; correspondence of, 149–51, 275–7; instructions to, 150–1, 274–5; accounts of, 151–4, 277–9; delay in payment to, 155 n. 2; refusal of payment to, 154–5; dismissal of, 155–6; method of choice, 158–61; nomination by governor, 162; salaries of, 166; relations with planters and merchants, 46–78, 174–214 *passim*; dissatisfaction in Bahama Is. with, 243; criticism of, by Governor of Barbados, 243; attitude of Colonial Office to, 242–3; abolition of, 241–5.
——, financial, see *sub nom.* Crown Agents
——, for "new colonies," see *sub nom.* Crown-Agents, Office of; Demerara; Trinidad.
——, personal of, Governors, 61, 105
Allen, James, secretary to West India Committee, 202
America, North, agents for, 165; merchants trading to, 203, 284–5; war of independence in, 203–4
Andrews, Jonathan, 28
Antigua, settlement of, 8; capture of, by France, 42; establishment of agency in, 67–8; act of appointing agents, 95–6, 128, 145, 267–9; election of members for General Assembly, 95; agents of, 251–2
Ashley, John, secretary to Planters' Club, 190
Atkins, Sir Jonathan, Governor of Barbados, 54, 55

Attorney-General, reference of colonial business to, 219, 224; payment of gratuity to, 226
Australian colonies, agency of, 245
Ayscue, Sir George, 21

Bahama Islands, proprietary rule in, 99–101; royal government in, 102–5; establishment of agency in, 106–7; acts appointing agents, 115, 128; committee of correspondence in, 141, 144–5; abolition of agency, 242; agents of, 253; correspondence with agent, 276–7
Barbados, establishment of assembly in, 4; position in 1660, 8–9, 24; political parties in, 14, 36–7, 39, 40–1, 81; establishment of agency in, 69–70 *et seq.*; acts appointing agents, 59, 128, 160; difficulties over agency, 80–8; method of nomination, 159–60; solicitation regarding laws, 129; appointment of assistant agent, 160–1; agents of, 250–1.
——, Gentlemen Planters of, in London, 47–53, 116, 163 (see also *sub nom.* Committee for the Concern of Barbados)
Barnes, William, agent for Antigua, 68, 126–7
Barré, Isaac, 172
Bayer, Bastian, commissioner for Leeward Is., 70, 251
Bayley, Nathaniel, 205
Beake, Thomas, clerk in Council Office, 168
Beauchamp, Lieut., secretary of Bahama Is., 105
Beckford, Julius, 176 n. 2
——, Richard, 176 n. 2
——, William, 176 n. 2, 182, 189
Beeston, William, agent for Jamaica, 73, 74, 152
Bennett, Sir John, agent for Bermuda, 248
——, Thomas, agent for Bermuda, 248
Bermuda, agency of, 247–9

311

INDEX

Bindloss, John, agent to Sir H. Morgan, 71
Blackman, Thurston, assistant agent for Barbados, 161
Blathwayt, William, secretary to Lords of Trade, 57, 65; payment of gratuity to, 226
Blenac, de, French governor of St. Christopher, 62
Board, Ordnance, reference of colonial business to, 219, 221; payment of gratuities at, 227
Board of Trade and Plantations (1696–1782), attitude to agency, 77, 87; clerks forbidden to serve as agents, 170; consultation of merchants by, 179–180; control of colonies by, 216; treatment of colonial business by, 217–223; records of, 297–8
—— (1784–6), 237; records of, 297
—— (1786 et seq.), 216, 217, 237; records of, 297
Bowden, Sir John, 58
Brathwaite, John, member of West India Committee, 213
Breda, Treaty of, 59
Brickwood, John, agent for Bermuda, 248
Bridges, William, agent for Barbados, 58, 84, 168, 171
Bristol, West India Club of, 288–9
Burke, Edmund, agent for New York, 166

Campbell, Alexander, member of West India Committee, 213
Canada, agency of, 80, 244–5; High Commissioner of, 245 (see also *sub nom.* Quebec)
Cardinal's cap, the, 178, 179, 183
Carlisle, Charles Howard, Earl of, Governor of Jamaica, 72, 73
——, John Hay, Earl of, proprietor of Caribbee Is., 21, 23, 26, 30
Carteret, John, Earl Granville, negotiation of agents with, 224
Cary, Richard, agent for Leeward Is., 70, 126, 251; agent for Antigua, 151 n. 1, 164, 251
Chalmers, George, agent for Bahama Is. and chief clerk to Board of Trade, 167, 237; writings of, 168; correspondence of, 276–7
Champante, John, agent to Lord Willoughby, 42, 47
Charge on Trade, 191–2, 197 (see also *sub nom.* Virginia)
Charlton, Edward, unofficial agent for Jamaica, 90
Chinese, emigration of, to West Indies, 211
Civil Servants, as agents, 167–9, 234

Civil War (1642–52) in West Indies, 14
Cleland, William, agent for Barbados, 84
Coffee houses and taverns, 177–182 *passim*
Colebrooke, Sir George, 112
Colleton, John, 15, 27, 28, 30, 33, 34, 40
——, Sir Peter, 40, 43, 54; agent for Barbados, 56–7, 250
Commander-in-chief, reference of colonial business to, 225
Commissioners of Customs, reference of colonial business to, 219
Commissioners for Leeward Is. (1690–7), appointment of, 69–71; payment of gratuities by, 226 n. 5
Committee of Privy Council for Trade and Plantations, (1660) 25–6, 33–4; (1667) 42–3; records of, 296
—— (1675–96), i.e. the Lords of Trade, attitude to agency, 55, 73–4; review of legislation by, 67; discussion of constitution of Jamaica before, 73; application to, by agents of Barbados, 129–30; consultation of merchants, etc., by, 179–80; control of colonies by, 216; records of, 297
—— (1786 et seq.), see *sub nom.* Board of Trade and Plantations
Committee for the Concern of Barbados, 51–3, 70, 182–4; minutes of, 260–2; correspondence of, 262–5 (see also *sub nom.* Barbados, Gentlemen Planters of)
Committees of Correspondence, 140–5 *passim*; records of, 142–4 (see also *sub nom.* Antigua, Bahama Is., etc.)
Convicts, importation of, 114, 126
Council of State (1649–60), authority of, in colonies, 21
Council for Foreign Plantations (1660), appointment of, 14; membership of, 34; attitude to agency, 34–5, 37; records of, 297
Council for Trade and Plantations (1670), 43–4; records of, 297
——(1672), records of, 297
Courteen, Sir William, 26
Cranfield, Edward, 17
Crispe, Joseph, agent for Leeward Is., 62–3, 126
Crosse, Epinetus, 18, 24.
Crown-Agents (financial), 169 n. 2, 234 n. 3
—— office of (1833 et seq.), origin of, 233–4; organisation, 234; use of, by West Indies, 244
Crown Colony System, 233–5
Cumberland, Richard, agent for Bahama Is., 106, 162, 169, 253;

INDEX 313

secretary to Board of Trade, 167;
agent for Quebec, 169, 234 n. 1;
crown-agent for Nova Scotia, 169;
playwright, 169

Defence, negotiations regarding, 129–31
Deficiency Acts, passed in Antigua, Jamaica, and St. Christopher, 188
Delafaye, Charles, agent for Jamaica, 90–1, 122 n. 2, 251; secretary to Duke of Newcastle and Under Secretary of State, 167, 170, 225
Demerara, appointment of agent by, 233
Dominica, cession of (1763), 110; activity of merchants trading to, 111; establishment of agency, 111–2; separation of government of, 121; committee of correspondence in, 148; capture by France, 204; agents of, 254
Douglas, James George, agent for St. Christopher, 188 n. 4, 252
D'Oyley, Colonel, Governor of Jamaica, 15, 24
Drax, Edward, 43
——, Henry, agent for Barbados, 16, 56–7, 250
——, Sir James, 28, 32, 34
Duport, Stephen, agent for St. Christopher, 92 n. 4, 164, 252; accounts of, 152
Dutch, possessions in West Indies, 7; trade to West Indies, 9

East Indians, emigration of, to West Indies, 211
Economic Reform in England, 236–7
Economy Movement in West Indies, 241
Elliot, Grey, chief clerk to Board of Trade, 237
Ellis, Charles, M.P., motion regarding Slave Trade, 230
——, John, agent for Dominica, 203, 254
Estwick, Samuel, assistant agent for Barbados, 161; M.P., 172; member of West India Committee, 205, 213; agent for Barbados, 251
Eyles, Francis, agent for Barbados, 84, 250

Fees and gratuities in Civil Service, payment of, by agents, 225–7
Four-and-a-half-per-cent. duty, imposition of, 31, 108; negotiations regarding, 114, 125; effect of, 174; repeal of, 240
France, possessions of, in West Indies, 7, 110–1; war with, (1666) 42, (1692–7) 91–2, (1756–63)

110–1, 124, (1793–1815) 232; Treaty of Neutrality with (1678), 62–3; fear of, in Leeward Is., 110; Treaty of Commerce with (1786), 209
Freeman, William, agent to Sir W. Stapleton, 60
Frere, Tobias, 28
Froude, Philip, secretary to Council for Foreign Plantations, designs on agency, 37, 159, 162
Fuller, Rose, M.P., 228
——, Stephen, agent for Jamaica, 164, 205; member of West India Committee, 199, 200–1, 213

Gambier, John, Governor of Bahama Is., 105
Gamiell, George, nominated as agent, 64–5, 162
Gardner, John, nominated as agent, 58
Gellibrand, Samuel, deputy-secretary to Board of Trade, payment of gratuity to, 226–7
Gerrish, William, nominated as agent, 93 n. 5, 164
Gilliam, Samuel, agent for Leeward Is., 70
Gookin, William, 178
Gorges, Ferdinand, absentee planter of Barbados, 40, 48, 51–2; agent for Sir W. Stapleton, 60; agent for Leeward Is., 63–4, 129, 251
Gracedieu, Sir Bartholomew, agent for Jamaica, 75–6, 171, 181
Graves, John, 102
Greatbach, Lieut., employed by Leeward Is., 62
Grenada, cession of (1763), 110; conditions in, 111; establishment of assembly in, 111; establishment of agency, 111; committee of correspondence in, 141; correspondence of Richard Maitland with, 275–6; agents of, 254
Grenville, Sir Bevil, Governor of Barbados, 84–5, 179
——, William, Secretary of State, relations with West India Committee, 207–8
Griffith, Sir John, agent for Jamaica, 71, 180
Guadaloupe, capture and restoration of, 110

Handasyd, Thomas, Governor of Jamaica, 221
Harris, Richard, unofficial agent for Jamaica, 122, 182
Hart, John, Governor of St. Christopher, 224–5

314 INDEX

Heathcote, Sir Gilbert, agent for Jamaica, 75, 90, 171, 180, 181, 251
Heysham, Robert, unofficial agent for Barbados, 84
———, William, agent for Barbados, 154, 171, 250
Hinchman, Thomas, 53
Holden, Robert, Governor of Bahama Is., 103
Holder, Melatia, agent for Barbados, 84, 250
Howard, Sir Robert, 117
Huggins, John, agent for Barbados, 160, 250
Hutchinson, Archibald, unofficial agent for Antigua, 93 n. 2

Interregnum, colonial development of, 20-2
Irish Resolutions (1785), negotiations regarding, 208

Jamaica, capture of, 6-7; Restoration settlement in, 18, 23, 24, 36, 45, 71; merchants trading to, 71; constitutional difficulties in (1677-80), 71-3; assembly of, 72; instruction to Governor, 73-4, 90, 265-6; appointment of agents by, 73-6, 128; difficulties over appointment, 88-91, 128; instructions to agents, 119-20; committee of correspondence, 140, 141-3, 152; method of nomination, 159; acts of appointment, 269-72; agents of, 251
Jamaica (and Guinea) Coffee House, 181-2, 202
Jeaffreson, Christopher, planter of St. Christopher, correspondence of, 12; influence on agency, 64-5; agent for St. Christopher, 65-7, 68, 126, 177-8, 252; commissioner for Leeward Is., 70, 251; payment of gratuities by, 226
Jeffries, Jeffry, commissioner for Leeward Is., 70
Jenkins' Ear, War of, 124
Jory, Joseph, agent for Leeward Is., 62-3, 126, 149, 251; instruction to, 274-5; agent for Nevis, 153-4, 164

Kendall, James, Governor of Barbados, 4, 58
———, Thomas, absentee planter of Barbados, 27, 28, 30, 31, 32, 33, 40
Kerby, Thomas, 93 n. 3, 164
Keynell, Christopher, Governor of Antigua, 18
King's Arms Tavern, 201-2
Knight, James, unofficial agent for Jamaica, 90 n. 6; correspondence and activities of, 182, 189; description of Virginia interest, 187, 279-80
Knight, Ralph, agent for Jamaica, 75, 127, 128

Langham, Purbec, agent for Grenada, 234 n. 1
Lascelles, Henry, planter and merchant of Barbados, 229; correspondence of, 282-4; papers of, 300-1
Laws, colonial, review of, by King in Council, 67, 218-9, 221-4; solicitations relating to, 127-9
Leare, Sir Peter, 34, 40
Leeward Islands, movement for separation from Barbados, 41-4; fear of French, 59-60; difficulties of defence, 114; appointment of agents by, 69-71, 91-5; General Legislature of all the islands, 69-70, 126, 146-8, 164; Governor-General of, 145-6, 149; agents of, 251; instruction to agent, 274-5 (see also sub nom. Antigua, etc.)
Leheup, Peter, agent for Barbados, 168, 250
Littleton, Sir Charles, agent for Jamaica, 74, 152, 251
———, Edward, agent for Barbados, 58, 250; author of Groans of the Plantations, 58, 174
Liverpool, merchants of, trading to Virgin Is., 107 n. 1; agent for Virgin Is. belonging to, 110, 205 n. 2
London, Lord Mayor of, attestation of agents' accounts before, 152
———, merchants of, 10-11, 24, 49, 111, 117, 118 (see also sub nom. Portugal, Virginia, West India Committee)
London Tavern, 201
Long, Beeston, Chairman of West India Merchants, 198, 202, 207
———, Edward, cited, 163
———, Colonel Samuel, of Jamaica, 72-3
———, Samuel, Treasurer of West India Committee, 202, 206
Lords of Trade, see sub nom. Committee of Privy Council for Trade and Plantations
Lucie, Jacob, 183
Lynch, Sir Thomas, Governor of Jamaica, 18, 24, 72, 74, 180

Magna Carta, 72
Maitland, Richard, agent for Grenada, Tobago, and St. Vincent, 121, 164, 199, 253-4; correspondence of, 275-6
Marine Society, offices of, 201
Marlborough, James, Earl of, 30, 34

INDEX 315

Marsh, George, absentee Planter of St. Christopher, 42
Martin, Captain George, 17
——, Samuel, agent for Antigua, Martinique, capture and restoration of, 110
Martyn, Joseph, commissioner for Leeward Is., 70
Maryland, agency of, 77
Massachusetts, agency of, 80, 87 n. 3, 106
Mathew, William, Governor of Leeward Is., 179
Mathias, Vincent, agent for Barbados, 248
Meredith, Sir William, 109
Micklethwaite, Joseph, agent for Barbados, 171, 250
Middleton, Thomas, 34
Modyford, Thomas, Governor of Barbados, 27, 28; partisans of, in England, 25, 33; leader of opposition in Barbados, 15, 31, 159
Molasses Act (1733), 122, 124, 187, 188; (1764), 195
Molesworth, Captain, 180
Monk, General, 27
Montague, Edward, agent for Grenada, 156, 254
Montserrat, settlement of, 8; capture by France, 42; agency of, 92, 93, 128, 140 n. 3, 145–6; committee of correspondence in, 140–1, 145 n. 2; agents of, 253; accounts of agent with, 277–9
Montserrat, and Nevis, 120, 150 n. 3, 155, 156, 161, 165, 172, 189
Morgan, Sir Henry, Governor of Jamaica, 71
Morton, Captain Roger, 18

Navigation Acts, 10–1, 22, 216; interest of Barbados in, 114; evasion of, 117, 118–9, 122; effect of, in West Indies, 121–2; enforcement of, 195
Neutrality, Treaty of (1678), 62, 126
Nevine, William, agent for Antigua, Montserrat, and St. Christopher, 93 n. 2, 129, 150, 251, 252, 253; supersession of, 155; negotiations regarding laws, 221–4; regarding French depredations, 224–5; payment of gratuities by, 226
Nevis, settlement of, 8; establishment of agency in, 92; appointment of agents by, 93, 128; committee of correspondence in, 141; agents of, 252
Newcastle, Duke of, relations with agents, 197, 224–5
New England, agency of, 34
New Providence, 99, 100, 103
New York, agency of, 77

Noden, Charles, agent for Bermuda, 247
——, Ralph, agent for Bermuda, 248
Noell, Martin, merchant of London, 11, 13, 16, 34
Nova Scotia, agency of, 169, 244–5

Oldmixon, John, *cited*, 58, 163
Osborne, Roger, Governor of Montserrat, 35
"Overture," of 1654, drawn up by Povey, 14

Painter, Sir Paul, 40, 48
Palatinate of Durham, 2
Paris, Peace of (1763), 124, 194
Parkes, John, Governor-General of Leeward Is., 107
Parliament, control of colonies by, 216; negotiation of agents before, 227–31; presence of agents in, 165, 171–2, 176; West India interest in, 227–9; influence of reform of, 236–7
——, Long, authority of, in colonies, 21
Pennant, Richard (Lord Penrhyn), Chairman of Standing Committee of Planters and Merchants, 205–6, 207
Phenney, George, Governor of Bahama Is., 104
Phipps, Captain James, planter of St. Christopher, 177
Pickering, Joseph, agent for Barbados, 155, 199, 250; assistant agent for Barbados, 160–1
Pigott, John, agent for Bermuda, 248, 254
Pikes, application for, by agents of Barbados, 54, 129–30
Pitt, William, the Elder, relations with Planters' Club, 191
——, the Younger, statement regarding West Indian absenteism, 175–6; relations with West India Committee, 207–9
Plantation Office, 219 n. 1, 221
Planters, West Indian, in London, consultation of, 14–15; difficulties with merchants, 49, 164, 178, 185–8
Planters' Club, establishment and organisation of, 189–91; disappearance of, 202–3
Pontack's, 178–9
Popple, William, secretary to Board of Trade, nominated as agent, 93 n. 2, 170; Governor of Bermuda, 248
Portugal, merchants trading to, 118
Postmaster-General, reference of colonial business to, 225

Povey, Richard, Secretary of Jamaica, 13
——, Thomas, London merchant, 11; correspondence with his brothers, 12–13; draft of "Overture" 14; correspondence with Virginia, Nova Scotia, and Barbados, 16; promotion of agencies, 16, 34–5, 37, 38–9, 41; member of Council for Foreign Plantations, 34; correspondence with Lord Willoughby, 47, 257–8; view on functions of agent, 116, 179; rivalry with Philip Froude, 159
——, William, Provost-Marshal of Barbados, 13, 61, 63
Pownall, John, Secretary to Board of Trade, 167; agent for Virgin Is., 109
Poyning's Law, application of, to Jamaica, 72
Privy Council, control of colonies by, 20–1, 54, 107, 216, 217, 220, 223, 237; reference of business to committees, 221; records of, 296–7. (For standing committees see *sub nom.* Committee of Privy Council.)

Quebec, agency of, 169, 234 n. 1

Ramsay, David, nominated as agent, 160
Rawlinson, Henry, agent for Virgin Is., 110, 171
Restoration, The, problems of, 20–3
Revenue Bill (1770), attempt of Jamaica to secure exemption from, 201
Riccard, Sir Andrew, 34
Robson, Thomas, agent to Sir Jonathan Atkins, 57
Rogers, Captain Woodes, Governor of Bahama Is., 102, 104, 105
Royal African Company, 71, 119
Royal Exchange, 13, 177, 181
Russell, Colonel James, Governor of Nevis, 25, 35
Ryswick, Peace of, 92

St. Christopher, centre of Leeward Is. Government, 8; capture of, by France, 42; negotiations relating to restitution, 59; establishment of agency in, 64–7; appointment of agents by, 92–3, 128; committee of correspondence in, 140; abolition of agency by, 241; agents of, 252; acts of appointment, 272–4
St. Leger, Sir John, agent for Antigua, 94, 148, 149, 155, 162
St. Lucia, capture and restoration of, 110

St. Thomas, 108
St. Vincent, cession of, 110; establishment of agency in, 111; constitutional difficulties in, 112–3; committee of correspondence, 141; agents of, 254
Scotland, Trade to, 125
Searle, Daniel, Governor of Barbados, 27, 178, 179; correspondence of Povey with, 16
Secretary at War, reference of colonial business to, 225
Secretary of State, control of colonies by, 218, 224–5
——, American Department, 217
——, Southern (after 1782, Home) Department, 217, 237
——, War and Colonies, 217, 237–9
Seven Years' War, see France, war with
Sewell, Robert, agent for Jamaica, 251; member of West India Committee, 213
Sharpe, John, agent for Antigua, Barbados, Jamaica, Nevis, and St. Christopher, 91, 120, 151 n. 2, 155 n. 2, 160, 168, 170, 188 n. 4, 189, 250, 251, 252; solicitor to Treasury, 167; M.P., 172; relation to Planters' Club, 191
——, William, clerk at Council Office, payment of gratuity to, 227
Shelley, Edward, 17
Shirley, William, Governor of Bahama Is., 106, 169
Sierra Leone Company, establishment of, 209–10
Sinecure Act (1782), 237
Slave Trade, movement for abolition, 125, 210–11, 229–31; conduct of, 216
Snow, John, 105
Society of West India Merchants, see *sub nom.* West India Committee.
Solicitor-General, reference of colonial business to, 219, 224; payment of gratuity to, 226
Spain, possessions in West Indies, 6
Spanish Succession War, 127
Spanish Town, 108
Spooner, Charles, agent for Montserrat, Nevis, and St. Christopher, 252, 253; member of West India Committee, 213
Standing Committee of Planters and Merchants, see *sub nom.* West India Committee
Standing Counsel to Board of Trade, reference of colonial business to, 219, 222; payment of gratuity to, 226
Stanhope, Lovel, agent for Jamaica, 251; Law Clerk to Secretaries of State, 168; M.P., 172; relations

INDEX 317

with West India Committee, 199, 200
Stanley, Sir John, agent for Barbados, 84, 162, 250; Commissioner of Custom House, 167-8
——, John, member of West India Committee, 213; agent for Nevis, 252
Stapleton, Sir William, Governor-General of Leeward Is., 60, 65; policy of, 69; personal agents of, 76
Stephenson, Alexander, unofficial agent for Jamaica, 90
Suckling, George, *cited*, 109
Sugar, duties on, 47, 49, 82, 117-8, 120, 188
——, prize, importation of, 121, 195 n. 4, 204
——, refiners of, 49, 116-7, 118
Sugar Act (1733), see Molasses Act
—— (1739), 123, 187
Sun Tavern, 177
Swan Tavern, 177
Symes, Captain John, agent for Leeward Is., 61-2

Tanner, E. P., *cited*, 231
Temple, Colonel, 16
Thompson, Maurice, London merchant, 11
Thornburgh, Edward, agent for Barbados, 51-4, 116, 117, 152, 183, 250
Tinker, William, Governor of Bahama Is., 105
Tobago, cession of, 110; establishment of agency in, 111; cession to France and reconquest, 113; re-establishment of agency in, 113; committee of correspondence, 141; representative institutions in, 233; abolition of agency in, 244; agents of, 253
Token feasts, 177-8
Tortola, 99
Trade, West Indian, organisation of, 9-11; depression in 1799, 175 (see also *sub nom.* West India Committee)
Trant, Patrick, agent to Sir W. Stapleton, 60
Treasury, reference of colonial business to, 219-20, 225
Trinidad, conquest of, 232; constitutional settlement of 233; appointment of agent by, 233
Tucker, Henry, agent for Bermuda, 248
Tutt, John, appointed agent for Jamaica, 76

Verney, Thomas, 12

Victualling Office, reference of colonial business to, 225
Virgin Islands, Dutch in, 7, 99, 107; under Leeward Is. Government, 99-100; relation with Liverpool, 107 n. 1; meeting of assembly in, 108-9; establishment of agency in, 109; acts of appointment, 128; committee of correspondence, 141, 145; abolition of agency in, 242; agents of, 253
Virginia, agency of, 2, 34-5, 77, 115, 187; merchants trading to, 117; 196-7; charge on trade levied by, 192

Walker, George, agent for Barbados, 155, 165, 172, 203, 251
Walpole, Sir Robert, nominated as agent, 166; negotiation of agents with, 123
Walrond, Edward, 28, 34
——, Humphrey, President of Council of Barbados, 31, 32
Walton, Captain John, Lieut.-Governor of Leeward Is., 107, 108
Ward, Captain Philip, Governor of St. Christopher, 25
Watson, Sir Francis, 72
——, Peter, 28-9, 48
Watts, Colonel William, Governor of St. Christopher, 27, 34, 35; relations with Povey, 35-6
West India Committee, early analogies and growth of influence, 174-93 *passim*, 196; Society of West India Merchants, 197-9, 201-2, 206-7; membership of agents, 199, 200-1, 213; General Meetings of Planters and Merchants, 199-200, 202, 204; Standing Committee of Planters and Merchants, 205-7; incorporation by Royal Charter, 206; negotiations with ministers, 207-10; attitude to Slave Trade abolition, 210-1; assistance to East Indian and Chinese immigration, 211; reorganisation in 1829 and 1843, 211, 212; abolition of Society of West India Merchants, 212; agents *ex officio* members, 213; records of, 202, 285-8, 299-300
West Indies, in 1660, 5-10; in 1763, 98-9, 110-1; at end of eighteenth century, 175; in 1815, 232; in early nineteenth century, 235, 239-40, 241
Wheeler, Sir Charles, Governor-General of Leeward Is., 44
Willock, Alexander, agent for Antigua, 252; member of West India Committee, 213

Willoughby, Francis, Lord, Governor of Barbados, 15, 17, 21, 26, 31, 33, 34, 40; relations with Povey, 35, 38
——, William, Lord, Governor of Barbados, relations with Povey, 38–9; difficulties with assembly, 40; negotiations in England, 47, 182
Wilmot, Henry, agent for Antigua, Montserrat, Nevis, and St. Christopher, 149 n. 4, 150 n. 4, 168, 169, 188 n. 4, 199, 252, 253
Windsor, Lord, Governor of Jamaica, relations with Povey, 36
Wine, excise on, in Barbados, 83, 86, 88 n. 2

Winslow, Edward, agent for Bermuda, 248, 254
Worsley, Charles, agent for Barbados, 160, 250; M.P., 172

Yeamans, John, agent for Antigua and Montserrat, 93 n. 5, 121–4, 146, 150 n. 2, 151 n. 3, 155 n. 2, 161, 165, 189, 221, 252, 253; payment of gratuities by, 226–7; accounts of, 277–9
Young, Sir William, agent for St. Vincent, 254; member of West India Committee, 213; activity relative to Slave Trade, 230

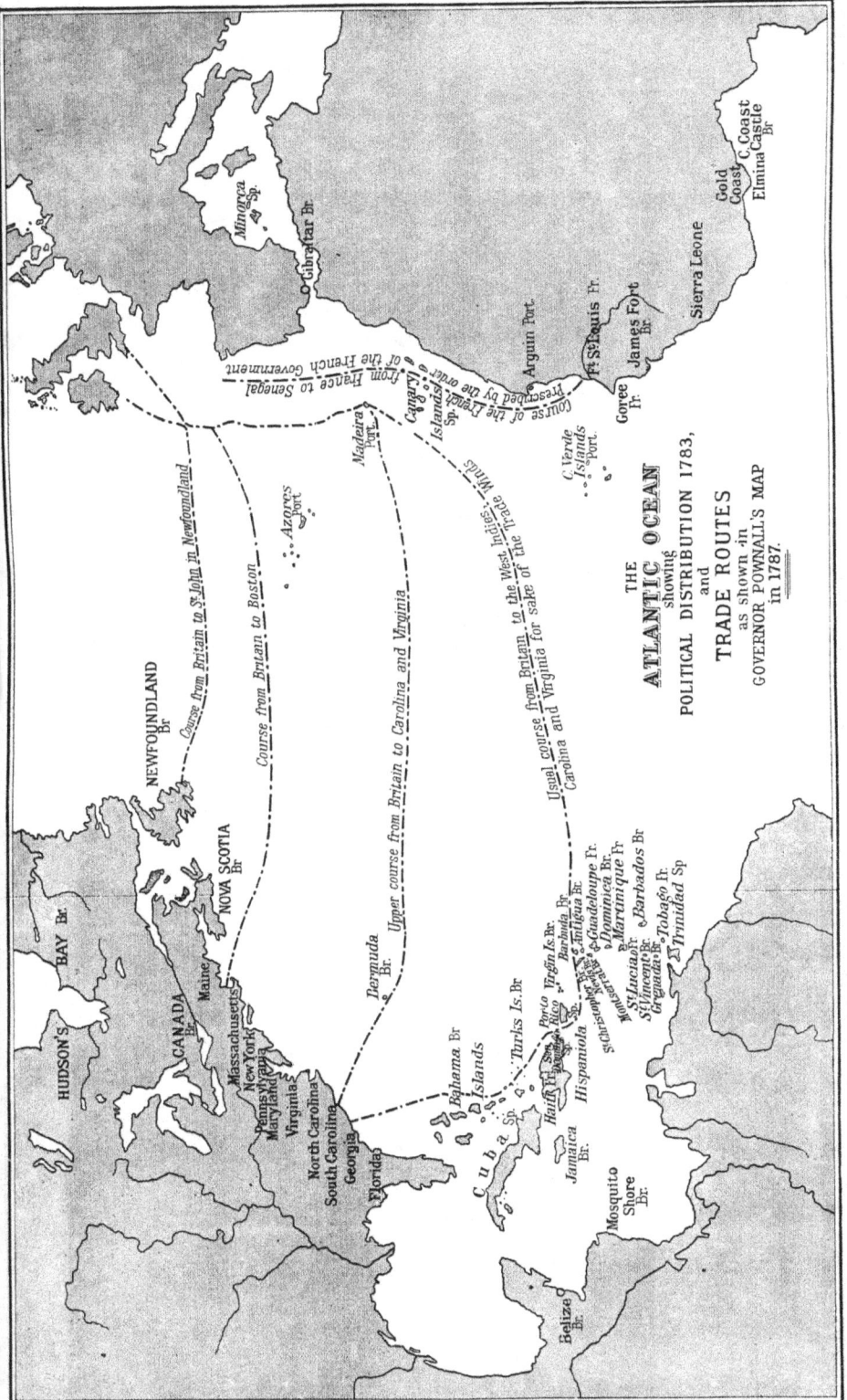

For Product Safety Concerns and Information please contact our EU representative GPSR@taylorandfrancis.com
Taylor & Francis Verlag GmbH, Kaufingerstraße 24, 80331 München, Germany

www.ingramcontent.com/pod-product-compliance
Lightning Source LLC
Chambersburg PA
CBHW052031300426
44116CB00024B/1162